**Hear
Our
Stories**

Hear
Our
Stories

Hear Our Stories

Campus Sexual Violence, Intersectionality, and How We Build a Better University

Jessica C. Harris

STANFORD UNIVERSITY PRESS
Stanford, California

Stanford University Press
Stanford, California

Printed in the United States of America on acid-free, archival-quality paper

Library of Congress Cataloging-in-Publication Data

Names: Harris, Jessica C., author.
Title: Hear our stories : campus sexual violence, intersectionality, and
    how we build a better university / Jessica C. Harris.
Description: Stanford, California : Stanford University Press, 2024. |
    Includes bibliographical references and index.
Identifiers: LCCN 2024012407 (print) | LCCN 2024012408 (ebook) | ISBN
    9781503635470 (cloth) | ISBN 9781503641051 (paperback) | ISBN
    9781503641068 (epub)
Subjects: LCSH: Rape in universities and colleges—United States. | Sexual
    assault—United States. | Sexual abuse victims—United States. |
    Minority women college students—Crimes against—United States. |
    Intersectionality (Sociology)—United States.
Classification: LCC LB2345.3.R37 H35 2024 (print) | LCC LB2345.3.R37
    (ebook) | DDC 378.1/9782—dc23/eng/20240515
LC record available at https://lccn.loc.gov/2024012407
LC ebook record available at https://lccn.loc.gov/2024012408

Cover design and art: Laywan Kwan
Typeset by Newgen in Guyot Text 10.25/15.5

Contents

Tables

Tables

Hear
Our
Stories

Introduction

> Many of the battles that we're fighting today are problems that grow
> out of intersectional failures from yesterday.... [Intersectionality] can
> help us provide a prism to find some of those failures, to repair those
> failures, and to create a basis for a far broader, deeper, more robust coa-
> lition towards the kind of world that we want to build.
>
> —*Dr. Kimberlé Crenshaw*[1]

We have long battled against the pervasiveness of campus sexual violence.[2] But in 2011, this battled erupted. Through the Obama Administration's April 2011 Dear Colleague Letter, the U.S. Department of
Education Office for Civil Rights addressed Title IX of the Education
Amendments of 1972, which states that sex discrimination is prohibited
by educational institutions and programs that receive federal funding.[3]
Through the Letter, the Obama administration aimed to enforce the
understanding that sexual violence is a form of sex discrimination and,
therefore, prohibited by Title IX.[4]

With the release of the Dear Colleague Letter, the issue of campus
sexual violence gained more attention from the U.S. government.
In March 2013, President Obama signed into law the Campus Sexual
Violence Elimination Act, or the Campus SaVE Act, which required

institutions to institute sexual violence prevention programming for all enrolled students and provide protections for survivors.[5] Nearly one year later, in April 2014, the White House Task Force to Protect Students from Sexual Assault released its first report.[6] In the report, the U.S. Department of Education Office for Civil Rights revealed a plan for releasing future documents that would guide best practices and compliance for campus sexual violence prevention and response.

Institutional leaders often attempted to comply with these new federal guidelines. Some institutions created or shifted the role of their Title IX Coordinator to align with the federal guideline that stated each institution must have a designated, trained, and neutral staff member available for victims.[7] Institutions also attempted to improve advocacy services for survivors.[8] Between 2002 and 2015, several colleges and universities increased their availability of on-campus counseling options and enhanced their messaging for off-campus sexual violence resources.[9]

Scholars were also compelled "to add their own research brains and resources toward finding solutions."[10] Research on campus sexual violence has increased over time and continues to focus on specific aspects of sexual violence, including victim and perpetrator risk factors, the role of alcohol and drugs in sexual violence, and campus prevention programming.[11]

And we can't gloss over the fervor of student activism. In April 2013, Dartmouth students marched through and disrupted a large prospective student event in protest of the college's inability to address both sexual violence and racism on campus.[12] Three months later, student activists from various college campuses converged at the U.S. Education Department in Washington, DC to deliver a petition urging the federal government to better enforce policies meant to keep students safe from campus violence.[13] Students from Swarthmore, University of North Carolina, Chapel Hill, Occidental College, and more, spoke out about the federal complaints they filed against their institutions for mishandling their allegations of sexual violence.[14]

Through it all—the increased governmental guidance, institutional efforts, scholarly focus, and the fervor of student activism—sexual violence remains a pervasive issue on campus.[15] "The conversation has grown fiercer, but not necessarily more productive," Sara Lipka, Assistant Managing Editor of *The Chronicle of Higher Education*, wrote about the heightened narrative concerning campus sexual violence.[16]

Sexual violence prevention efforts continue to fall short. Approximately one in four women students will experience nonconsensual sexual contact while in college; this number can be higher or lower depending on institutional environment and students' identities.[17] For instance, I recently worked with a private university in the southern U.S. to explore different, more effective approaches to preventing sexual violence on campus. Leaders at the university had recently received the results of their sexual misconduct climate survey. They were concerned. Over 40% of undergraduate women experienced sexual violence while attending the university. That number increased to over 50% for undergraduate women students who identify as lesbian, gay, bisexual, and/or queer. And the percentage shifted once again when accounting for student survivors' race, gender, *and* sexuality.

Improving institutional response to sexual violence has also proven unsuccessful. The Obama Administration's May 2014 list of 55 higher education institutions under investigation for Title IX violations has, as of 2023, grown to approximately 155 institutions currently under investigation.[18] This does not include the hundreds of other cases at institutions that have been opened and closed between 2014 and today.[19]

We continue to fight today's battle against campus sexual violence because of the intersectional failures of yesterday.[20] Intersectional failure occurs when intersectionality is absent, denied, forgotten, or intentionally distorted within spaces and places where the effects of multiple systems of oppression are present.[21] The stories in this book expose many of these intersectional failings and demonstrates why we continue to fall short in preventing and responding to campus sexual violence. But the stories in this book also contain implications for addressing these failures that move us closer to more effective campus sexual violence prevention and response.

Over the span of several years, I spent time with 34 Women of Color survivors of campus sexual violence.[22] Because Women of Color experience multiple and compounding forms of oppression they often develop an "epistemic advantage" that provides them with critical insights into the practices of their oppressors, as well as knowledge of their own oppression.[23] Jennifer Nash, a scholar of Black feminism, explained, "Marginalized subjects have an epistemic advantage, a particular perspective that scholars should consider, if not adopt, when crafting a normative vision of a just society."[24] Women of Color are uniquely positioned to speak deeply and directly to intersectional failure because these women are often the most impacted by and conscious of these failures.

Through our conversations, the 34 survivors demonstrated how sexual health education, institutional reporting policies, prevention programs, resources for healing, and more, were riddled with intersectional failures. These policies, programs, and procedures that were meant to prevent and respond to sexual violence often failed to account for how intersecting systems of domination, specifically racism and sexism, influence Women of Color survivors' experiences with and needs for addressing campus sexual violence.

The ultimate intersectional failure, however, is that we rarely listen to the stories of Women of Color. Their "epistemic advantage" has been ignored throughout the battle against campus sexual violence. Instead, scholars, policymakers, and practitioners often take a race-evasive approach to violence, which denies the significance of race in sexual violence and focuses on the significance of gender.[25] This race-evasive lens has helped to create a uniform, one-size-fits-all approach to prevention and response that perpetuates "a paradigm that implicitly highlights the white female experience . . . and ignores other racial ethnic groups."[26] Because the stories of Women of Color have been ignored (the ultimate intersectional failure), many other intersectional failings remain unnoticed. Evading intersectionality in our work on campus sexual violence results in intersectional failure; this is why we're still here, fighting this battle.

Yes. This book is about intersectional failure. But it is also about intersectional repair. While intersectionality is helpful in exploring what may be wrong with the current approaches to addressing campus sexual violence, it also pushes us toward what is right, or what is intersectional, inclusive, and more effective.[27] At the 2020 MAKERS Conference, Dr. Kimberlé Crenshaw explored how intersectional failure is the reason "why we are not done."[28] Crenshaw continued:

> Intersectionality is a prism. It's a framework. It's a template for seeing and telling different kinds of stories about what happens in our workplaces, what happens in society, and to whom it happens. Now, some part of why we're not done is predicated on what we haven't been able to see, what's not remembered, the stories that are not told. So, intersectionality is like training wheels to get us to where we need to go. It's glasses, high index glasses, to help us see the things we need to see.[29]

Crenshaw ended her MAKERS Conference Keynote by stating that intersectionality "can inspire us to get shit done."[30]

When we pay attention to the stories that have been erased by intersectional failure, we begin to repair some of the damage done by this failure. Women of Color's stories provide tangible information and implications for how we can repair intersectional failures through sexual violence prevention and response efforts that attend to intersectionality, which attends to the needs and experiences of *all* students.

Women of Color survivors' stories push us to where we need to go— they help us "to get shit done."[31]

Intersectionality and Intersectional Failure Explained

In 1989, with her legal article, "Demarginalizing the Intersection of Race and Sex: A Black Feminist Critique of Antidiscrimination Doctrine, Feminist Theory and Antiracist Politics," Dr. Kimberlé Crenshaw introduced the term "intersectionality" to the academy.[32] Although Crenshaw coined the term "intersectionality" in 1989, the concept "provided a name for a pre-existing theoretical and political commitment" that had long existed within the scholarship and knowledge of Women of Color, such as the Combahee River Collective, Gloria Anzaldúa, and Cherrie Morága.[33]

In a recent *NPR* podcast, entitled, "What Does Intersectionality Mean?" Crenshaw defined intersectionality as a frame that "deals with the interactive effects of multiple forms of discrimination, racism, patriarchy, sexism, misogyny, homophobia . . . we are looking where all of these 'isms' converge."[34] Intersectionality is a metaphor for how multiple forms of oppression can be compounded to influence various experiences and needs for different groups and individuals.[35] Intersectionality also provides a "prism" for identifying intersectional failures.[36] Intersectionality, then, is not just about intersecting systems of domination, it is about what happens—the failures that occur—when intersectionality is not accounted for when addressing specific problems, such as campus sexual violence.

In "Demarginalizing the Intersection of Race and Sex," Crenshaw laid the groundwork for us to better understand intersectionality and intersectional failure. Crenshaw theorized how single-axis frameworks that center either race *or* gender and operate in antidiscrimination law, feminist theory, and antiracist politics result in intersectional failures that "theoretically erase" Black women from these spaces.[37] Here, Crenshaw introduced her now-infamous analogy of the traffic intersection to illustrate how Black women can experience discrimination from multiple directions. Yet dominant frameworks, which are based on the experiences of individuals who are not multiply minoritized, assume that discrimination is unidirectional for Black women. Since Black women's experiences exist at the intersections of race *and* gender, many structures meant to protect Black men or white women cannot and do not protect Black women who are multiply minoritized.[38]

Two years later, with "Mapping the Margins: Intersectionality, Identity Politics, and Violence against Women of Color," Crenshaw expands our understandings of intersectionality by demonstrating how racism and sexism intersect to influence Women of Color's experiences with battering and rape. In "Mapping the Margins," we are introduced to three forms of intersectionality: structural intersectionality, political intersectionality, and representational intersectionality. The forms demonstrate "the various ways in which race and gender intersect in shaping structural, political, and representational aspects of violence against women of color."[39]

Structural intersectionality explores how the experiences of Women of Color with violence are qualitatively different from white women's experiences and are rarely accounted for within the structures of U.S. society, such as the U.S. legal system or campus sexual violence resources.[40] Resources and policies that are meant to respond to survivors of sexual violence often view Women of Color's needs and experiences as the same as white women's needs and experiences. For example, some rape crisis centers allocate a significant portion of their money and time to attend court with victims.[41] Yet, due to racist and sexist stereotypes that position Women of Color as un-believable and, at times, unrapeable, these women are often less likely than white women to have their cases pursued in court. Therefore, resources allocated for court services may be "misdirected" in Communities of Color.[42]

Political intersectionality focuses on the ways that Women of Color fall into a chasm created by competing discourses of resistance, specifically antiracism and feminism. Antiracist discourse often focuses on Men of Color and falls short in addressing patriarchy. Influenced by antiracist discourse, Women of Color are often expected to remain silent around issues of domestic violence to preserve the image of the community and to prevent the perpetuation of racist stereotypes attributed to Men of Color.[43] Furthermore, reporting to police and other governmental services is often not an option for Women of Color, who hesitate to place their trust in systems that are systemically racist and hostile toward Communities of Color. Yet feminist resistance movements that are meant to empower all women may disempower and subordinate Women of Color because privileged, cisgender, heterosexual white women often dominate and dictate single-issue concerns for these movements.[44]

Competing discourses have also shaped conceptualizations of rape that erase Women of Color from these discourses and their concerns for sexual violence. Socio-historical stereotypes often construct Women of Color as hyper-sexual, dirty, and sexually permissive and, therefore, unrapeable.[45] These racialized and gendered stereotypes of unrapeability are woven throughout the fabric of the United States and continue to influence the lives of Women of Color.[46] Colonizers, for instance, justified the rape of Indigenous land and Indigenous women's bodies by claiming that these lands and bodies were polluted, dirty, and, therefore, unrapeable.[47] Yet feminism and antiracism do little to address these stereotypes for Women of Color and, instead, often focus on the social constructions of Black men and privileged white women in discourses of rape. Historically, "real" sexual violence has been cast as a violent act perpetrated by Black men against privileged white women.[48] This paradigmatic violence influences antiracist movements to center Black men in their concerns for race and rape, and feminists to center privileged white women in their concerns for gender and rape. The chasm that these competing discourses create influences why the rape of Women of Color is often viewed as less important and less believable than the rape of privileged white women.[49]

Representational intersectionality focuses on the ways cultural representations reproduce violence against Women of Color. Rap music, with its "misogynistic imagery" transmits racist-sexist stereotypes of Women and Men of Color to U.S. society broadly, but also, to young "Black women who, like young men, are learning that their value lies between their legs."[50] Crenshaw drew upon "The 2 Live Crew controversy" to demonstrate that rap music may empower the Black community in the U.S., but it is also demonstratively misogynistic and devalues and dehumanizes "those most directly implicated in rap-Black women."[51] Representational intersectionality centers not only how violence against Women of Color is reproduced through cultural representations, but also how Women of Color are further marginalized when Communities of Color defend these cultural representations as cultural traditions or as a core component of the culture.

Intersectional Failure and Campus Sexual Violence

Jennifer Nash stated, "Intersectionality invites scholars to come to terms with the legacy of exclusions of multiply marginalized subjects from feminist and antiracist work, and the impact of those absences on both theory and practice."[52] Intersectionality, then, helps us uncover intersectional failure as it relates to current approaches to campus sexual violence prevention and response.

Scholars, for example, often approach sexual violence research from a race-evasive framework that may result in intersectional failure. In reviewing 540 scholarly articles that focused on campus sexual violence, Linder and colleagues found that only 15 articles explicitly centered race in their analysis.[53] Still, other researchers draw on samples with majority white women, resulting in some scholars' decisions to drop Women of Color respondents from their analysis.[54] In what scholars might consider a foundational study on the prevalence of campus sexual violence for women students, Gidycz and colleagues explained, "Given that the sample was predominantly Caucasian women, race and ethnicity were not entered into the model."[55] This approach to research denies intersectionality, or the significance of the interactive effects of race and racism and gender and sexism, in sexual violence to capture what violence means for singularly-minoritized students, that is, cisgender, heterosexual privileged white women students.[56]

Federal and institutional sexual violence policies are also riddled with intersectional failures. These policies do not often include any indication that race, let alone racism, might influence a student's experience with violence.[57] Title IX is a, if not *the*, central policy guiding campus sexual violence response. Recently, Wadley and Hurtado found that some institutional sexual violence and harassment policies, issued by a university Title IX Office, does not mention race *or* gender, resulting in an identity-and-power-devoid approach to sexual misconduct on campus.[58] This race-evasive approach negates how Women of Color students often have unique experiences and needs with reporting campus sexual violence. Racist and sexist structures that have positioned the bodies of Women of Color as hypersexual, promiscuous, and, therefore unrapeable, continue to influence Women of Color students' hesitancy to report their assault to formal outlets.[59] Asian American women students, for instance, may not report rape to authorities because of stereotypes that paint them as hypersexual, passive, and not "the white norm."[60] Women of Color students may not label their experiences with violence as "rape." If one did not experience rape, then

there is nothing to report.[61] Black women's hesitancy to label assault
may be influenced by the understanding "that the community will not
support them as victims or survivors."[62] But federal and institutional
policies often evade these racialized and gendered realities.[63]

Intersectional failure can also exist alongside sexual violence prevention programs and practices. Bystander intervention, for example,
is promoted as an effective sexual violence intervention that has been
adopted by many institutions of higher education.[64] Yet the effectiveness of bystander intervention may be influenced by students' racial
identities and their racialized and sexualized understandings of violence.[65] White women students may be less likely to intervene in a risky
situation when the victim is a Black woman compared to a victim of
an unknown race.[66] Due to racist and sexist stereotypes that position
Women of Color as hypersexual, "White women in college may choose
not to help Black women at risk for sexual assault."[67] And some Students of Color perceive a risk to engaging in bystander intervention,[68]
particularly when this intervention might take place on a campus with
a hostile racial climate.

Although some scholars and educators have pointed out the dearth
of intersectional approaches to campus sexual violence,[69] most scholarship, policies, and practices that aim to improve campus sexual violence
prevention and response continue to be riddled with intersectional failures. The stories in this book explore these and other intersectional failings, but they also demonstrate how to address these failings, moving
us toward intersectional repair.

Women of Color Survivors' Stories and Moving Toward Intersectional Repair

In the fall of 2017, I started what I thought would be a small,
two-to-three-month research project. My initial intention was to use
intersectionality to explore 10–15 Women of Color student survivors'
experiences with sexual violence at City University (CU), a large public
university in the U.S. The stories I heard that fall were illuminating,
infuriating, and inspirational. After completing my interviews with

survivors at CU, I had an immense desire to hear more. And I wanted others—I wanted you—to hear more.

By spring 2019, I expanded the project to two additional institutions: Mountain University (MU) and River University (RU). All three institutions are large public universities in the U.S.[70] Over a three-year period, and with the help of Nadeeka Karunaratne, a graduate student at UCLA who had worked in campus survivor advocacy, I spoke with 34 Women of Color undergraduate students who had experienced sexual violence at one of the three institutions.[71] We interviewed all but two survivors twice, for a total of 66 interviews that each lasted approximately 90 minutes.[72]

In our first interview together, I asked women about their academic, social, and familial experiences prior to college, their academic and social lives on campus, and their experience(s) with sexual violence, including reporting, healing, and immediate responses to the violence. I used this first interview to build rapport with each survivor and to gain a better understanding of their identities and the systems and structures that influenced their identity-specific experiences with violence.

In the second interview, I followed up on the in/consistencies, on individual and group levels, from the first interview. For example, in the first interview, survivors consistently hinted at the poor sex education they received before enrolling in college. Prior to the first interview, I had not thought about the connection between survivors' K-12 sexual health education and campus sexual violence. So, in the second interview, I asked women to expand on their informal and formal sex education prior to arriving on campus and how this sex education impacted their experiences with violence. Through the second interview, I also dug deeper into women's experiences with intersecting systems of domination, which, I was coming to find, could not be divorced from the institutional context.

Throughout both interviews, Women of Color survivors openly shared stories about the intra-racial politics of reporting, the influence of structural racial diversity on their decisions to disclose, and how intergenerational and historical trauma acted as a precursor to experiencing sexual violence. These were stories I rarely, if ever heard in campus conversations concerning how to prevent and respond to campus sexual violence. Many of the survivors were also aware that society and institutions did not center their stories. At the tail end of our final conversation, Raquel stated:

> I literally hear nothing about African women ever. . . . I never hear that story. . . . It's not well known. No one ever talks about it. And for years, I thought I made it up. It's pretty awesome getting to say it and be proud of it and identifying it as, "This is real. This is different from what you've heard. And just because you don't hear it a lot doesn't mean it's not there and not real."[73]

These stories are different, and they certainly are real.

Intersectional Failure, Intersectional Repair, and Institutional Context

While interviewing women across the three institutions, my intersectional "high index glasses" allowed me to see how intricately and intensely intersecting systems of domination were woven throughout institutional structures.[74] These structures and systems sometimes varied across the three institutions. At CU, for example, I observed how institutional values upheld an ethos of gender inequity and racist sexism on campus that influenced campus rape culture and Women of Color survivors' decisions to report their assault to the institution. At MU, however, survivors did not often relay a hesitancy to report their assault, nor did they speak at length about experiencing racism on campus. I concluded that the community-oriented, racially diverse MU campus environment may have encouraged survivors at MU to report their assault. Women of Color survivors' stories demonstrated how institutional context matters when examining intersectional failure and intersectional repair. Scholars of intersectionality agree.

During a talk at the 2016 Women of the World Festival, Crenshaw stated:

> Intersectionality is not primarily about identity. It's about how structures make certain identities the consequence of and the vehicle for

vulnerability . . . you've got to look at the context. What's happening? What kind of discrimination is going on? What are the policies? What are the institutional structures that play a role in contributing to the exclusions of some people and not others?[75]

To root out intersectional failure and engage more fully in intersectional repair, it was imperative that I focus on the institutional context. And more so, the intersectional within the institutional. While interviewing the 34 participants, particularly during the second interviews, I interrogated how institutional policies, procedures, values, and other structures upheld intersecting systems of domination that influenced survivors' experiences with campus sexual violence.

With my growing interest in exploring the connection between the intersectional and the institutional, Nadeeka and I began to collect over 120 documents across the three institutions. The documents included: institutional sexual violence and harassment policies; policies that concern diversity, equity, and inclusion; local and campus newspaper articles about incidents of campus sexual violence; public Facebook posts concerning sexual violence and/or racism on campus; campus "secrets" pages that were mentioned by Women of Color survivors, and more. The documents provided additional context for survivors' stories at the three institutions. But I continued to want more information that might illuminate the institutional context, intersectional failings, and possibilities for repair at an institutional level.

In the spring of 2019, while interviewing women survivors at RU, I began to interview staff members who worked at RU, MU, and CU who had knowledge about women students and/or sexual violence at their respective campus. In the 60-minute interviews, I shared with staff members some of the initial findings about sexual violence I had generated from Women of Color students' narratives. Staff participants provided reactions, as well as more information and context for survivors' narratives. For example, at RU, several survivors mentioned how the institution responded inadequately to an incident where a Black woman student was drugged and raped. I relayed these perceptions and this incident to RU staff. Some RU staff members provided more information about this alleged incident and the institutional response to the incident. In the end, Nadeeka and I interviewed 23 staff members across the three institutions, including Deans of Students, Title IX Coordinators, Sexual Violence Resource Center Directors and Advocates, Directors of the Campus Counseling Center, and Directors of Fraternity and Sorority Life.[76] In this book, staff members' narratives are used to support and further animate Women of Color student survivors' stories of campus sexual violence.

Overview of the Book

Hear Our Stories unapologetically centers the stories of 34 Women of Color survivors. Each chapter demonstrates how intersecting systems of domination influence survivors' experiences with and needs for effectively addressing campus sexual violence.

The chapters are ordered in a way that, for me, tells a story. The first chapter explores the 34 survivors' experiences with sex and sexual violence prior to and immediately after arriving for their first year on campus. It focuses on sexual violence prevention and offers alternate narratives from what is often discussed, for why sexual violence remains pervasive on the college campus. Here, I draw on all 34 Women of Color survivors' stories to demonstrate the failings and possibilities for campus sexual violence prevention.

Chapters 2, 3, and 4 take an intersectional turn toward the institutional context of River University, Mountain University, and City University, respectively. To learn more about the institutional characteristics of each university and their environments, please visit the Appendix. The three chapters explore how the campus environment influences survivors' experiences with sexual violence. Subsequently, each chapter centers on the stories of the 10–13 survivors I spoke with at each institution. Women of Color survivors' stories demonstrate how the campus environment influences campus rape culture and how this same environment can discourage or encourage reports of violence. The three chapters are not comparative analyses of sexual violence at three universities. Instead, they demonstrate how key aspects of a campus environment can influence various experiences with and perceptions of sexual violence, intersectional failure, and intersectional repair.

In these institution-focused chapters, you will become familiar with the concept of institutional betrayal, or "when an institution causes harm to an individual who trusts or depends upon that institution."[77] According to the federal government, college students and their communities should be able to trust that their institutions take immediate and effective action to end sexual violence on campus.[78] But when institutions do not adequately engage in sexual violence prevention and response, the institution betrays students.

Institutional betrayal can occur through acts of omission, which may involve negligence or oversight, such as a failure to notify all students of institutional resources for sexual violence prevention. Institutional betrayal can also exist in more active manners through acts of commission, such as purposefully underreporting acts of violence to the campus community and to the federal government.[79] Institutional betrayal can exist as an isolated incident, for example, the institution dissuades one student from reporting their assault, or as a systemic problem, for example, the institution consistently dissuades students from reporting their assault. Betrayal can be carried out by individuals within an institution, such as faculty and staff, and by institutional structures such as policies, programs, and procedures.[80]

Some survivors and staff members also explored institutional courage. Institutional courage is the antidote to institutional betrayal.[81] With institutional courage, colleges and universities can address how they fall short in preventing and responding to sexual violence. For example, institutions can exhibit courage by responding sensitively to survivors' disclosures, educating leaders about sexual violence research, and complying with federal and local policies and procedures that concern sexual violence.[82] Like institutional betrayal, both individuals within institutions and institutional structures can enact institutional courage.[83]

The concept of institutional betrayal emerged throughout my interviews. Institutions often betrayed Women of Color survivors by failing to account for intersectionality within sexual violence prevention and response. For example, although institutions offered mandatory prevention education to all new students, this education was devoid of an intersectional understanding. Therefore, several Women of Color survivors did not see their experiences reflected in this prevention education—they often felt disconnected from the sexual violence scenarios, refusal skills, and resources offered through these programs. Intersectional failure, then, was well-acquainted with institutional betrayal.

Chapter 5 turns away from focusing on a specific institution and turns toward an exploration of how intersecting systems of oppression influenced 34 Women of Color survivors' decisions to disclose and report their experiences with sexual violence.

Chapter 6 demonstrates the various, often beautiful ways that Women of Color survivors heal from campus sexual violence. Although healing is the subject of the final chapter of this book, I do not suggest that all 34 survivors' stories ended in healing or that the final chapter of survivors' stories is about healing. Instead, this final chapter offers stories and suggestions for how we might explore the concept of healing in ways that are more expansive and inclusive for all students.

At the end of all six chapters, and through the book's conclusion, I offer implications for how we can move toward intersectional repair and institutional courage.

Taken together, this book moves us closer to where we need to go. My hope is that it "can inspire us to get shit done."[84]

One

"Why Does it Happen?"

RISK FACTORS FOR CAMPUS SEXUAL VIOLENCE

Alcohol use. Membership in a Greek letter organization. Prior victimization. First-year student status. Engaging in risky sexual behaviors. These are some of the most cited risk factors for experiencing sexual violence in college.[1] For example, some scholars have explored how prior victimization—including experiencing child sexual abuse—increased college women's risk of experiencing sexual violence.[2] Scholars also focus on the risk of the "red zone," an early period of students' lives on campus when they may be more likely to experience sexual violence.[3] This focus on few, specific risk factors is concerning. Particularly because this research often falls short in accounting for intersectionality.

Take alcohol use, for example. It is one of the most-studied risk factors for experiencing campus sexual violence.[4] Nearly half of all cases of campus sexual violence involve alcohol,[5] suggesting a connection between alcohol and perpetrating or experiencing violence. This large body of scholarship tends to guide institutional prevention programming that focuses on the connection between alcohol and drug use and sexual violence.[6] Yet this scholarship and programming may be "misdirected" for many Students of Color.[7] White students may drink more frequently, and experience more alcohol-related violence, than Students of Color.[8] Systems of domination can influence this racialized difference in alcohol consumption; some Students of Color, for example, perceive that heavy alcohol use may exacerbate race-based police violence.[9] Scholars have also focused on how women students' sorority membership influences greater alcohol use, increased risk-taking behavior, delayed assessments of risk, increased contact with fraternity men,[10] greater number of sexual partners,[11] and attendance at coed Greek social events with alcohol[12]—all factors that predict an increased risk of sexual violence.[13] Yet this scholarship rarely captures the experiences of Women of Color students who, due to racism and sexism, are often excluded from membership in Panhellenic sororities.[14]

Most of the Women of Color survivors I spoke with did not perceive alcohol as a main risk factor for experiencing sexual violence. And while a few survivors were members of sororities, these same women did not indicate that membership in their sorority was a precursor to experiencing violence. Survivors also did not identify prior victimization, first-year student status, or engaging in risky sexual behaviors as primary risk factors for experiencing sexual violence.

So why, according to the 34 Women of Color survivors, does campus sexual violence happen? I asked each woman survivor and each staff member this question. My hope was that participants might provide me with a prolific answer to this age-old question we've been asking and answering in similar manners for decades. Their answer: a lack of sexual health education.[15]

"There's just not enough education about it," Monae answered in response to my probe, "Why does campus sexual violence happen?" "There's so much that people need to be educated [on] about consent," she continued. Monae and her peers were under-educated about the concept of consent, which, according to Monae, was a far more complex topic than institutions and individuals might think.

"I think because there is a lack of education on [sex], it doesn't help in decreasing or increasing an understanding of [sexual violence]," Terri claimed.[16] She acknowledged that first-year college students are suddenly exposed to more sexual experiences than ever before. But the increase in sexual experience was not the issue. It was the lack of education surrounding how to navigate these experiences.

A lack of sexual health education, which includes education on sex, sexual relationships, sexuality, and sexual violence, is a significant risk factor for experiencing campus sexual violence. As the survivors point out, this lack of education is a systemic issue woven throughout the U.S. educational system and is often exacerbated by the dearth of sexual health education students receive at home. Many women survivors, then, turned to alternate outlets to better understand sex—albeit "misconstrued" understandings of sex. These outlets included YouTube, television, books, and social media. They also learned about sexual health by observing their parents' and grandparents' relationships, some of which involved trauma and violence. By reading about Women of Color survivors' stories of sexual health mis/education, this chapter demonstrates how a lack of information and knowledge about sexual health—not alcohol, sorority membership, or first-year student status—often placed women students at risk for experiencing campus sexual violence.

"I Don't Think My Sex Ed was Great": Sexual Health Education in U.S. Schools

At 18 years old, Jane moved on to the RU campus with very limited knowledge of sex. She recalled her feelings about sex at the start of her college journey:

> The lack of education on [sex], I didn't know how to approach it. I didn't know how to have safe sex. I don't know what to do if safe sex doesn't happen. . . . I was just like, "Oh just don't do it. That's the best thing." That's what I've been taught. And even when I got here, I'm still learning about it now. And it feels so stupid. But it's kind of how we've been socialized.

Prior to moving to college, Jane participated in a ninth-grade sex education course that socialized her to believe that, when it comes to sex, "the best way is abstinence." If Jane did not abstain from sex, she was taught that whatever happened because she had sex, including violence, was her fault. Abstinence education was the only formal sex education Jane received prior to enrolling at RU. In fact, most of the survivors I spoke with encountered abstinence-only education at some point in their formal schooling. Abstinence education "teaches young kids not to have sex at all rather than how to have sex safely."[17] Many have problematized abstinence-only education for withholding information that is necessary for individuals to make fully informed decisions about sexual health.[18] Abstinence-only education contributed to Jane's lack of knowledge of how to have safe sex and what to do if she did not experience safe sex, that is, sexual violence. At the age of 20, after experiencing sexual violence, Jane was "still learning" about sex.

Abstinence-only education influenced women's vulnerability to experiencing campus sexual violence. These educational programs often promote a culture of fear, shame, and silence around sexual health, and fail to prepare students to recognize and engage in healthy adult relationships.[19] They can also reinforce sexism, heterosexism, racism, rape culture, and victim blaming,[20] or ideologies that imply there is something inherently wrong about the victim or their behaviors that leads to their victimization.[21] Sneen explained that abstinence-only curriculums "often propagate gender stereotypes with strong undertones of female responsibility and shame for male sexuality" which can uphold rape culture.[22] Through this education, men are not often held accountable for their sexual behaviors, which may include sexual force and coercion, and women are seen as culpable for their sexual behaviors.[23] In short, abstinence-only education does not often teach students to recognize sexual violence victimization *or* perpetration, influencing vulnerability to this violence throughout the lifespan.[24]

Recently, some scholars have explored how sex education that does not teach abstinence-only and, instead, teaches students how to say no to sex (i.e., refusal skills training) may act as a protective factor for experiencing sexual violence in college.[25] In one of the most comprehensive studies about sex and sexual violence on the college campus, Hirsch and Mellins found that women students at Columbia University who received pre-college sex education that involved refusal skills training were half as likely to experience penetrative assault while in college than students who did not receive this training.[26] Hirsch and Mellins concluded, "Receipt of school-based sex education promoting refusal skills before age 18 was an independent protective factor; abstinence-only instruction was not."[27]

Although refusal skills training may be effective in preventing sexual violence, it often focuses on individual-level behaviors, does not focus on perpetrators' actions, and places the burden and blame for refusing assault with the survivor.[28] Focusing on refusal skills as the *only* protective factor learned from sexual health education can result in victim blaming, as if sexual violence happens because survivors did not say "no" in a skilled or forceful manner. Therefore, refusal skills training should be one component of many within sexual health curricula that accounts for individual, institutional, and societal-level factors that contribute to sexual violence victimization and perpetration.[29] Unfortunately, almost all women survivors I spoke with did not receive education on refusal skills, or other aspects of sexual health, prior to entering college. Instead, most women relayed how their education revolved around abstinence-only, which solely taught them not to engage in sexual activity.

Most survivors readily recalled the inadequacy of their formal, sex education in middle and high school. Tessa, for example, took one semester of health in high school that covered sexually transmitted infections, the process of giving birth, and puberty. But, Tessa concluded, "I don't think my sex ed was great." Tessa blamed the U.S. public education system for the sexual mis/information students brought into college. "Public school health systems are not great," Tessa stated.

According to SIECUS: Sex Ed for Social Change, only 29 states and the District of Columbia mandate sex education in public schools.[30] Sixteen states offer abstinence-only education, and many other states require schools to emphasize abstinence through sex education.[31] As many as 13 states do not require sex education to be age-appropriate, medically accurate, culturally responsive, or evidence-based/evidence-informed. Twelve states and the District of Columbia teach about consent within sex education courses.[32] Only three states require comprehensive sex education, or education on relationships, decision-making, human development, communication, and access to reproductive health services, to be taught in all schools. The lack of uniformity across state-level requirements for sex education means that many young adults experience a lack of access or no access to comprehensive sex education.[33]

Students of Color may be disproportionately impacted by this variation in education. The Women of Color Sexual Health Network and SIECUS emphasize how there exists "less comprehensive sexual education programming offered in schools and districts, particularly in the south and with disproportionately higher populations of Black and Latinx students, perpetuating gaps in information, learning, access to services, and support for these youth."[34] Students of Color also report experiencing racialized assumptions about their sexual behaviors within the sexual health curriculum.[35] Some teachers assume that Black and Hispanic students are hyper-sexual, lack the willpower to abstain from sex, and are, therefore, already sexually active. Subsequently, these teachers do not often provide Black and Hispanic students with basic sexual health information and, instead, tell students to use condoms with no instruction on how to do so.[36]

The state of sex education in public schools is bleak. But survivors who attended religious educational institutions, most of which were privately controlled, also described subpar sex education. These religious institutions almost always implemented abstinence-only-until-marriage education. This form of sex education aligns with conservative Christian values and teaches abstinence from all sexual behavior outside of marriage, providing no information about contraception.[37]

Eliza, for example, attended a Christian elementary school where "basically sex didn't exist." Because there was an assumption in the school that all students would abstain from sex until marriage, Eliza never received any information about sex. But a lack of information about sex did not stop Eliza from being curious about the topic. To learn more, she searched for information on the internet. "Guys would message me and they would say they wanted to do things, which is really horrible. Then I would be like, 'Oh, what's that?' Then I would look it up." But Eliza did not "actually get [sex]" until she became sexually active in middle school.

Mary went to a Catholic school that was "very hush about [sex]. Like, you're not supposed to know what this is." From the school's health course, Mary did learn that females have eggs and males have sperm, but there was no conversation about how eggs and sperm related to sex. "It was rough," Mary jested about her Catholic school sex education.

Like Eliza, Mary's self-guided sex education also took place on the internet. "There was always that division of, I can't talk about it with my parents or anyone around me or [at] school. There's no place to talk about it except for the internet." Mary received a dearth of information about sex from the people around her, including her family, friends, and teachers, but she did receive an overwhelming amount of information from the internet. She described her internet sex education:

> There's just so much stuff [on the internet] where it's like, "Okay, maybe I should have been talking to the people in real life to get more of a realistic idea." Instead, it was just this stuff about the most horrible acts you can do and all this really explicit stuff. That's where I mostly learned about sex in general.

Mary's internet education did not provide her with a realistic understanding of sex. But it did help fill a gap in knowledge that her formal schooling, and her home environment, created. Mary did not receive sex education at school. She also did not receive this education at home. She could not talk to her teachers or her parents about sex. In concluding her thoughts about sex education, Mary shared that she and her peers negotiated the college campus with an inability to "navigate sex in a healthy way."

"We Didn't Talk About It": Sexual Health
Education in the Home

Margaret could not recall where she learned about sex. Perhaps it was from her friend in 8th grade? Or maybe it was from the internet? She could, however, recall where she did *not* learn about sex. It was not through formal schooling. And it was certainly not from her parents. Margaret subtly laughed as she recalled her parents' attitude about sex:

> My parents literally didn't talk about [sex]. Ever! Literally. Never! Didn't speak about it. It didn't exist in my house. I knew marriage and that kind of stuff. But literally, sex was just not a thing. We didn't talk about it. I couldn't ask them questions.

As a 20-year-old college student, Margaret's parents remained silent about sex. "My parents?" Margaret asked jokingly, "Still to this day we don't talk about it."

Although many parents are not the primary sex educators for their children,[38] there often exists some discussion in the home of sex, such as STIs and condom usage.[39] But Margaret, and most other Women of Color survivors relayed that their parents remained silent on the topic of sex—there was no sex education in their homes. Margaret was certainly not the first or the last survivor I'd talk to that described how their parents remained silent about sex. So, I feigned surprise at Margaret's joking comments and asked, "What is that about? Why?"

"They're older so that might have something to do with it and it might just be uncomfortable talking about it," Margaret answered me nonchalantly. But then Margaret paused and took another moment to think about my question. After a short silence, she responded with another suggestion. This time, she spoke slowly, working out her thoughts as she answered:

> Hispanic parents are just weird. They're just weirdly strict and they're just weirdly against a lot of things. So really, sex just wasn't a topic of discussion. . . . If we didn't talk about [sex], then we wouldn't know about it and it would never happen.

As Margaret implied, her parents' approach to sex education related in some ways to "Hispanic" culture. Influenced by a history of forced colonization, some Latino cultural values dictate that Latinas "be modest in behavior, know little about sex, and not enjoy intercourse in order to maintain her family's esteem."[40] If Margaret's family provided her with sex education, it might compromise Margaret's perceived sexual modesty and the family's esteem.

Monae also explored how Latino culture influenced her parents' silence on sex:

> When I came to MU, I was clueless about everything, because I feel like [for] a lot of people [sex] is such a taboo. And you would think, in 2019, it's not. But for me, I didn't really know anything about sex, sexual violence, consent. Specifically, too, because of my family. They're conservative. They're Catholic. They're Mexican. It's all something we don't talk about.

For Monae, the intersection of Mexican culture and the Catholic religion influenced her family's conservative approach to sex. Over 80% of the population in Mexico identifies as Catholic.[41] According to the Pew Research Center, "Mexico has the globe's second-largest number of Catholics, and a larger majority of Mexicans have remained tied to their Catholic faith compared with people in many other Latin American countries."[42] Consequently, Catholicism and the Catholic Church continues to dictate what is right and moral in Mexican culture, particularly as it relates to sexuality.[43] For many conservative Catholics, sex is reserved for heterosexual marriage and solely for the purposes of reproduction.[44] Following the teachings of the Catholic Church, Monae's family took an abstinence-only-until-marriage approach to sex in the home. As a result, Monae arrived at college under-educated about sex. She perceived that her lack of knowledge about sex had consequences. "When I came here, I didn't really know much about [sex]. And so I feel like I was even more vulnerable because I didn't know about the resources. I didn't know I can say 'No,'" she stated. Monae perceived she was more "vulnerable" to sexual violence because she did not have adequate knowledge about consent, refusal skills, bodily autonomy, sexual violence, or sex.

It was not just survivors from Latino cultures, such as Monae and Margaret, that named the connection between culture, religion, and a lack of sex education in the home. "Catholicism" was the one-word answer Queenie gave when I asked her why her mother refused to speak to her about sex. According to Queenie, Catholicism in Vietnamese culture led to a hyper-fixation on Vietnamese women's purity. Any mention of sex in the home would compromise this purity. Raquel explained that her parents never spoke to her about sex because it was "prohibited" by the Islamic religion practiced by her African tribe. And several South Asian women connected Hinduism and South Asian culture to their lack of sex education in the home. Rayn, for instance, first acknowledged, "Talking about sex. Period. Like relationships, is just not something that happens in my community. It's a very taboo topic." Moments later, Rayn relayed that her mis/conceptions about sex stemmed from gendered ideologies that she learned within her South Asian community, which intersected with being "raised very Hindu."

"A Misconstrued View on What Sex Is": Alternate Modes of Sex Education

Survivors often did not receive sexual health education at school or at home. So, they looked elsewhere for this sex education. Many women consciously and consistently turned to media to explore sex. YouTube and Google were some of the most visited sites for self-guided sex education. Noelle, for instance, learned about sex through "viral videos" on YouTube that were "not exactly insightful." Survivors also explored sex by watching television and movies. Coraline learned about sex by watching sensationalized news programs with her family, while some others mentioned their foray into sex with the crime drama, 'Crime Scene Investigation,' or CSI. Several South Asian women pointed to Bollywood, the nickname given to the Indian film industry based in Mumbai,[45] as a main component in their self-guided sex education.

Survivors were aware that these alternative educational outlets were not ideal sources for sex education. Terri spoke about the influence that her media sex education had on her mis/understandings of sex:

When you don't talk about [sex]. When you're young and you don't understand it. When you're young, you get the idea of what sex is supposed to be like from media, from everything else that you see. Because
your parents aren't talking about it. Your friends aren't really talking
about it. . . . It's such a misconstrued view on what sex is.

To fill the gaps created by a lack of sex education at home and at school,
survivors often turned to media for knowledge of sex. But this media
created a "misconstrued" understanding of sex for most Women of
Color I spoke with.

Tessa, for instance, demonstrated how Bollywood movies taught
her to believe that women are men's property, which normalized sexual
violence:

In a lot of Bollywood movies, the woman exists for the man. . . .
Growing up seeing things like that, that really shifts your mentality
and then you start to think of yourself as an accessory to whatever the
guy is doing. I think having that kind of mentality, growing up with
that kind of media, and then having something like [sexual violence]
happen to you, it's very natural to think that it's okay. He did what he
wanted to, and that was fine. I could be put in that position and it was
okay.

Because Tessa did not receive comprehensive sexual health education
at home or at school, Bollywood became her sex education. But Bollywood influenced the transmission of deleterious messages to South
Asian women that normalized, if not glorified sexual violence. Tessa,
and many other Women of Color survivors, entered college with these
"misconstrued" views of sex that they learned from the internet, television, books, social media, and elsewhere.

"Where Did I Learn this From?" Intergenerational Trauma

There existed one additional, perhaps, more influential mode through
which survivors learned about sexual health—intergenerational trauma.
Intergenerational trauma is the concept that adaptive behaviors to, and

psychological impacts from, traumatic experiences will be passed from one generation to the next.[46] Although many survivors' families did not talk about sex, these same families often transmitted sexual lessons through intergenerational trauma, also known as the intergenerational transmission of trauma.

The intergenerational transmission of trauma captures how children are often affected by their parents' trauma and trauma responses.[47] Parents' experiences with traumatic sexual violence can be transmitted to their offspring, increasing the child's risk for experiencing sexual violence. Young women may be at an increased risk for sexual abuse if their mothers experienced sexual abuse or domestic violence.[48] Exposure to domestic violence in the household, for instance, places children at risk for experiencing domestic violence as adults,[49] and mothers' experiences with sexual victimization can be associated with their adolescent daughters' experiences with sexual victimization.[50]

In the only study I could locate that focused on college students and the intergenerational transmission of trauma, Brownridge found that several college women who witnessed domestic violence as children experienced intimate partner violence while in college.[51] Witnessing parental violence as a child may have an impact on women students' experiences with sexual violence in college.[52] Although helpful, most of this research is quantitative and draws on majority white samples; the literature does not explore how or why the intersections of race, gender, and other minoritized identities might influence students' experiences with the intergenerational transmission of trauma.

The survivors I spoke with demonstrated how the intergenerational transmission of trauma was often present in their experiences with violence and unique for them, as Women of Color. Survivors expanded the concept of the intergenerational transmission of trauma, citing how trauma was passed from *multiple* generations, not just from parent to child, to influence their experiences with campus sexual violence. Women of Color also expanded on the intergenerational transmission of trauma by demonstrating how historical trauma intersected with intergenerational trauma. Historical trauma is the "cumulative emotional and psychological wounding over the lifespan and across generations, emanating from massive group trauma experiences,"[53] including the transatlantic slave trade, American Indian genocide, and Japanese-American "relocation" camps.

Padma, for instance, described how her grandmother's and mother's experiences with domestic violence influenced her own experience with sexual violence:

> I'm falling into the same patterns as my mom, as my grandma; that relationship was also really abusive. And who knows how many generations it goes back. And I'm exactly the same. I'm just someone who men can do whatever they want to and get away with it.

Padma was aware that she was falling into a pattern of intergenerational trauma and violence. She, like her mother and grandmother, were survivors of sexual and domestic violence. She, like her mother and grandmother, were expected, as South Asian women, to cater to the needs of men, including fathers, uncles, brothers, and husbands.[54] Men were allowed "to do whatever they want" to Padma, and to the previous generations of women in her family. Padma demonstrates how the intergenerational transmission of trauma, across multiple generations, taught her about sex and sexual relationships and made her vulnerable to experiencing sexual violence on campus.

After naming how intergenerational patterns of trauma influenced her life, Padma added, "Especially People of Color, we hold onto generations of trauma." Padma went on to condemn a history of colonization in both the U.S. and in India for positioning Women of Color as "inherently rapeable and being property." As Padma pointed out, colonization continues to structure, and is structured by the sexual violation of Women of Color's bodies.[55] For instance, the rape of land and Indigenous women's bodies "was the first act to establish the United States."[56] Colonizers justified this violence by claiming that Indigenous women's bodies were polluted, and, therefore rapeable.[57] This settler colonial structure continues to influence sexual violence, as well as health, wealth, and employment for Communities of Color.[58] For Padma, this colonization was the foundation for why most women in her family were "cursed" with experiencing "really abusive relationships."

Here, Padma explored how intergenerational trauma intersects with historical trauma. In response to historical trauma, many individuals display a historical trauma response or "the constellation of features in reaction to this trauma."[59] The historical trauma response can include resilient responses as well as destructive physical, social, and psychological responses, including domestic violence, child abuse, depression, anxiety, and substance abuse.[60] The historical trauma and the learned responses to this trauma (intergenerational trauma) can pass from, and influence, multiple generations (intergenerational transmission of this trauma). Sotero summarized this cycle, "The symptoms of historical trauma as a disease are the maladaptive social and behavioral patterns that were created in response to the trauma experience, absorbed into the culture and transmitted as learned behavior from generation to generation."[61]

"When people say that People of Color are violent, or within their family life there's always domestic abuse, I think it goes back to colonization, and the fact that this has been a learned thing," Faye stated as she began to speak of her experiences, and her mother and grandmother's experiences, with domestic violence. She continued, "I can visualize my mom's experience, my grandmother's experience, all these women. We have always been violated, and by so many people." For Faye, intergenerational violence was rooted in historical trauma, specifically, the colonization of India, a massive group trauma experience.

From a young age, Faye consistently observed her father physically and emotionally abuse her mother. At some point, Faye's father began to abuse Faye. Yet the family remained silent about the abuse. Faye's mother and grandmother showed Faye, "This is how it is in our culture. This is just how it is. Just don't fight it." Faye despised this component of her culture, but she was also aware that she had adopted some of these problematic cultural ideologies, for example, South Asian women must submit to men. And these cultural ideologies influenced her experiences with sexual violence while in college.

Faye explained the connection between her socialization to Indian cultural values, the intergenerational transmission of trauma, and her experiences with violence:

[Indian women] always want to see the best in those people. And [that's] why I always think about little things he did during that encounter that could be like, "Oh, he didn't mean to. It was okay." And that connects so deeply—my response and my reaction to my assault is very similar to how I've cut my dad a lot of slack, and how I see my mom. I was so mean to my mom growing up, like "Why are you doing this? Why are you letting him? Why are you still here?" And I stayed with this person. I kept talking to him for at least a couple months after this event. It's because you don't want them to be hurting.

Faye's mother accepted her father's violence, which influenced Faye's acceptance of and justification for her perpetrator's violence; this is what they were socialized to as South Asian women. Faye, and her mother and grandmother, were socialized "to be dutiful daughters, loyal wives, sacrificing mothers, and obedient daughters-in-law . . . wherein women assume and internalize their subordinate roles in an attempt to ensure harmony in the household."[62] Faye recognized that her socialization to sex and sexual relationships through her family influenced more than just her response and reaction to experiencing violence. It placed her at risk for experiencing violence. "When I got to CU, I remember telling one of my friends, 'It feels like I'm waiting to be assaulted.' . . . It's just like I was waiting [for it to happen] because every woman in my family had been assaulted," she shared. To Faye, the trauma was historical, and it was intergenerational, making it almost inevitable that she would experience violence.

Historical trauma, intergenerational trauma, and the intergenerational transmission of this trauma, coupled with a lack of sexual health education, were risk factors for experiencing sexual violence. Many scholars have focused on how prior victimization, in one student's lifetime, increases that student's risk for experiencing sexual violence on campus.[63] Scholars, however, have not explored how prior victimization across generations, that is, intergenerational trauma, may contribute to students' risk for experiencing sexual violence on campus. And historical trauma is near absent from scholarship and conversations concerning campus sexual violence. Women of Color survivors' stories encourage a more expansive approach to "prior victimization" as a risk factor that accounts for historical, intergenerational, and individual traumas experienced across generations and geographies.

The Institution "Could Have Made Us More Aware": Sexual Health Education in College

Like many college students, most survivors in this research entered college with little to no understanding of sexual health,[64] which includes understandings of sexual violence.[65] And the sexual understandings that survivors brought to campus were often "misconstrued" and unhelpful within their college environment. Abstinence-only sex education poorly prepares college students for many of the sexual situations they encounter on campus.[66] Unfortunately, higher education institutions did little to correct or enhance students' knowledge of sexual health. A lack of adequate sexual health education for college students, including education on how to recognize and prevent sexual violence, is institutional betrayal.[67]

"I didn't really find out the extent of sexual assault and sex on campus and things like that until I was actually in the environment," Ananya shared. Intrigued by Ananya's comment, I asked her how she eventually learned about sex and sexual violence on campus. She replied with detail:

> It surprisingly wasn't the programs. You know that interactive slideshow that we had to go through? I didn't learn anything from that. You don't learn statistics. When I started going to parties and things like that [is when I learned]. Actually one of my closest friends in my hall, she had experienced sexual assault, and I was there. . . . I saw it firsthand. And I saw it [happen] to multiple people . . . I'm thinking to myself, "Well, where did I hear that statistic that it only happens to a small percent of the population, when it's happening to literally everyone I know?" That was just such a shock to me coming into college. I felt very ignorant of that fact after my freshman year. How could I have come in thinking that I would have been safe going to parties? . . . They could have made us more aware, the institution itself. . .

All three institutions required new students to complete at least one training on sexual and relationship violence prevention prior to or during their first semester on campus. Depending on the institution, and the year that each participant first enrolled, this training encompassed one online module, ranging from 45 minutes to 2 hours, and/or attending an in-person educational session during new student orientation. Students who did not complete the online course were subject to a hold placed on their registration.

Ananya, however, critiqued the online prevention programing that MU required her to complete as a new student. After attending the mandatory program, she remained unaware about the realities of sexual violence, as well as sex, on campus. It was only through other students' experiences with sexual violence that Ananya began to grasp the magnitude of the issue. Ananya did not share what, exactly, about the program was ineffective, but several other survivors shared why they perceived institutional prevention programming to fall short.

Monae was unable to recall receiving sex education at home or at school. When she arrived at MU, she sat through a 10-minute in-person presentation about consent. "That was it," Monae stated. She continued, "You would think [consent] is straightforward, but since we're not teaching that in schools, even elementary schools . . . then it just gets lost on people." Because Monae was not educated about sex or consent prior to college, nothing about sex or consent in college was straightforward. Yet the institution continued to approach sexual health education as straightforward, which may be why the topic of consent only warranted a 10-minute presentation at the start of one's college journey. But this 10-minute presentation was the first time that some students heard about, or were allowed to talk about, consent.

Some Women of Color survivors named the intersectional failures that were present in prevention programming. Erika, for instance, referenced a sexual health education video "made with all these frat people." She continued, "All of [the actors in the video] were white. All of them were heterosexual. And [they] spoke in a way that assumed everyone was just like them." Erika, who was not involved with Fraternity and Sorority Life and did not identify as white, had a hard time identifying with the video. Erika suggested that the institution have Survivors of Color, like herself, come in to talk about their experiences with violence so that other Students of Color might relate to the experience.

Similarly, Queenie was frustrated by the lack of intersectionality in both the in-person and online orientation prevention programming. The programming did not account for how Women of Color students might respond to and disclose sexual violence in different, nonlinear manners. Queenie shared:

> I think for that skit, thinking back to it, in the orientation, the thing was [the survivor] went to a friend and then cried and then instantly she reported it, you know? There's a very interesting linear message in the story.... For a lot of times, for the stories, of all the MeToo things, a lot of it, for Women of Color, takes a long time to process.

Queenie perceived that Women of Color survivors' processes of disclosure and reporting violence were different from the linear story CU offered in their prevention education.[68] For example, influenced by a history of police brutality against Communities of Color, some Women of Color students are hesitant to report their assault to police.[69] And some Women of Color must remain silent around issues of violence that occur within their racial communities to prevent the perpetuation of racial stereotypes attributed to Men of Color.[70] Yet the institution continued to educate students in a way that portrayed reporting and disclosure as linear processes that were not influenced by racist and sexist structures.

Prevention programs were not only brief and punctured with intersectional failures, but they were also impersonal. Alice recalled her attendance at a large in-person prevention program during her first year at CU:

> There was that orientation presentation I guess, but a lot of people don't take that *seriously* [emphasis added] . . . you're forcing hundreds of people in the same room to watch this movie about it. It's weird. You can't actually talk to people around you about what you're seeing.

Using similar language, Rayn acknowledged how the "Orientation prevention programming was just so surface level because it was so many people." Rayn explained that talking about sex and consent with "800 other people" influenced students "to laugh at the presentation and not take it *seriously* [emphasis added]." Because this was the first time that many students were able to learn and talk about sexual health, some survivors preferred to do so in an intimate setting where they might explore the topic in more depth. Unfortunately, the three institutions did not offer this small group setting for educating new students about sexual violence.

Online prevention programs did not land any better with staff and survivors than the in-person programs. "There honestly wasn't much else that I can remember. . . . I don't think MU did much that was effective," Tessa recalled about the required online training module she "hacked" through during her first few days at MU. At RU, Margaret was also required to complete online training during her first semester on campus. The training provided an overview of, "Is this consensual?" But Margaret and her peers did not take the training seriously. "Everyone thought it was funny because we were freshmen. We were like, 'Haha! They're talking about consent.' So, that was that," Margaret shrugged.

The lack of seriousness many women felt for these programs was influenced by a lack of institutional commitment for, and a lack of institutional importance given to, sexual violence education. Ann an Advocate at the CU Sexual Violence Resource Center (SVRC), stated outright, "The online prevention stuff, that's a joke. Honestly. It really is." Ann explained that institutional leaders did not dedicate enough time, staff, or money to adequate prevention education. It was "a joke" how much the institution expected SVRC to do with the little that they were provided.

Arlene, the Director of CU SVRC, was also not impressed by large group prevention education sessions. "I can't dialogue with 500 people, because there's so much risk that someone's going to say something really problematic. And I don't want any confusion when we walk out of the room about what was okay and what wasn't," she complained.

Arlene was attempting to improve CU's prevention education, but she continued to struggle against the immense organizational constraints of the institution. "The workload here is not humane . . . the workload that we're expecting people to do is cruel," Arlene relayed. Two SVRC Advocates were expected to serve over 800 clients in one year. At the same time, SVRC staff were tasked with educating the entire campus community about sexual violence prevention. With demand far exceeding supply, Arlene believed it was unethical to label the education SVRC currently provided as "prevention education."

SVRC staff pointed to how Title IX guidelines influenced a high institutional demand for prevention education. In the 2011 Dear Colleague Letter, the U.S. Department of Education recommended that institutions of higher education "take proactive measures to prevent sexual harassment and violence."[71] The federal government suggested that schools include education programs in new student orientations and that these programs encompass "a discussion of what constitutes sexual harassment and sexual violence, the school's policies and disciplinary procedures, and the consequences of violating these policies."[72] The Title IX guidelines are contained within a 19-page document. Guidelines concerning sexual violence prevention are outlined in only three paragraphs of this 19-page document. The remainder of the document is dedicated to institutional compliance for reporting and adjudicating cases of sexual violence. The guidelines tend "to focus attention on limiting liability concerns through crime statistics reporting and investigatory practices" while missing an opportunity to be student and survivor-centered.[73]

Ivonne, the Director of MU SVRC, consistently struggled to find sufficient institutional resources to comply with federal guidelines:

> I think one of the challenges is the mandates around education or advocacy and trying to balance this idea with capacity. We have one violence prevention coordinator and 4,000 incoming students. How do you cater advocacy or prevention to 4,000 students when you only have 30 minutes with them at a time? And not being able to go in-depth talking about advocacy or talking about sexual assault in its many forms. . .

Ann the CU SVRC Advocate, also bemoaned the guidelines: "The thing that is challenging with the prevention [education] is the mandate. It's mandated that we talk through consent, and the definitions, and the stats and all of that stuff." Ann continued her critique by exploring how CU's commitment to prevention education conflicted with the federal mandates:

> They expect us to go through all of this stuff. This isn't something, as you know, that you can just go through. In order to have an effective presentation, you have to have a smaller group of people in a discussion. It's a problem that the campus isn't willing to commit.

There was an institutional expectation, influenced by federal guidelines, that SVRC present specific information about sexual violence to thousands of students. But the institutional commitment to meet these expectations often fell short across the three institutions. Institutional leaders did not often provide SVRC with sufficient human and financial resources to effectively educate the campus community. Time was also a scarce resource. Institutional leaders at CU had recently cut SVRC's New Student Orientation timeslot from 45 minutes to 30 minutes. And they now shared this 30-minute time slot with Title IX. On all three campuses, there existed a "lack of institutional priority in abuse prevention," influencing institutional betrayal via "absent, lax, or pro forma policies on training or educating their members on how to recognize and prevent abuse."[74] Educating new students about campus sexual violence, let alone providing these students with comprehensive sexual health education, was not an easy task—but it was certainly a necessary one.

Where Does Intersectionality Take Us?

While writing this chapter, the Florida House of Representatives considered House Bill 1069. The Bill stipulates that sex education can only be taught to youth in grades 6–12. No earlier. If the bill passes, students in grades 5 and below will not have access to sexual health education. For the young adults in grades 6–12 who would have access to sex education, the curriculum would center abstinence-only and socialize students to "the benefits of monogamous heterosexual marriage."[75]

House Bill 1069 is the antithesis of how politicians and institutions should be thinking about sex education. Blocking access to sexual health education and instituting abstinence-only education ensures the permanence and prevalence of campus sexual violence. Comprehensive sexual health education can work to prevent sexual violence.[76] According to SIECUS President, Christine Soyong Harley, "High-quality CSE [comprehensive sexual health education] programs include age, developmentally, and culturally appropriate, science-based, and medically accurate information on a broad set of topics related to sexuality, including human development, relationships, personal skills, sexual behaviors, including abstinence, sexual health, and society and culture."[77] Comprehensive sex education must be allowed in schools so that students of all ages can discover their values around sex, develop skills concerning sexual health, and actively explore new information concerning sex, relationships, and sexual violence.

All sexual health education curricula across the U.S. should be comprehensive, but these must vary according to the needs and demographics of each school district and the communities they serve. School district leaders must shape sex education curricula to fit the identities, backgrounds, and needs of community members. Women of Color survivors, for instance, demonstrated how culture and religion intersected to influence parents' silence around sexual health. The content of some school curricula can address how sex is approached within the home— why might this silence exist? How might students navigate this education with parents and caretakers? Pedagogically, teachers must remain conscious of how this silence might influence students' ability or willingness to learn about sex within the classroom environment. In short, all sexual health curricula must be comprehensive and account for the intersections of students' identities and community needs.

Higher education institutions must view comprehensive sexual health education *as* sexual violence prevention education. Prevention, then, is not just about consent, alcohol awareness, or bystander intervention. Prevention involves teaching students about refusal skills, healthy relationships, bodily autonomy, communication, the social construction of gender roles, sexual behaviors, contraception, human development, and more.[78] Institutional leaders must commit to this comprehensive education. But as institutional staff suggested, institutional commitment is often tied to federal mandates concerning campus sexual violence. Federal guidelines, then, must be more detailed, and more radical, in how campuses educate students concerning the prevention of sexual violence. Federal guidelines must encourage institutions to offer comprehensive sexual health education.

Intersectional sexual health education in college will provide students with multiple spaces and places to discuss and unpack the mis/ education they may have brought with them to college. Institutions must provide space for students to discuss the intergenerational transmission of trauma on both theoretical and personal levels, how religion, culture, and family intersect to inform sexual understandings, and how media, including Bollywood movies, rap music, and telenovelas, might normalize sexual violence.

The delivery methods of comprehensive sexual health education must also shift. One 30-minute large group seminar and/or one online course that students "hack" through is ineffective for preventing campus sexual violence. Colleges and universities must implement both academic and extracurricular courses that offer students sustained engagement with sex education. Although many universities offer human sexuality courses,[79] some students remain unaware, disinterested, or unable to enroll in these courses.[80] Multiple academic departments can offer various academic courses on sexual health, allowing students to explore diverse perspectives and approaches to sexual health, for example, social, gendered, historical, psychological, and medical. Academic departments can cross-list or co-teach these courses with other departments, which will offer students varied experiences within one course, for example, the racialized history of sexuality in the U.S. or the socio-geographical determinants of sexual health. To increase enrollment in these courses, institutions must provide academic credit for course completion, publicize the course widely, and offer multiple sections of each course.[81] As survivors and staff hinted, these courses should be discussion based and enroll a small number of students. Institutions might also offer several online sexual health courses for students who wish to remain anonymous as they discuss what may be a taboo topic.[82]

Institutional staff demonstrated how sexual violence education fell to one, maybe two, offices on campus, that is, SVRC and Title IX, stifling the effectiveness of this education. Sexual health education and sexual violence prevention must be conceptualized as a campus-wide effort. Institutions must require most academic and student affairs units to educate the student body about sexual health. Institutions can encourage these units to program a minimum number of events and workshops concerning sexual health education. Like the academic curriculum, these events can explore various, identity-specific issues concerning sexual health that might pique various students' interests. To involve the campus community and include diverse perspectives, students, community members, and faculty and staff should be involved in planning and leading these programs.

The narratives of the 34 Women of Color survivors made it abundantly clear that comprehensive sex education is a key component to effectively addressing campus sexual violence. It is imperative that policymakers and institutional leaders take note of the effect that comprehensive and intersectional sexual health curriculum—which includes explorations of intergenerational trauma, refusal skills, gendered and racialized stereotypes, bodily autonomy, and consent—can have on the lives of students and on the broader campus environment.

Two

River University

"WHERE NOTHING MAJOR HAPPENS"

"I could totally see myself just being here," Felecia immediately decided after taking a springtime tour of the River University (RU) campus.[1] A few months later, Felecia transferred to RU from her local community college. But the magnetic pull Felecia felt toward River yielded to a months-long struggle to find a sense of belonging on campus. She was searching for a "home away from home," preferably one that reflected her Latina culture. It took Felecia almost six months to find this new home. But she eventually found belonging with the RU Latino Business Organization:

> You know how they have all these tents on the main campus road? One time I saw "Latino Business." And I was like, "Me, business! Me, Latino!" I was like, "Let me go." . . . I went and the first thing that happened was the two young men that I first met, they were really friendly. They were like, "Oh what's your name? We've never seen you around before. Where are you from?" And all this stuff. And just really inviting.

From that first meeting, Felecia was consumed with the Latino Business Organization and its members. She attended nearly every weekly meeting and all the community socials and service events. Felecia was elected to the Board of the organization shortly after her first meeting. The organization quickly became her RU family.

After describing her passion and love for the Latino Business Organization, Felecia paused for a moment and stated, "I feel like I have kind of strayed away from the organization because . . . I had a situation with them that I wasn't very comfortable with. And ever since then it was just never the same." Felecia clarified that it was three separate "situations" with three different Latino men in the organization. But the third situation, which Felecia later labeled as sexual violence, was the most impactful.

Felecia described her relationship with Jake, a fellow Board member, as friendly, "more than just club affiliate[s]." After a night out with members of the organization, Jake offered Felecia a ride home and Felecia happily accepted. On the way home, they stopped at a friend's party and had more to drink. Friends observed that Felecia was not feeling well and encouraged Jake to take her home. Jake walked Felecia back to her residence hall room. "Do you want me to spend the night?" he asked Felecia as they entered her room. "No. I'm fine. I'm here," Felecia replied. After responding "No," Felecia thought Jake would leave. Jake, however, got into bed with Felecia—who was falling asleep—and started kissing her. Jake then sexually assaulted Felecia.

Felecia woke up the next morning a bit disoriented, but quickly surmised, "I guess last night actually did happen." Then fear set in. Jake might tell their friends in the Latino Business Organization that they had consensual sex. Felecia began to worry about her reputation in the organization. Members might think she was "super easy." To avoid embarrassment, and to avoid Jake, Felecia stopped going to meetings and events for several months. But she quickly realized that avoiding the organization meant losing her campus family. After a few months away, Felecia hesitantly returned:

> I went back to the Business Organization and they were like, "Oh, we haven't seen you in a while. Where have you been?" I was like, "You know, just like, things happen." That's what I said. And then when I

first saw [Jake], it was really awkward. And I was just really nervous. Like it's weird. But it took about a solid month for me to process and be okay with being around him.

While Felecia was happy to be back together with organization members, she also felt uncomfortable when Jake was around. She became even more uncomfortable when she learned that Jake had slept with three other women students while they were intoxicated. Felecia saw a pattern to Jake's behavior and began to recognize that the situation may be more severe than she had believed.

But Felecia continued to tell herself "Maybe it's not that bad" and "I could move on with this." Felecia minimized her assault to maintain her RU family. Minimization refers "to the perception that the assault itself and/or the impact of the assault on survivors' mental or physical well-being is not 'serious enough'" to warrant reporting or disclosing.[2] Some of this minimization worked to maintain Felecia's relationship with the Latino Business Organization. But Felecia also minimized her experience because she perceived there was nowhere for her to turn for help. Reporting to the institution or seeking help from campus resources was "pointless" for Felecia. She explained:

> [RU leadership] don't really believe you, or they just dismiss it. . . . I've seen other things on campus. I remember this girl. I think [men students] tried poisoning her or something, and they didn't do much about it. I think there was another sexual assault and they didn't do much about it either. I was just like, "It's pointless."

In talking about why she did not report her assault to the institution, Felecia described the above story about the "girl who got roofied" and how the institution "dismissed" the case.[3] To Felecia, the institution engaged in institutional betrayal by being slow to respond to, or even cover up, some campus crime.[4] Felecia then launched into a litany of other violent incidents—a stabbing and attempted rape, a student death, suicides—that RU leadership consistently "swept under the rug." If the institution swept these severe incidents under the rug, what would they do with Felecia's minor/minimized experience with Jake?

"It's not that big of a deal" or "it did not rise to that severity" or "it wasn't that bad" was a strong pattern throughout Women of Color survivors' narratives at RU. *Individual* minimization, where survivors frame the incident as not "serious enough," or the outcomes of the violence as not bad enough to warrant a report or the use of support services is well documented in research.[5] But RU survivors' individual minimization was often influenced by *institutional* discourses that minimized sexual violence. In other words, individual minimization was directly related to institutional minimization. Felecia described this institutional minimization of violence at RU:

> The institution just probably [tries] keeping it under the rug because they don't want stuff to get out there. . . . The university just doesn't want a bad look on them and that's all they're ever doing. It comes down to big things . . . did you know that somebody recently passed away from here? It took them two days to release a statement on that and I'm like, "Are they trying to cover it up?" I don't know. It just seems like they are always trying to [say], "Nothing major like this happens."

According to Felecia, RU's tagline should be, "River University: Where nothing major happens." In the end, Felecia did not report her assault to the institution. In fact, no Women of Color survivors I spoke with at RU reported their experiences with violence to the institution.[6]

This chapter explores how the institutional minimization of sexual violence at RU often compelled Women of Color survivors to minimize their experiences with violence. The incident must be truly severe—a stranger rape—to be labeled by RU, and subsequently by survivors, as important enough to report. This minimization maintained a campus environment where most instances of sexual violence were normalized, common, or simply did not qualify as sexual violence.[7] Minimization was a key component in maintaining the campus rape culture at RU. Institutional minimization influences the perpetuation of campus sexual violence because it allows campus leaders to say, "Sexual violence does not happen on this campus. It is not a problem on this campus."[8] Minimization makes it difficult for institutions to address sexual violence as a legitimate campus issue.[9]

Rape Culture at River University: An Institution
that "Glosses Over" Sexual Violence

One evening, a week before the end of the semester, an RU student was walking her dog near a cluster of student apartment complexes when she felt someone swiftly approach her from behind. Out of nowhere, a large man appeared and began to attack her. He first attempted to remove her clothing. He then hit her in the head and began to stab her. The student struggled against her attacker who, moments after the attack began, fled on foot. Shortly after, around 10pm, the stabbing was reported to police.

The RU Police Department used an emergency text and email system to alert the campus community to the incident. The first communication stated that the police were actively searching for the suspect. It was best to secure in place. That same night, the Police Department sent two additional alerts to the campus community. The second cancelled the secure in place order, although the suspect had yet to be apprehended. The third and final alert came shortly after the second. The police had swept the campus and did not believe the suspect was on the premises.

The RU Police Department sent a community alert email the next morning. The message summarized the previous three emergency alerts and provided "safety tips" and resources to the community, including "do not walk alone" and "avoid dimly lit areas." Police and news outlets confirmed later that week that the perpetrator had attempted to sexually assault the student while she was walking her dog.

Several Women of Color survivors I spoke with pointed to this attempted assault to demonstrate how the institution "swept issues under the rug" to maintain their reputation as a low crime/high safety institution, or, as one survivor described, a "perfect utopian society institution." Naomi, for example, stated that the institution does not "publicize anything bad that happens. Everything is kind of hush." She continued:

> I know that a lot of things happen. I don't know if you heard, the stabbing happened.... One time was the stabbing and the two [other] times

were break-ins. . . . Those things were maybe like one word touched on in the emails and no parents ever heard about it. Just things like that, to where our campus can actually be pretty dangerous. They don't want anyone to know. I definitely think that things like that, they just don't like to put out there and let people know that things could possibly go wrong.

Moments later, Naomi added her opinion as to why the institution continued to minimize instances of crime, including sexual violence: "If it seems like a very prestigious and safe environment, then [institutional leaders] have reason to be able to make it a more expensive place to live and be around."

Students were not alone in thinking that the institution minimized sexual violence to protect their reputation. When Mollie, the Director of the RU Women's Center, heard that some survivors were concerned about the silence and cover ups around crime on campus, she stated flatly, "[The institutional leaders] have to keep the optics. Because then it tarnishes their number one reputation, it impacts their sales. . . . The students had it right for sure."

Undercounting or minimizing instances of sexual violence on college campuses is an "ordinary practice."[10] Corey Rayburn Yung found that higher education institutions often report higher incidents of sexual violence while being audited by the federal government.[11] These rates are lower before and after federal audits, suggesting that many institutions do not accurately report rates of sexual violence when there is little-to-no oversight. Yung asserted that under-reporting works to maintain an institution's reputation and sustain prospective students' interest in attending the school. Cantalupo agreed, stating, "Potential/current students and their parents are the ultimate audience schools are concerned about when they face the dilemma of encouraging victim reporting but looking like a dangerous campus."[12] Unfortunately, this institutional minimization also works to maintain campus rape culture. Minimization allows "administrators to ignore sexual violence as a problem, resulting in failure to address it as a legitimate problem."[13]

RU, however, did not have a "number one reputation" to protect. The institution did not hold a number one ranking on the *U.S. News and World Report*'s list of best colleges or *Washington Monthly*'s College Guide and Rankings. From what I observed, RU's reputation was connected to the image of an exceptionally safe campus. Too much (publicity around) crime would tarnish this reputation.

Women survivors, and other RU students who were interviewed by local journalists, were extremely disappointed with the lack of institutional communication about the stabbing and attempted assault. At the first alert, some students felt terrified. With the second and third, many were confused. Students relayed that they did not receive adequate information from the institution about this crime. They remained in the dark.

The institutional obscurity around this specific assault was not unique. Daisy explored how the lack of institutional communication about the stabbing was one of many examples of the institution "glossing over" crime and betraying the campus community:

I feel like River University mentions these things happening, but then, after that, they don't really mention anything else. Like, "Oh yeah, this happened." But the school itself, I feel like it glosses over a lot of these things that do happen.

She continued:

Sexual assaults are important for our campus to know, [for] our campus to be aware about. But [institutional leaders] kind of want to gloss over it . . . something like this happens and they don't really talk about it or talk about what's happening.

Daisy grew even more frustrated when she described how the institution had the capacity to clearly communicate with students, but only when advantageous for the institution. Daisy had just received an institutional email congratulating the RU Men's Basketball Team on a recent victory. But "when important things like [sexual violence] happens, there isn't much follow up."

Jennifer, the Interim Director of Fraternity and Sorority Life also mentioned, "I have gotten three emails alone today about how many

Olympians we have." But when it came to student deaths and campus safety issues, Jennifer noticed that institutional communication went "significantly silent." She suggested that some of this silence was due to the high staff turnover the institution had recently seen and due to institutional policies concerning confidentiality. The silence around crime and assault "sets the tone" for how the institution and the institutional community view and respond to sexual violence.[14]

After sharing with the RU Title IX Director that several women survivors perceived that the institution minimized and swept issues—sexual violence, student deaths, a drugging—under the rug, the Director responded, "We just have to eat that perception." Speaking specifically about the RU woman student who was allegedly drugged and raped, the Director shared that she knew "other information, another side of the story" that she would not and could not release to the RU community due to issues surrounding confidentiality. The Title IX Director lamented:

> It sort of looks like the institution doesn't care or is being silent or is brushing things under the rug, but at the same time . . . this is the shittiest part of my job, and how you can't defend yourself. Ever. And it would be wrong to.

Due to institutional and federal policies, the Title IX Director could not offer additional or detailed information to the campus community about these cases. According to the institutional policy on sexual violence and sexual harassment, the university must protect the privacy of individuals involved in a report of sexual misconduct. Title IX Guidelines also stipulate that complainants can request that their identity and identifiable information remain confidential from the alleged perpetrator,[15] let alone the institutional community. These policies aim to protect survivors and alleged perpetrators, but they may also position staff members between a rock (protecting students' identities and information) and a hard place (appearing to hide or minimize violence).

Some other RU staff members acknowledged that federal and institutional sexual violence policies might be more hurtful than helpful.

Gwendolyn, the Director of the RU Cultural Center, referenced two previous incidents where she felt that the institution fell short in their communication. One incident involved a first-year student who recently died of alcohol poisoning and the second, which Felecia also mentioned, involved a woman student who was allegedly drugged and raped by several men students:

> I understand that there are some protections with confidentiality, but there's no follow-up. This thing happened and the institution put out an email. If there was a resolution, or follow-up, or update, those things don't happen [at RU]. I think people feel like they don't get official notice or information from the university unless it's about a college ranking or something like that.

Gwendolyn noted the disjointed institutional communication at RU; messaging around crime and violence was spotty, while communications about rankings or wins were common and clear. Like Jennifer, she perceived that some of this lackluster communication from leadership may relate to "protections with confidentiality." Gwendolyn also relayed that she did not know much about the state of violence on campus. She did, however, know that the institution was required by the U.S. government to publish and disseminate an Annual Security Report. But Gwendolyn could not recall seeing institutional communication about when or how the report was released or where it might be "housed" so that she could view the report. Slightly annoyed that she, too, was uninformed about crime on campus, Gwendolyn concluded, "There's no discourse around it. If just sending an email is the only thing that you're doing, that's not enough. . . . The compliance approach is not good enough."

Gwendolyn hinted at "compliance" with the Clery Act, a federal act that "requires colleges and universities to report campus crime data, support victims of violence, and publicly outline the policies and procedures they have put into place to improve campus safety."[16] The Clery Act is named after Jeanne Clery, who, in 1986, was a first-year student at Lehigh University. During her second semester on campus, Jeanne was raped and murdered in her residence hall room by another student she did not know. Upon learning of her death, Jeanne's parents, Connie and Howard Clery, were stunned. Connie was in disbelief that Jeanne was murdered on a college campus, "the safest place she could have been."[17]

The Clerys put their trust in Lehigh University, but the institution betrayed them—or did it? In 1986, no guidelines or laws existed that required institutions to alert the campus community to crimes that took place on or near campus. There were no legal expectations that institutional leaders would alert the campus community to the "rapidly escalating crime rate" at the institution.[18] Thirty-eight violent crimes occurred on the Lehigh campus the three years prior to Jeanne Clery's rape and murder, yet most students and parents remained unaware of this violence. The lack of transparency surrounding campus crime reinforced, as Howard Clery said, "the medieval myth that colleges are safe."[19] After Jeanne's death, her parents lobbied for state- and federal-level policies that would make colleges and universities safer, more transparent environments for students. In 1990, the Clerys' lobbying resulted in the passing of the federal Crime Awareness and Campus Security Act, now known as the Jeanne Clery Act.

Under Clery, institutional leaders are asked to evaluate any "serious or ongoing threat" to the institution and communicate this threat, via a timely warning, to students and staff. In speaking about the stabbing near campus, Christine stated bluntly, "I was shocked that [the institution] even responded because usually they don't respond to things that aren't serious. . . . There's a lot of things that happen on campus, and always, you see it swept [under the rug]." Christine was stunned that institutional leaders viewed the incident—a stabbing and attempted assault—as serious enough to publicly acknowledge and warn students of a threat. But it was not necessarily the institution's decision to alert the campus community about the crime. Institutions must issue a timely warning for any Clery Act crime that occurs on or near campus and is "reported to campus security authorities or local police agencies" and/or is "considered by the institution to represent a serious or continuing threat to students and employees."[20] The stabbing and attempted assault was first reported to the RU Police

Department: the institution was legally obligated to issue a timely warning to the campus community.

But issuing timely warnings for crime "considered by the institution to represent a serious or continuing threat" is less objective.[21] The Clery Center acknowledges this complexity, stating, "institutions are constantly weighing the needs of individuals versus the needs of the overall community when making decisions about how and when to issue such warnings."[22] This complexity is evidenced in the many institutions that continue to misunderstand and misinterpret Clery policy every year, contributing to their noncompliance.[23]

In 2019, for example, the U.S. Department of Education required Michigan State University to pay a $4.5 million fine for Clery noncompliance. Months later, the Department charged the University of North Carolina, Chapel Hill with $1.5 million in fines for noncompliance. Shortly after, the University of California, Berkeley was required to pay $2.35 million for violating Clery Act policy.[24] While several areas of Clery noncompliance were identified at each school, all three of these institutions failed to issue timely warnings in accordance with federal regulations.[25] If RU was not complying with Clery, they would, unfortunately, not be the first. This noncompliance may occur through institutional acts of omission, that is, misinterpretation of Clery policy. Yet noncompliance through acts of commission remains a possibility, particularly because there has been little governmental oversight or incentive to comply with Clery.[26]

At RU, most women survivors and some staff believed there was "significant silence" around sexual violence, and crime in general. Crime was minimized and swept under the rug unless it was severe enough—attempted assault, at knifepoint, perpetrated by a stranger—to alert or discuss with the campus community. This institutional minimization of sexual violence is a form of institutional betrayal; it maintains a false sense of safety on campus and creates a narrative that severe sexual violence is the only form of sexual violence that occurs at RU.[27] Subsequently, institutional minimization upholds campus rape culture by allowing campus leaders to deny that sexual violence is an issue that must be addressed and prevented.[28]

"What Happened to Me Wasn't Extreme": The River University Scale of Severity and Reportability

The institutional minimization of sexual violence constructed an "unspoken spectrum of sexual violence" that positions stranger rape, or when a stranger attacks a victim with physical force, as the only real form of sexual violence.[29] The spectrum operated like a scale at RU. Women survivors measured their experiences with sexual violence on this scale to help them decide the severity and, subsequently, the reportability of the experience.

Both staff and survivors acknowledged the presence of the scale of severity at RU. "There's what the campus says [about campus crime] and then there's a bunch of things that I think go unreported because they don't, maybe, elevate to that *scale* [emphasis added]," Gwendolyn, the Director of the Cultural Center, suggested. It was unclear who Gwendolyn believed was underreporting—institutional leaders, students, or both. But it was clear that she perceived that RU operated on a scale that elevated extreme incidents to a serious, reportable level, while incidents that lacked severity might be minimized and go "unreported."

Most Women of Color survivors at RU used this scale to decide if they should report their experiences with violence. Anastasia, for example, recalled how she made her decision to not report assault:

> I know River University. It's a calm environment. Not a lot happens. It's either an extreme, a medium, or [low]. . . . I feel like we're in between the medium and the low. So, yeah, people go through things, but they're not extreme. So maybe people feel like . . . "I wasn't raped. I was still sexually assaulted. But I shouldn't report." Because it was not as extreme as someone who actually has been through a lot.

According to Anastasia, students at RU have medium to low experiences with sexual violence, but extreme experiences, such as rape, were rare at RU. If someone *were* to experience an extreme experience, such as rape, it would warrant reporting. All other (medium-to-low) incidents of sexual violence did not warrant reporting.

Survivors at RU, such as Anastasia, often perceived that their experience was less severe because the assault did not align with "the stereotype of a real rape," that is, committed by a stranger, involving a struggle, resulting in injuries.[30] Understandings of stranger rape as the only real form of violence are entrenched in racist and sexist historical understandings of rape.[31] Historically, the U.S. legal system defined rape as an illegal act only if physical force was used and the survivor did not provide consent.[32] This definition, and its use in criminal courts, is intertwined with classed and racialized understandings of "consent and character."[33] Many Women of Color are viewed by the courts as more likely to consent than white women, that is, they are seen as more promiscuous than white women.[34] And white men's sexual desirability and trustworthiness signifies that women almost always consent to sex with white men. Therefore, "even in modern cultural imaginaries, the paradigmatic 'real rape' involves the violent vaginal penetration of a chaste, unmarried, wealthy, cisgender, heterosexual, white woman by a stranger, typically portrayed as a Black man."[35]

When survivors view their assault as less severe they are often less likely to seek help for or report the assault.[36] Therefore, the RU scale of severity dissuaded many survivors from recognizing their experiences as assault and, subsequently, from reporting these experiences.[37] Robin, the SVRC Advocate, confirmed this observation, suggesting, "Students will have experiences and not recognize it's something they can report if they wanted. They don't define it as, 'Oh. This was sexual assault.' It's either minimized or, I don't know?"

Anastasia did not report her assault to the institution. She *did*, however, experience rape—an extreme on the RU scale of severity. During her first semester on campus, Anastasia was hanging out with her roommate and her roommate's boyfriend, Daniel. At one point in the night, Anastasia left the residence hall room to give her roommate and Daniel "their time." When Anastasia returned, Daniel sexually assaulted her. Anastasia did not report her assault because she believed, "What happened to me wasn't extreme. People have gone through worse. You know?"

Although Anastasia first described how rape was an "extreme" that warranted reporting, she did not report her rape because it was not "extreme" enough.[38] It was possible that Anastasia was not educated on the definition of rape. She did not know that what she had experienced was, in fact, rape and, therefore, a reportable offense according to the RU scale of severity. Anastasia may have minimized the assault because it did not involve forced vaginal penetration and the perpetrator was an acquaintance, not a stranger. Within the RU environment, these possibilities were probable; RU often failed to communicate with and educate students about the various ways, beyond stranger rape, that sexual violence might occur on the college campus.

"No One Would Ever Talk About That Here": Re/Constructing the Scale of Severity and Reportability at RU

Up until this point, we've observed how the scale of severity and reportability was constructed by the institutional minimization of campus sexual violence, which maintained a false sense of safety on campus. This minimization perpetuated the belief that severe sexual violence is the only sexual violence that exists, and therefore warrants reporting, at RU.[39] But there was one additional, powerful way that the scale of severity and reportability was constructed and maintained at RU—through institutional education on campus sexual violence. Women of Color survivors often demonstrated how this education perpetuated the myth of stranger rape as the only valid and reportable form of sexual violence.

Jane, for instance, called out RU administrators for failing to educate students on more "nuanced" forms of sexual violence—beyond stranger rape:

> [The institution] never, ever said anything, even to this day. I don't remember any space in terms of classroom or educational, institutionalized space where they talk about, "What if it happens from someone you love, someone like a partner, domestic partner kind of thing [perpetrates sexual assault]?" It was always talked about like, "Oh some random stranger is going to come for you." Not that that doesn't

happen. But I think it's more often the case, "Well these people who are in your life, like your close network kind of thing." How do you deal with that? And those nuances?

Jane's suspicions were correct. Ninety percent of campus sexual violence occurs between acquaintances and involves multiple other forms of non-penetrative sexual contact.[40] Yet the institution continued to push discourse that supported the "random stranger" rape narrative. By focusing on only stranger rape, all other forms of sexual violence that occurred at RU, for example, groping, acquaintance rape, coercion, were not often talked about or seen as legitimate forms of violence. In constructing this narrative, RU was engaging in institutional betrayal by misrepresenting sexual violence in manners that "serve to invalidate victims and fail to educate consumers."[41]

Jane was skeptical of the stranger rape discourse that permeated RU's sexual violence education. What about other forms of sexual violence? Do they not happen on campus? Do they not matter? Jane was particularly concerned about the answers to these questions because her experience with sexual violence, like all other women survivors' experiences at RU, was not stranger rape and therefore did not qualify as a reportable form of sexual violence on the RU scale of severity.

Jane met Justin through an RU mentoring program that aimed to educate other RU students on issues of diversity and social justice. Jane and Justin became immediate friends. Jane was drawn to Justin because he espoused strong values for social justice, equity, and diversity. After several months of friendship, Jane and Justin began a romantic relationship. Jane quickly relayed to me that the relationship was unhealthy. "At first it was a lot of guilt tripping, like emotional trauma and abuse. And after that it was, guilting me into having sex with him and stuff," Jane began to describe the beginning of the end of her relationship with Justin.

Jane hesitated to label what happened between Justin and her as "rape." She explained, "It's not that serious. I don't want to make it serious. For me, I wouldn't call my instance a rape. I still hesitate calling it 'sexual assault' because I feel more accurately it's 'non-consensual sex.'"

Jane's hesitancy to label her experience as rape or sexual assault is, unfortunately, unsurprising. From what she could recall, RU's sexual
violence education covered only stranger rape, not intimate partner
violence. Jane may have minimized her experiences with intimate partner violence because her institution was mis/communicating to her
that this form of violence was not sexual violence.

In our second conversation together, Jane reiterated, "I didn't have
a right to claim, 'Oh, this is a sexual assault.'" Instead, she settled on,
"Oh, he was just a really shitty person." Jane knew she was using euphe-
misms to help her minimize her experience with Jake. But Jane's euphe-
misms did not capture her experience. "It was a lot more intense than
that," she murmured.

"What do you mean by, 'I might not have a right or I didn't have a
right [to claim sexual assault]?'" I asked.[42] Without missing a beat, Jane
responded that her definition of sexual assault involved "strangers,
people jump at you at night kind of stuff." But since she did not experience stranger rape, she did not experience sexual assault. "I was like,
'Oh, well that didn't happen to me, it was just a miscommunication. . . .
That's kind of what I told myself. It wasn't that bad. Don't make it a big
deal." On the institutional spectrum of severity, Jane's assault was not a
big deal. She was not attacked by a stranger—the most severe, valid, and
reportable form of violence on the RU campus.

Jane was frustrated with the inadequacy of her sexual violence prevention education, suggesting that the institution "reconstructs how
they approach sexual assault, in terms of not leaning on those comments of 'make sure you don't walk home alone.'"[43] Jane wanted variation in the institutional education, beyond the stranger rape scenario,
of how sexual violence might happen on the college campus. If students
saw more possibilities for how, when, where, and between whom sexual
violence can happen, then they may be more able or willing to identify
and report these experiences as assault.

Carrie also wanted to see more diversity within sexual violence
education at RU. She first pointed out how institutional leaders "don't
make [sexual violence] as urgent as it should be. And so, people just
don't know too much about [sexual violence] because they don't hear

a lot about it. . . . Having the lack of representation in that doesn't help, either." Wanting clarity on her statement, I asked Carrie, "What do you mean by representation?"

"Representation, as in the sense of different ways people are assaulted," Carrie instantly answered. She wanted to see and learn the various ways that sexual violence can happen, beyond "the stranger rape," as she described it. She continued, "You hardly see anything where the person is being talked into it and coerced. You don't really see that." More diverse representations of sexual violence within prevention education might disrupt the narrow scale of severity that was operating at RU. On this current spectrum, Carrie was unwilling, if not unable, to define and report her experience as sexual violence.

"That's kind of the main reason why I didn't speak about it a lot," said Carrie, beginning to explore why she did not report her assault to the institution. She continued, "I was just like, 'Nobody's going to believe that.' It's not the horror story that maybe some other people have experienced, where it's like, 'Oh, the person, their clothes were ripped off of them.'" Continuing, Carrie began to describe the recent incident that occurred near campus: "A girl was assaulted. She was walking her dog and someone stabbed her from behind and stuff." This, of course, was not the first time I was hearing about this incident. I lifted my eyebrow with interest, hoping Carrie would continue without interruption. She continued:

> [Institutional leaders and campus police] are going to definitely believe
> that she was hurt because she was stabbed and everything. But if it was
> me and it was like, "Oh, well, someone was in your dorm room and y'all
> were friends before. Do we really believe that? You sure it wasn't you
> just regretting it?"

During her first year at RU, Carrie was watching YouTube with a friend in his residence hall room when he began to force Carrie to engage in sexual activities. Reporting was never an option for Carrie because she did not view the experience as assault. It was not a "horror story." It did not involve a stabbing, a stranger, or her clothes being ripped off. Being assaulted by an acquaintance, someone you were hanging out with, was not a reportable offense. It was minimized by the institution. Carrie, in turn, minimized, the severity of the assault.

It was not just prevention education that perpetuated the prevalence of the stranger rape narrative that maintained the scale of severity and reportability at RU. The institutional education concerning response to sexual violence was also often problematic. Naomi had recently spent a weekend visiting her best friend at another public institution in the same state as RU. While visiting the institution, Naomi and her friends went to a party at a fraternity house. Prior to entering the home, a fraternity member provided the women with information about consent and about institutional resources for sexual violence. Naomi acknowledged that the doorway chat with the fraternity member was to "cover [the fraternity's] butts," but was also "so that we know if something happens, that we should [and] can talk to someone." Naomi returned to the present moment and stated, "There's nothing like that at River."

With a sarcastic tone, Naomi speculated that there was no need to talk about sexual violence resources at RU because the institutional environment is "very calm and there's no way [sexual violence] could happen because we're so anti-Greek. We're not crazy." Naomi continued:

> After that party we were just laughing. We were like, "This is so nice."
> ... We thought, "I'm glad that [the fraternity] brought this up, because at least someone is talking about it." No one would ever talk about that [at River]. No one. Ever. They would never want to say, "Oh, if something happens, please report it." They would just be like, "You got too drunk. You hooked up with someone. You fell. You were a DAB [dumb ass bitch]."

RU's calm, not-a-party-school environment seemingly precluded its students from experiencing sexual violence. Because the environment supposedly disallowed for assault, it was unnecessary to educate or talk with students about sexual violence. It was also unnecessary to offer students options for reporting. If students do not report their assault, RU remains "not crazy." If someone *were* to report their assault, institutional leaders might minimize the incident *for* the survivor: it was just a hook-up gone wrong. This minimization has "a direct silencing effect (e.g., victims withdraw complaints) but [can] also feed back into the institutional culture to discourage future reports."[44] Subsequently, institutional and individual minimization perpetuates campus rape culture by allowing administrators to deny or ignore that sexual violence is an issue that must be addressed on campus.[45]

Where Does Intersectionality Take Us?

"First of all, things need to be talked about more," Daisy succinctly responded to my question "What can the institution do to better address campus sexual violence and support you, a Woman of Color survivor?" Moments later, Daisy added, "There needs to be more support and more openness to talk about these issues. . . . We just want awareness about these things that happen." Women of Color survivors and several staff were eager for more information about preventing and responding to sexual violence on campus. They also desired more information about the sexual violence that occurred at RU, but they perceived was often swept under the rug.

Survivors had several ideas for how their institution might speak "more publicly," as Naomi suggested, about sexual violence. Naomi advocated for RU leaders to start talking about sexual violence in their meetings with one another. These leaders should invite students into the meetings to have conversations about sexual violence on campus. These conversations would allow students to gain more information about the state of sexual violence at RU. They would also allow leaders to better understand the prevalence and realities of sexual violence on campus for students.

Naomi's recommendation for institutional improvement aligned with Robin, the RU SVRC Advocate's suggestion that institutional leaders hold more town halls, where they communicate to RU students, "Hey, we wish we could tell you that, but XYZ are the reasons we cannot. How can we work around that?" Instead of their current communication of, "We just can't tell you. That's what it is." Survivors and staff were asking for more transparency that sexual violence, beyond just stranger rape, occurred on campus.

Naomi also suggested that the institution put more information about sexual violence in the campus newsletter. The RU newsletter was delivered to subscribers daily and contained information on events, news, and education happening at RU and the surrounding community. Felecia also mentioned the utility of the RU newsletter in improving institutional communication around sexual violence. She suggested that the institution use the newsletter to convey to students, "We support you through this." Felecia continued:

> I know it takes a lot for them to say things. So, that would be a big way to [support] me. I'd be like, "Oh wow." That's actually like they're taking it serious because they're addressing it to every single student around here with their newsletters.

The newsletter could include information on allegations of campus sexual violence, sexual violence programing and education, the definition of sexual violence, and information about Clery and the Annual Security Report. For Felecia, the newsletter was a place to remind students of the available resources concerning sexual violence. Institutional leaders could write: "Oh, you can go to these places, and we have People of Color, women, men, whatever you feel comfortable talking to. And they're there for you." This messaging and support would convey to students that the institution took sexual violence seriously—that it would not minimize this violence.

Jane offered another suggestion for how the institution might take sexual violence "seriously." "Treat sexual assault as seriously as you do plagiarism," she quipped. Jane perceived that the institution treated plagiarism as a more serious crime than sexual violence. Students had to complete several workshops on plagiarism. Plagiarism policies were on almost all course syllabi. Faculty went over the definition of and recourses for plagiarism at the start of each course, every semester. The institution was a "hardass" about plagiarism but not about sexual violence. To take sexual violence as seriously as plagiarism, faculty and instructors must talk about sexual violence at the start of every semester and place sexual violence resources and policies on course syllabi.

The institution must respond to allegations of sexual violence in the same way they do plagiarism—with consequences.

Finally, institutional leaders must talk candidly about sexual violence in manners that demonstrate the various ways that this violence can occur. Margaret suggested:

> Maybe if they gave us more examples. . . . I feel like they should talk more about alcohol being involved. Or if it's just not a stranger, but someone you're not dating. Maybe just more examples that specifically pertain to us might've hit home a little closer because we've all been there, you know?

Margaret wanted prevention programs that explore the realities of acquaintance rape, which accounts for approximately 90% of campus sexual violence.[46] She also suggested that the institution provide more information on alcohol-involved sexual violence.[47] Less focus should be dedicated to stranger rape, including a hyper-focus on self-defense, not walking home alone, and use of the campus' emergency blue light system. Prevention and education programs must spend time on the definition of sexual violence, stressing the various ways that this violence can occur.

Women of Color survivors were imploring their institution to have institutional courage; to talk candidly about violence, to be more transparent and forthcoming about crime on campus, to offer better, more relevant education around prevention and response, and to not minimize the realities of sexual violence on campus.

Three

Mountain University

"GUYS JUST FEEL LIKE THEY CAN DOMINATE"

Katrina's story of campus sexual violence revolved around the Brotherhood, an unofficial club for Black men students at MU. The men involved in the Brotherhood were also often involved in the MU Black Student Union. While MU recognized the Black Student Union as an official student organization, they did not recognize the Brotherhood as a formal student organization. Regardless of its unofficial status, the Brotherhood was well-known within the MU peer environment.

According to Katrina, it is common knowledge that the men in the Brotherhood "regularly finesse girls for sex." They are "known for picking on freshman girls . . . they will try to sleep with you. If you do sleep with them consensually, you end up on 'The List.'" After a woman joins The List, she is no longer important to the Brotherhood. "You're used meat," Katrina declared. But the number of names on The List remained important. Brotherhood members consistently updated and shared The List with one another to brag about their sexual conquests on campus.

Katrina's first encounter with members of the Brotherhood occurred the second semester of her first year at MU. In January, four different men in the Brotherhood were simultaneously pursuing Katrina. She described their pursuits as "relentless."

> No matter if I told them to stop talking to me or leave me alone, to go away, they'd come back the next time they see me. They would make kissy faces at me, rub their hands on my butt when I walk by, stay in my Instagram DMs.

The harassment from the Brotherhood influenced how Katrina navigated the campus environment that winter. She began to avoid the dining halls, where Brotherhood members were notorious for hitting on first-year women students. Katrina did not hang out in her residence hall lobby and avoided going to campus parties. Outside of her cramped dorm room, she felt "targeted" by the Brotherhood.

After a few months of dodging these men, Katrina grew tired of avoiding spaces on campus that were important for her social life. In March, she decided she was done with hiding from the Brotherhood. With her mind made up, Katrina went to an off-campus party. She knew all the members in the unofficial club and made sure to steer clear of them that night. Once at the party, Katrina noticed a man. And the man noticed her. She'd never seen him before, but Katrina knew he was not a member of the Brotherhood. They began to dance. His name was Samuel. They immediately hit it off. A few hours after meeting, Katrina and Samuel walked outside to the front porch for fresh air. Once outside, Samuel noticed the chilly March weather. "We can keep talking in the car," he suggested.

"Okay. When you get in the car, make sure you lay down the ground rules. If he tries to do something, you just make sure he knows you're not about it," Katrina thought to herself as she walked with Samuel to his car. The first ten minutes in the car were okay. There was lively conversation and music playing in the background. But then, Samuel quickly and forcefully grabbed the back of Katrina's neck and shoved her head into his crotch. Katrina immediately pulled back and screamed at Samuel, "What are you doing?" Samuel responded, "No, no. Come on, come on." He grabbed her neck again and slammed her head into his crotch. Katrina yelled, "NO!" as Samuel attempted to control her head.

Katrina pulled away and stated flatly, "I'm not about that. I'm gonna go back to the party." Samuel asked why they couldn't just get into the backseat and have sex. Katrina reiterated that she had only wanted to talk. She was going back to the party.

Later that night, Katrina learned that Samuel was in fact a member of the Brotherhood that she had so strategically attempted to avoid the past few months. She felt immense guilt and shame. "I was so crushed that I messed up," Katrina sighed, blaming herself for the assault. But then, Katrina challenged this internalized victim blaming. "But, if a girl wants to wear a skirt to a party, that's not an invitation. And if she says, 'No,' she says 'No.'" Katrina stated that her encounter with sexual violence at MU was not her fault—it did not occur because of her behaviors or her attire. Instead, rape culture on the MU campus existed because men students at the institution were playing a game of "Who has a bigger dick? [A game of] how many girls, how many bodies, he can get and then you look like 'The Man.'"

Katrina was not the first or the last Woman of Color survivor to describe how campus rape culture at MU revolved around men students engaging in competition, domination, heterosexual promiscuity, and sexual aggression so that they are seen as real men or "The Man." This is toxic masculinity, or the "problematic attitudes and behaviors associated with hegemonic forms of masculinity that cisgender men are socialized into" to fit into societal and community expectations for what it means to be a man.[1] It is not men or masculinity that are inherently toxic, but rather the gendered constructs that men are socialized to perform to be labeled as "real men."[2] To think of masculinity as either healthy or toxic is a false binary framing of masculinity.[3] Masculinity is fluid in nature, and toxic masculinity is one of several possible gender expressions that one can engage.[4]

A strong current of toxic masculinity vibrated throughout the MU peer environment. The Brotherhood, and the Brotherhood's List, was just one example of how MU students engaged in toxic masculinity, which contributed to the campus rape culture. Women of Color survivors at MU whom I spoke with placed a great amount of responsibility on their peers to intervene in these displays of toxic masculinity.

Because MU was a community-oriented campus, students often looked to their peers to engage in bystander intervention, such as interrupting the telling of rape jokes or intervening in situations that could lead to sexual violence.[5]

Unfortunately, peers did not always intervene before assault (primary bystander intervention) or during assault (secondary bystander intervention), which may have maintained toxic masculinity and campus rape culture. But survivors *did* perceive peers to engage in bystander intervention post-assault (tertiary bystander intervention),[6] influencing many Women of Color survivors' decision to formally report their experiences with sexual violence to the institution. For instance, during her second year at MU, Katrina disclosed to a friend a second experience with assault perpetrated by an MU man student (not in the Brotherhood). "There's no guarantee that he won't do it again. There's no guarantee that he hasn't done it before," the friend responded, encouraging Katrina to contact MU Title IX. That same day, Katrina reached out to Title IX to explore her options. Existing scholarship suggests that negative reactions to disclosure can act as a barrier to survivors' reporting and psychological well-being.[7] But I observed a contrasting phenomenon at MU. Peers' positive reactions to informal disclosures often encouraged Women of Color survivors to seek help post-assault.

Eight women survivors visited the MU SVRC and five of those eight survivors reported their assault to the institution, that is, MU Title IX and/or MU Campus Police.[8] Peers were one of the main reasons that survivors were connected to or reported to these resources. In other words, peers often displayed individual courage within their institution by listening to and supportively responding to survivors' disclosures post-assault.[9] When survivors visited and used SVRC, often at the encouragement of their peers, Women of Color frequently experienced additional institutional courage enacted by individual staff and institutional structures.[10] This courage often worked toward the disruption of toxic masculinity and rape culture on campus.

This chapter, like the chapter before and the chapter after, explores institutional betrayal on the college campus. But this chapter, and the

MU environment, demonstrate moments and examples of institutional courage—the antidote to institutional betrayal.[11] Women of Color survivors' stories reveal how institutional betrayal and institutional courage can occur on an individual level, wherein individuals within institutions display courage and betrayal. These stories also demonstrate how institutional betrayal and institutional courage can co-exist on one campus to influence the maintenance and the deconstruction of toxic masculinity and campus rape culture.

Rape Culture at Mountain University: "Whoever Can Have Sex with the Most Girls is the Hottest"

On September 25, 2017, actor, comedian, and writer Aziz Ansari and a 23-year-old Brooklyn woman, Grace (pseudonym), went out together on a dinner date. After dinner, the pair returned to Ansari's apartment and the following, according to Grace, occurred:

> They kissed. He performed oral sex on her. He asked her to do the same. She briefly did. He was eager to have sex. She says she would try to move away from him and used, quote, "verbal and non-verbal cues" to show she was uncomfortable with the situation. Yet he kept trying. She eventually says she's going to call a car. He gets her an Uber, and she leaves. And she feels violated.[12]

The next day, Grace and Ansari exchanged text messages. Grace stated, "I just want to take this moment to make you aware of [your] behavior and how uneasy it made me."[13] Ansari responded, "Clearly, I misread things in the moment and I'm truly sorry."[14] Some view this now very public incident as a misunderstanding between two consenting adults, while others assert that Ansari perpetrated sexual violence.[15] Some have connected Ansari's behavior that night to toxic masculinity; men, such as Ansari, are socialized to "be assertive, take charge in the mating and seduction ritual. The message was clear: Make the first move, be persistent, don't back down. All of this . . . was part of toxic masculinity."[16]

Several Women of Color survivors spoke about Grace's encounter with Ansari in relation to the MU campus rape culture. Tessa, for example, connected the "Aziz Ansari thing" to her observations of toxic masculinity at MU:

> I think the whole Aziz Ansari thing is very reflective of things that I see happen on this campus . . . just the way [men] can be so desensitized to other people's experiences and feelings. If you're doing something that intimate, there's just no excuse for having those blinders on. I definitely see that parallel [here]. . . . I just feel like a lot of guys just feel like they can dominate. It's their responsibility to initiate. It's their responsibility to take it to there.

An inability to read, or care about women's feelings stems from many men's myopia to dominate women, to take charge of the sexual situation. Tessa perceived that this socialization and mentality influenced men at MU to view heterosexual sex as their "own and not a shared experience."

Noelle explored in more depth what toxic masculinity looked like on campus and how it influenced rape culture at MU. "You've got to party really hard, drink like a champ, and then also sleep with all these girls, get all these girls. Whoever can have sex with the most girls is the hottest." Seconds later, Noelle clarified that experimenting or having sex with a lot of people was part of the college experience. But for many men at MU, sex was a "trophy." "You need to go and get [sex]. It's not something that you can just expect someone to consent to. You go and you take it," Noelle stated.

Noelle asserted that the men who win the trophy become "the hottest" men on campus. Jasmine also drew a line between men students' attractiveness, their toxic behaviors, and rape culture at MU. "I'm not saying that everybody that sexually assaults is ugly. But you see other guys getting girls and ['ugly' guys] are just like, 'Well, I'm going to get it on my own terms.'" Jasmine continued:

> Men just get frustrated. Especially how men [to other men] are just like, "Oh well, you're probably still a virgin," type of thing. You know? It's seen as something you should be embarrassed about, especially with men. I just think it's the culture that leads them there.

The "culture" that Jasmine referenced is a culture of toxic masculinity, wherein men compete in the game of masculinity to receive a trophy of recognition; their trophy allows them to be seen as attractive, real men.[17] Men often engaged in the game regardless of women's consent. Some Women of Color survivors expressed that it was U.S. society, not necessarily MU, that was at fault for men students' games of toxic masculinity. Noelle, for instance, didn't think the institution could do much to disrupt toxic masculinity because "that's how society is conditioned to think."

In a 2019 article, *The Problem with a Fight Against Toxic Masculinity*, Criminology professor Michael Salter explained why men might feel they need to "take" sex on their "own terms." Salter explained, "Falling short can make boys and men insecure and anxious, which might prompt them to use force in order to feel, and be seen as, dominant and in control."[18] Being a virgin, not having enough sexual partners—this is viewed as falling short of manhood in a culture steeped in toxic masculinity. Salter cautioned us from seeing toxic masculinity as an individual behavior or issue. Instead, "it comes from these men's social and political settings, the particularities of which set them up for inner conflicts over social expectations and male entitlement."[19]

Although some Women of Color survivors acknowledged that toxic masculinity was a societal issue that was bigger than the individual, they simultaneously viewed the disruption of toxic masculinity as an interpersonal, peer-level issue. The onus placed on peers to disrupt toxic masculinity often stemmed from the community-oriented campus.[20] As Joy, the SVRC Prevention Educator stated, the MU student body is "an incredible group of students that are community based . . . they're very community minded." Influenced by this community mindedness, survivors expressed that it was the community's responsibility to disrupt toxic masculinity. Specifically, Women of Color survivors expected their peers to engage in bystander intervention—a tactic that can be used to disrupt toxic masculinity and campus rape cultures.[21]

Bystander intervention frames sexual violence as a community issue, in which everyone and anyone can disrupt violence before it happens.[22] Since the MU environment was community-centered, it made sense why survivors might expect their peers to engage this community-level intervention. At MU, all new students were required to complete a training about bystander intervention through the new student prevention programming. As mentioned, bystander intervention can take place on three different levels: primary (prior to assault), secondary (during the assault), and tertiary (after the assault).[23] It is important to differentiate between the levels of intervention because each may present a different amount of risk, ranging from high-risk situations, such as saying something to a student who is leading an intoxicated student into a bedroom, to low-risk situations, such as making a comment to a student who told a rape joke.[24] Subsequently, students may be differently able and willing to engage in each level of intervention at any one time.

While survivors' expectations were high for peers to engage in bystander intervention at MU, survivors also perceived that peers did not often engage primary and secondary interventions. Many peers, however, *did* engage tertiary intervention. Ananya described one experience where peers did not intervene in an incident that might lead to sexual violence at an off-campus party (secondary interventions):

> I've been to parties where I wish I didn't see the things that I saw. I saw students just really not in a good place and by themselves in a corner, and there was no one helping them. You just think to yourself, "How can this happen? How is nobody stopping and helping this individual?"

Ananya was hinting at how students' drug and alcohol use may position them in "not a good place" when it came to preventing sexual violence. To be clear, drugs and alcohol are not the root cause of sexual violence, but these substances often make it easier for perpetrators to dominate, control, and "take" other's bodies without consent.[25] Although Ananya expressed her disbelief that peers did not intervene in potentially risky situations at parties, *she* herself did not mention intervening in these situations. Ananya's contradiction suggests that intervening as a bystander may be easier said than done. There are many reasons why students might hesitate to engage bystander intervention. Some students feel that they lack the necessary education and skills to intervene,[26] while others may be wary of disrupting the toxic masculinity that structures social life and social status on campus.[27] Therefore, there often existed larger societal and institutional structures, such as the pervasiveness of toxic masculinity and a lack of prevention education, that dis/allowed for peers' engagement in bystander intervention.

Peers also rarely intervened in ideas and beliefs that supported toxic masculinity and sexual violence (primary intervention). Tessa was particularly concerned with how the telling of rape jokes was normalized within the campus peer environment:

> I just think that we need more people who, even if you know in the back of your head that something's wrong, why don't you say something about it? Even if it's just a joke. Like rape jokes and stuff like that. Why don't you just say, "That's not funny"? That really normalizes it.

Rape jokes reinforce toxic masculinity and normalize rape culture.[28] Pérez and Greene explained, "The rhetorical function of patriarchal rape jokes is ostensibly to convince the audience of the idea that rape, a brutal and violent act, can be funny, entertaining and unserious."[29] Responding to a rape joke is a political act.[30] Yet if a man intervenes in the telling of a rape joke, other men may perceive that he is challenging toxic masculinity and, subsequently, these men may label the man as feminine, less masculine, not a real man.[31]

Many peers *did* engage in tertiary intervention. Samantha explained "cancel culture" by referencing an episode of Sunday Gems, a podcast hosted by the singer/songwriter Kehlani and her best friend Reyna:

> Kehlani just taught me this yesterday. She mentioned something called "cancel culture" and her and Reyna were going back and forth about it. It's like, say I tell someone that there is this guy. I don't have to say he sexually assaulted me, but saying someone made me feel very uncomfortable and I feel very unsafe around them. Then that friend that I told, they would immediately be like, "Okay, he's done, he's canceled, we're done. I won't ever speak to him again. Thank you for telling me so now I know that he did that to you and he makes you feel unsafe."

Cancelling a person, place, or thing is "a last-dich appeal for justice."[32] Individuals and groups collectively cancel culture as a final effort to disrupt systemic ideas and behaviors, such as toxic masculinity, that organizations and institutions, such as colleges and universities, have failed to disrupt.[33] Cancel culture, then, may have offered MU students a direct response to the failure of MU and society to disrupt toxic masculinity.

The concept of cancel culture has its roots in Black vernacular, queer Communities of Color, and Black Twitter. Recently, however, "social elites" have co-opted cancel culture, turning it into a tool used for public shaming, expressing intolerance for opposing viewpoints, and modern day "witch hunting."[34] Cancel culture, at its (Black) roots, "is an expression of agency, a choice to withdraw one's attention from someone or something whose values, (in)action, or speech are so offensive, one no longer wishes to grace them with their presence, time, and money."[35]

Samantha connected her newfound understanding of cancel culture to her experience with sexual violence, toxic masculinity, and the MU peer environment:

> I feel like we lack cancel culture. . . . I encountered people who were like, "Okay, we're done. I'm never gonna talk to him again now that I know he's trash." Then there were the other boys in [perpetrator's] frat who found out about the situation, but they were okay with it and they still talked about him, hung out with him and stuff.

Samantha's story captures the duality of tertiary intervention at MU. Several MU students did, in fact, engage in tertiary intervention and cancel toxic masculinity on campus. For example, Samantha disclosed her assault to her sorority sister who immediately connected Samantha with campus sexual violence resources. The sorority sister's support influenced Samantha's decision to eventually report her assault to the institution.

But some students did not fully engage in tertiary intervention, which may have upheld toxic masculinity. Samantha also disclosed to one of her best friends at MU, Jason. Jason was in the same fraternity as the man who sexually assaulted Samantha. Once Samantha decided to report her assault to MU Title IX, Jason hesitated to support her through the reporting process. Jason did not want to accompany Samantha to court "because he was afraid of his image in Greek life." He explained to Samantha, "Oh I just don't think I should be there because what if [the perpetrator] sees me and we're like bros?" Like students who may not intervene in rape jokes, Jason was hesitant to compromise his relationships with other men on campus. He did not want his manhood to be questioned. If Jason aligned himself with Samantha, he risked deviating from the norms of toxic masculinity—he risked not being seen as a real man who supported male dominance and sexual aggression.

Jason's behavior is not particularly surprising. College men are less likely to intervene in sexual violence within environments rife with misogynistic peer norms—their intervention may be viewed as preventing another man from winning his sexual trophy.[36] Women, such as Samantha's sorority sister, are often more willing to intervene than men students.[37] By intervening, men may compromise their social position, and their masculinity, on campus.[38] Toxic masculinity, then, often influences men's proclivity to perpetrate violence, as well as men's hesitancy to intervene in this violence.

In the community-oriented campus context of MU, survivors' expectations for peers to intervene made sense. Students who have a greater sense of campus community report a higher intent to engage in bystander intervention.[39] But intent did not always translate to action. This may be because the situation, for some, was too risky to intervene.[40] But there was another reason for why some peers fell short in engaging bystander intervention—inadequate prevention education.

As we learned in Chapter 1, MU, like CU and RU, did not comprehensively educate the student body about sexual violence, including bystander intervention. "I don't know if the campus breeds sexual violence, but I think because there is a lack of education on it, it doesn't help in decreasing or increasing an understanding," Terri stated. Also speaking about the lack of sexual violence education at MU, Monae shared, "If we're not teaching that regularly or making requirements for stuff like that. . . . There's just not enough education." Different, more effective sexual violence prevention education may have helped to disrupt toxic masculinity *and* influence students' willingness to intervene in sexual violence.[41] Students who engage in sexual violence education may be more likely to engage in bystander intervention, whereas[42] students who feel they lack the skills to intervene may be hesitant to engage in bystander intervention.[43]

"This is What We're Gonna Do": Peers' Influence on Reporting at Mountain University

Within the first few moments of visiting the MU campus on a high school tour, Tessa could imagine herself as an MU student, living and learning in the diverse, community-oriented campus environment. She was even more excited to attend the institution after speaking with students enrolled in the Business School. After her tour, Tessa was intent on enrolling at MU and majoring in Business.

During her first semester on campus, Tessa immediately joined the MU Business Fraternity. Later that same year, Tessa became the Chair of Recruitment for the fraternity. As Chair, she was required to interview all MU students who were interested in joining the organization. This is how Tessa met Adam, a second-year South Asian man student who was interested in joining the fraternity. Adam stood out to Tessa. He was incredibly accomplished. And almost everyone in the Business Fraternity wanted him to join their organization.

One night, during recruitment, Tessa ran into Adam at a campus event for South Asian students. There, he invited Tessa to a party he was hosting at his apartment that same night. Tessa struggled to contain her excitement. Adam was impressive, older, and popular. When Tessa told her friends about the invitation they responded, "Oh my God. You've gotta go. He's totally hitting on you!"

Tessa remembers some "weird moments" from the party. At one point, Adam was pouring alcohol in Tessa's mouth without her consent. The next moment, everyone had suddenly left the apartment except for her and Adam. "It was definitely coercion," Tessa stated. Tessa was clear with Adam that she did not want to hook up. Tessa tried to force Adam off her, but, as she described, there was only so much she could do. Adam sexually assaulted Tessa that night. The next morning, Adam acted as if everything was consensual. Tessa was confused. Or maybe she was in shock. Perhaps she was blowing things out of proportion? Was she to blame? She said nothing to Adam as she left the apartment.

Shortly after the assault, Tessa learned that Adam went through her phone that night while she was unconscious. He was looking for inside information about his pledging process with the Business Fraternity. Adam told some fraternity members that Tessa willingly gave him the confidential information. The members reprimanded Tessa for sharing the information with Adam. Tessa began to feel even more confused. Adam was lying. But he was also well-liked and supported by the fraternity. Who would the members believe—this popular man, or her?

When the fraternity reprimanded Tessa, she reached a breaking point. "Enough is enough, I'm telling someone what happened," Tessa declared. Tessa went to her big sister in the Business Fraternity and disclosed the assault:

> I was just like, "I don't know if I'm overthinking this or what's going on." And, she was like, "No, that's not okay." And then she immediately made that appointment with the SVRC Advocate without even asking me. She was like, "I am telling you that this is not okay." I didn't even know myself. And it took me a long time to convince myself that it was sexual assault and I'm not just blowing things up in my head.

Tessa deeply appreciated her friend for being "someone stronger" than she was in that moment; someone who told her outright, "These are your next steps, this is what we're gonna do." Tessa's friend connected her to SVRC, but also helped Tessa recognize that, by definition, she had experienced sexual violence. Because of her friend's reaction to her disclosure, Tessa visited MU SVRC and shortly after, she filed a report with MU Title IX.

Scholars have consistently explored how reactions to disclosure impact various health outcomes for survivors[44] and a few scholars have interrogated how reactions to disclosure can lead to sexual violence resource referrals.[45] But it remains somewhat unknown how peers' reactions to disclosure influence survivors' willingness to *use* sexual violence resources or to *report* their assault. For most survivors I spoke with at MU, the connection between peers' reactions to disclosure and survivors' use of institutional resources was clear. Tessa's story was not unique to the MU environment. Women survivors often disclosed their assault to peers, and peers met survivors with validation and resources. Peers displayed individual courage within the context of their institutions.[46] This courage influenced several survivors' ability and willingness to seek resources and/or report their assault.

Melanie, for instance, experienced continuous sexual harassment and assault from her track coach throughout her first year on campus. Although Melanie "felt grossed out" about the unwanted touching and attention, she attempted to let the feelings go. Melanie did not know where to turn for help or if the unwanted comments and touching were even a big deal. The harassment became a normal part of Melanie's life on campus.

But after one particularly uncomfortable meeting with her coach, Melanie called her teammate. "He touched my butt. He said this at practice. He did this," she disclosed. Her teammate immediately responded, "You should report it. If you really don't feel comfortable, you should say something." The next day, Melanie began the process of reporting the sexual violence to MU Title IX. "I don't think I realized how much it sucked until after I told someone," Melanie reflected.

Previous research suggests that survivors use campus services at low rates.[47] For example, only 3% of the student survivors in Walsh and colleagues' research[48] used a campus service after experiencing sexual violence. Individual-level factors, such as feelings of shame, guilt, or embarrassment often act as barriers to survivors' service use.[49] Reporting rates are also low for student survivors; approximately 4% of women survivors report sexual violence to campus officials.[50] But service use and reporting amongst the survivors I spoke with at MU did not seemingly align with these low rates; eight women survivors used campus resources, and five of these reported their assault to a formal outlet.[51]

As I continued to talk with survivors at MU, I began to recognize this peer support as institutional courage. Smidt and Freyd explained that although "not every member of an institution can demonstrate the same level of institutional courage . . . at every level of any institution

exists an opportunity to demonstrate institutional courage."[52] Peers
may have been limited in their ability to demonstrate institutional courage in some forms, for example, primary and secondary interventions,
but they often engaged individual courage within their institutions by
responding sensitively to victim disclosures and creating pathways for
individuals to discuss violence (tertiary intervention).[53] Peers' courage
to engage tertiary intervention was integral to MU survivors' willingness to use campus services and report the assault. Subsequently,
the courage that peers displayed often led survivors to encounter even
more courage, but this time from some campus administrators, at the
institutional level.

"I Really Felt Empowered": Institutional Courage and Betrayal in the Reporting Process

Shortly after Tessa's big sister helped her make an appointment with
MU SVRC, Tessa met with a SVRC Advocate. She relayed to the advocate a general retelling of the assault and vague details about Adam,
the perpetrator. From there, the advocate guided Tessa through her options for moving forward. Tessa recalled her feelings in that first meeting with SVRC:

> The best thing about that meeting was how reassuring [the advocate]
> was. That everything was going to be okay. Everything was in my con-
> trol. We would only do as much as I was comfortable with. And I really
> felt *empowered* [emphasis added] by that meeting. I also felt like not ev-
> erything [is] falling apart. Things are still in my hands. That was really,
> really comforting.

After meeting with the advocate, Tessa concluded that she had two options moving forward—pursue an on-campus no-contact order and/or
make a formal report to MU Title IX.

Although she felt empowered while meeting with the advocate,
Tessa remained hesitant to bring action against the perpetrator. She
did not want to "ruin" Adam's life, a barrier to reporting that we explore in depth in Chapter 5. But Tessa gained clarity after she spoke,
once again, to her big sister. Her big sister questioned, "If he wasn't so

concerned about you, why do you have the responsibility to be so concerned about him?" Tessa responded immediately, "You're right!" In that moment, Tessa decided to pursue the no-contact order and make a formal report to Title IX. The Title IX process, however, "sucked." Tessa explained:

> It's supposed to take like 60 days or something of investigation, and my case is still not closed. This happened spring of my freshman year. I went through three or four different Title IX investigators.

Tessa, then a junior at MU, had only recently received a decision. But then, Adam found errors in the report, so the Title IX Officer had to re-write the report. Then Adam appealed the original decision that found him responsible. At the time of our conversations, the appeal was finally "wrapping up" with the decision remaining that Adam was responsible.

Tessa wrote a letter of complaint to the MU President about her Title IX process. Many individuals who make complaints within their institutions often end up "making complaints about how their complaints were handled."[54] In the letter, she recounted how many days the process took and the other aspects of Title IX that were broken. Sara Ahmed has labeled this prolonged complaint process as "dragging" or when "a complaint keeps dragging on, taking up more and more time . . . the longer it takes the heavier it becomes."[55] The dragging of the Title IX process weighed heavy on Tessa and had a negative impact on her grade point average, which fell from a 3.9 to a 2.4. Tessa concluded her letter to the MU President stating that the institution had "failed" her. The institution had betrayed her.

"I feel like the institution really did fail me," Tessa stated. But with her next breath, Tessa quickly clarified that the SVRC Advocate did not fail her. It was quite the opposite:

> The advocate was right there with me. She was pointing out things that I should be more outraged with. She was taking all these notes. She was taking tally marks every time that the [Title IX] investigator asked me unwarranted questions like, "What were you wearing?" . . . I wouldn't

group the advocate with the institution. . . . She wasn't thinking about
the school at all. She was only thinking about my best interests. I really
did have an ally in her.

According to Tessa, the advocate was not part of the institution because
the advocate was student centered—something the institution was not
able, or perhaps willing, to be. MU SVRC Advocates were responsible
for providing survivors with institutional and community resources
post-assault. This included exploring survivors' options for reporting
the assault and accompanying survivors to subsequent meetings. Tessa's advocate was fulfilling the duties of her job. But the advocate was
also fulfilling these duties in ways that empowered Tessa. With the support of her advocate, Tessa stated she was able "to take something awful
and turn it into something that was empowering."

Student survivors do not often use campus advocacy services, but
the survivors who *do* use these services often perceive them to be the
most helpful of all campus sexual violence resources.[56] Campus-based
advocacy services are rooted in community-based advocacy models,
which often approach care from a trauma-informed lens, or a lens that
"recognizes the ongoing impact of past and current trauma on survivor
needs" and includes principles of safety and support.[57] Student survivors
may be more interested in accessing campus advocacy due to their focus
on trauma-informed care, including confidentiality, validation, control
over the reporting process, and a focus on identity and social justice.[58]

Although research with student survivor experiences with campus
advocacy services continues to emerge, community-based advocacy
services, and their trauma-informed approach to care, have been found
to positively influence survivors' engagement with the criminal justice
system.[59] Survivors who are assisted by a community advocate are more
likely to have police reports taken, less likely to be treated negatively by
the police, and report less distress from their experiences with the legal
system.[60] This was often true for the women survivors at MU who used
SVRC and went on to report to the institution. Each woman explored
how SVRC, in some way, was integral to the reporting process, often

acting as a buffer or defense against institutional betrayal that may permeate the Title IX experience.

Katrina recalled being nervous as she walked into the Title IX Office with her SVRC Advocate. The Title IX Officer's first question for Katrina did not help to calm her nerves. "Why are we having this meeting? . . . You already have this no-contact order in place. As far as that goes, there's really nothing more we can do for you," the Officer gazed blankly at Katrina.

Katrina was shocked. "That's not why I'm here," she stumbled over her response. The Title IX Officer curtly responded, "So what is it you're here for then?" Katrina felt that she had to justify why she, a survivor of sexual violence, wanted to pursue justice. As Katrina began to feel smaller and more nervous, she looked to her advocate and half-asked, half-stated, "I think I'm making the right decision by making an investigation. I don't know how that sounds to you. How does that sound to you?" "Yeah," the advocate responded with confidence. Katrina turned to the Title IX Officer and stated with more confidence, "Yup. That's what I'm going to do."

The Title IX Officer was "chilling." But with her advocate, Katrina felt more able to navigate the reporting process. She felt justified, even empowered, in reporting the assault. Katrina wondered why the Title IX Officer was so cold and disempowering and why the advocate was so warm and empowering—was it training, personality, or both? Regardless, Katrina was grateful that her advocate was able to be a "safe space" and have a "holding capacity" for her and other survivors at MU.

I brought Katrina's wonderings into my conversation with Ivonne, the Director of MU SVRC. Ivonne also served as an SVRC Advocate. What exactly was SVRC's philosophy on supporting survivors? And how did she, the founding Director of SVRC, come to this philosophy?

Before working in survivor advocacy, Ivonne worked with campus cultural centers that were dedicated to empowering Students of Color. When she entered advocacy work, she brought her focus on student empowerment with her. Ivonne explained how she "married" her cultural center work with her advocacy work:

I've viewed survivors, no matter what race or ethnicity they were, as beings that needed to be provided care and services that were geared toward what they were experiencing. And for me, it's like a survivor takes a huge hit in their identity, right? They stopped trusting themselves. They don't feel like they belong. All these things that I feel like sometimes Students of Color in general also go through. They don't feel like they belong. They don't trust the institution. . . . They don't trust us. When I initially started doing advocacy programs that was kind of the mentality that I brought to it.

While working in cultural centers, Ivonne provided Students of Color with empathy, validation, a listening ear, and resources—concepts that aim to empower students. These were also core concepts that allowed Ivonne to practice individual courage within an institution.[61] Ivonne carried this philosophy and courage with her from institution to institution and from job to job. But Ivonne felt she was able to fully actualize her philosophy within the MU environment because of the racial diversity of the student body.

At MU, Ivonne interacted with and supported more Survivors of Color than she had at her other institutions. The racial diversity of her clients made Ivonne's sessions with survivors at MU different than those at the institutions she had previously worked. She was less prescribed at MU. Ivonne, for example, connected with Spanish-speaking survivors by speaking Spanish in some sessions. As a Woman of Color, she could tell Survivors of Color, "Yes, I understand that experience." Ivonne's identity and her empowerment approach to advocacy offered a "connection" with the many MU survivors who walked through her door. Ivonne attempted to embed this empowerment model throughout SVRC policies, procedures, and practices. For example, the professional and student staff that worked in SVRC were trained in and used an empowerment approach to advocacy. Ivonne displayed individual courage within the institution while simultaneously institutionalizing this courage at MU.

Women of Color survivors often felt the influence of this empowerment framework. Tessa used the words "empower" and "empowerment" to describe her interactions with the SVRC Advocates. Katrina also demonstrated how her advocate empowered her to file a report, despite the coldness of the Title IX Officer. Raquel, who worked alongside SVRC as she navigated the Title IX process, praised the support she received from the advocates:

> They heard something. They didn't doubt. They didn't question. In fact, I doubted and they believed in me when I didn't believe in myself. . . . They were the ones that said, "No, you're more than that. And we are gonna correct it." And they did correct it. And they showed me that it doesn't matter what happens to me. If I want to do something, and if I wanna get something done, I can.

Overwhelmingly, Women of Color survivors who used SVRC felt empowered by the institutional resource. SVRC engaged in institutional courage with "accountability, transparency, actively seeking justice, and making reparations where needed."[62] This institutional courage displayed to some students that the institution will care for and protect them, making it easier for students to encourage other students to use SVRC. Ivonne was aware that this was an effective way to get more survivors to use SVRC. She explained, "Surveys tell us the first people that students reach out to are their friends. I think the more that you fulfill services that have empathy and build empowerment for students, the more they'll gravitate toward accessing them."

Ivonne's comment sparked an "aha!" moment—the more institutional courage that MU displayed, the more courage that individual students might be willing and able to display within their institution. Although I observed this cycle of institutional courage at MU, I also observed how institutional betrayal throughout the Title IX reporting process might work against, or challenge, this courage. Institutional betrayal and institutional courage are not mutually exclusive; both can be present and interacting within one environment. Ivonne acknowledged how the Title IX process is often "dehumanizing" for survivors. These policies claim to be neutral and fair, ignoring the role identity, power, and history play in the adjudication process.[63] Title IX, then, often has an oppositional mission to advocacy, which focuses on validation, empowerment, identity, and social justice.[64] Fortunately, at MU, most survivors relayed how the courage from SVRC mitigated the betrayal from Title IX and not the other way around.

Where Does Intersectionality Take Us?

Institutional courage was present at MU. Although institutional betrayal was also present on campus, institutional courage, at times, undercut this betrayal. The possible influence of this institutional courage was observable in some survivors' answers to my question, "What can the institution do better?"

Noelle shrugged her shoulders and replied, "Overall, they are doing really well." Jasmine was also at a loss for suggestions. After chewing on a few incomplete thoughts, she offered, "I don't know. There's a lot of resources already." Several survivors at MU did not have ready suggestions for how their institution could better approach campus sexual violence. According to some survivors, the institution was already doing a lot.

While many women were content with their institution's approach to sexual violence prevention and response, some offered suggestions for improving sexual violence education, specifically as it related to bystander intervention. Tessa wanted MU to offer more education on secondary bystander interventions:

> If there was education that teaches people how to conduct themselves in situations, not only to get out of them if you are the person something's being done to, but to know how to be present and be like, "This person's intoxicated, now is not the time," etcetera. That would've been great, too.

Tessa thought it important for peers to know how to intervene in situations that might lead to sexual violence. While Tessa wanted more education about secondary interventions, Samantha was interested in her peers learning more about tertiary bystander intervention:

> I think we could really make a light-hearted video where someone hits someone and that person is like, "Now I feel unsafe around this person

and we can't be here." I feel like we could push it and then show that it's important for you to support one another and understand that, that person feels unsafe and uncomfortable enough with that person. . . . We're in this together.

Samantha desired for her peers to be knowledgeable about what counted as violence; that this violence is not okay; and that disrupting violence is a community issue. Samantha concluded her recommendation with the community-centered nature of the MU campus in mind: "We're in this together."

Although MU SVRC offered students bystander education, it was often a brief overview included within a larger, very short orientation program. The institution must provide more opportunities, within academic, community, and co-curricular spaces, for students to engage in bystander intervention education. These programs must also differentiate between the three different intervention types.[65] Focusing on this variation in bystander interventions will help to educate students on specific types of intervention that are lacking on campus (in the case of MU, primary and secondary intervention) and take advantage of the types of intervention that are often present and effective on campus (at MU, tertiary education).

Prior to interviewing women at MU, I was weary of the hyper-focus that institutions may place on bystander intervention to disrupt campus rape cultures. Most bystander intervention programs have not been found to impact rates of sexual violence perpetration.[66] But at MU, because of the community-oriented peer environment, survivors may have viewed bystander intervention as the key to disrupting toxic masculinity and the campus rape culture. The effectiveness of bystander intervention, then, depends on the campus context and may not be as effective or appropriate at all institutions. These interventions may be more effective on campuses where students have a high sense of belonging and responsibility to their community.[67]

Beyond bystander intervention, Women of Color survivors also hinted at the importance of embedding an empowerment approach to sexual violence throughout MU structures. Monae, for instance, stated that the institution could do better if they "prioritize us as survivors." Monae continued with her suggestion:

> I think it's cool that we have SVRC, but it's like a tiny, little office. It's really hard to find. They should have their own building. . . . I feel like they're so inaccessible because you never hear of them until you actively search and dig or know someone who uses their services. I think just paying more funding for them and just for them to be more mainstream.

Institutional leaders must allocate more resources toward SVRC. To maintain clients' privacy, however, it may be important for SVRC's physical space to remain somewhat obscured from the center of campus. But with additional human and financial resources, SVRC could put on more educational events that reach more students, increasing their presence within the MU environment. A more "mainstream" position on campus might increase students' awareness of SVRC, mitigating students' need to search for, or be told post-assault, about the institutional resource.

It is also imperative that the institution embed the empowerment model throughout other campus resources and structures. Ananya posited:

> I remember when I did go to Title IX, I felt very discouraged, as I had mentioned last time, and I think that there could have been more. I wouldn't be able to say exactly what could have been done, but I feel that there was some gap in between what was done, and what should have been done. I really felt that I was discouraged from coming forward or naming the person that had done this.

Ananya perceived that Title IX discouraged her from pursuing a formal report against her perpetrator. This discouragement is the opposite of empowerment.[68] Although Ananya did not explicitly suggest that Title IX use an empowerment approach to their work, she recommend that there could have been more encouragement in the formal reporting process.[69] Recommendations for a more empowering reporting process are explored in greater detail in Chapter 5.

SVRC often offered the encouragement that survivors sought, which worked to counter some of the discouragement felt from the Title IX process. It is integral that other campus actors and programs, such as the Women's Center, Residential Life, and Athletics, are educated about and use an empowerment approach with all students. The empowerment approach must be embedded into institutional structures, such as sanctioning and conduct procedures, and leave of absence policies. This approach includes listening to students' concerns and disclosures, offering students empathy and validation, and providing resources and other areas of support to students. This empowerment approach demonstrates institutional courage, which is imperative for decreasing (the effects of) institutional betrayal that can concurrently exist on campus.

policies. This approach includes listening to students' concerns and

Four

City University

AN INSTITUTION THAT "VALUES THE ATHLETES MORE THAN ANYTHING"

Leyla's first semester at City University was relatively uneventful—she
made several friends, went to a few student organization meetings, and
studied diligently. During her first week back on campus after winter
break, however, Leyla and a friend decided to venture off campus to
attend a party. But this wasn't just any party. This was "an athlete football player party." Several CU football players were hosting and attending the exclusive event.

Once at the party, Leyla spotted Adam, a football player who had
pursued her for a "hook up" throughout the fall semester. Leyla made
it clear, to both me and to Adam, that she was not interested in hook-
ing up. She consistently and clearly met Adam's sexual advances with
"No!" But Leyla's clear and constant refusals the previous semester did
not stop Adam from making a beeline to Leyla as soon as she entered
the party.

Mid-way through telling me about her entrance into the party, Leyla
paused, took a moment to think, and doubled back. She wanted to clar-
ify something prior to saying more about that night:

I chose to get drunk with my friend. I didn't know that she was such a heavy drinker and had such a high tolerance. She wanted me to match her. I was drinking something I'd never drank before in my life.

I knew what was happening here. I'd heard it too much throughout my time working with survivors. Leyla was wrapping her story in internalized victim blaming. Victim blaming, however, is damaging. It takes the focus off the perpetrators and institutional systems that allow for perpetration and places the blame on those who have little to no agency in these situations. Although Leyla was couching her story in her own culpability, she was also fully aware that the assault was not her fault. The precursor for her experience with assault was much larger than Leyla. It was societal. It was institutional.

Alcohol merely made it easier for Adam to corner Leyla at the party, take her into a bathroom, and rape her. Shortly after the assault, Leyla slipped out of the party and made her way back to her residence hall room. Much to Leyla's disappointment, the friend that she went to the party with had left earlier in the night. Over the next few weeks, Leyla slowly began to tell select friends that Adam raped her. Her peers' responses shook her:

> People were saying that it probably wasn't even rape because Adam is a football player. "You were lucky." That type of thing. I was like, "No. He knew. Even if I wasn't drunk, he knew." They were like, "It was probably because you were drunk. Maybe you did want it. Maybe you said it was okay." I was like, "No, I wouldn't have said it was okay because I told him it wasn't okay while I was sober, before I got drunk, and the day before, and the day before that, and the week before that."

Leyla was confident that what she experienced was rape; she did not consent to having sex with Adam. Leyla's peers, however, believed that there was no way a "hook up" with a NCAA football player could be non-consensual; she *had* to want it. A few days after disclosing to her peers, several football players confronted Leyla, reminding her, "No one would believe it was rape because Adam was a football player."

They threatened Leyla that life on campus would be "hell" if she continued to tell people about the assault.

Leyla grew even more frustrated by an interaction she had with Adam a few weeks later. One afternoon, Adam approached Leyla in a public campus space and whispered, "Ever since that night I feel like we had a spark." Leyla was furious with Adam and the ways that he, and his teammates, oozed privilege and power. According to Adam and his peers, all women students want to have sex with CU football players. All sex with these football players is consensual. "They all decided that it wasn't rape," Leyla stated, infuriated by the situation.

"City University values the athletes more than anything. The athletes are their main income." Leyla began to connect her experiences with sexual violence, and her peers' behaviors, to her perceptions of the institution's values. Leyla perceived that CU leadership provided men students, specifically men athletes and fraternity members, with unlimited privilege, power, and resources on campus because these men and their organizations generated significant amounts of income and prestige for the university.[1] Women students at CU did not share the same elevated status as these men. The differential value and privilege that the institution gifted many men students influenced pervasive gender inequities on campus that worked to maintain campus rape culture.

Scholars have long stressed the connection between gender inequity and sexual violence.[2] In 1983 Ellis and Beattie suggested, "Deep-rooted social traditions of overwhelming male domination of all important sociopolitical and economic activities in a community or society (and the consequent exclusion of women) is the primary and ultimate factor responsible for rape."[3] More recently, some scholars have explored how policies, procedures, and regulations at colleges and universities reproduce gender inequity and, subsequently, campus rape culture.[4] The connection between institutional structures, gender inequity, and campus rape culture was particularly pertinent on the CU campus.

According to Leyla, institutional policies and procedures at CU contributed to "a social structure [on campus] that athletes are to be praised at all times and that they can be excused from their homework and all this shit." Leyla hinted that "all this shit" included crime. Due to the reputation and prestige athletes brought to the institution, the institution sometimes "excused" these men from perpetrating crime, including sexual violence. The possibility to commit assault with impunity provided even more privilege and power to men students on campus. Leyla suggested that CU was often more concerned about its elite status and reputation than caring for (women) students' well-being and safety.

The pervasiveness of gender inequity at CU also influenced survivors' decisions to report their assault. Many survivors and some staff perceived that the institution would not hold men, particularly those that were valued by the institution, accountable for perpetrating sexual violence. Survivors were often hesitant to report their assault to the institution for fear that they would not be believed. Or rather, that the institution would *choose* not to believe and protect survivors over the men who may perpetrate assault. These hesitations were informed not only by the gender inequity and sexism that permeated campus, but also by racial inequity and racism. Several survivors acknowledged that, due to racist and sexist conceptualizations of sexual violence,[5] the institution treated Women of Color as less credible, less valuable, and, therefore, less deserving of justice than some white women students and most men students. When it came to reporting sexual violence, the institution did not provide justice to women survivors, particularly if they are Women of Color.

This chapter explores how structures related to athletics and Fraternity and Sorority Life (FSL) at CU fostered gender inequities that influenced the campus rape culture. Although most survivors' perceptions of campus rape culture point toward athletics and FSL, athletes and fraternity members were not the only perpetrators of sexual violence. In fact, only two survivors experienced sexual violence within the context of FSL. And Leyla was the only CU woman student that I spoke with to name a student athlete as her perpetrator. This, however, does not negate survivors' observations of how athletics and FSL influenced and maintained the campus rape culture. Rather, survivors' stories demonstrate how CU policies, procedures, and values that concern athletics and FSL influenced gender inequities that deeply permeated the campus environment. In other words, many Women of Color survivors that I spoke with at CU experienced violence from cisgender men who exist in an environment that often values and provides these men with more resources, privileges, and power than most women. The privileging of athletics and FSL played a key role in maintaining the institution's elite status—it also played a key role in maintaining campus rape culture and institutional betrayal. When men enjoy an "elevated role within the community or society, their potential to perpetrate or facilitate abuse can be obscured."[6]

Rape Culture at City University: The Institution that "Gives Guys the Permission to do Everything"

"Gender inequity does seem to be the single highest predictor. It is the strongest correlate to sexual violence anywhere," Arlene stated succinctly. Although Arlene, the Director of CU SVRC, suggested that gender inequity predicts sexual violence on many college campuses, she pointed out the specific structure that influenced gender inequities at CU—Fraternity and Sorority life. Arlene described how fraternities and sororities are single-gender social organizations that reinforce a strict gender binary. The separation between fraternities and sororities strengthens socially constructed gender roles, or "what's appropriate for these groups [fraternities and men] versus these groups [sororities and women]." Arlene continued to explain how FSL at CU upheld gender inequity:

> Fraternities are allowed to throw parties. Sororities are not. Everyone has to immediately go to a fraternity party as opposed to staying in the house that is home-field advantage for the women. The structure of fraternities and sororities, which is huge here at City University, is a contributing factor. But, also, indicative of the larger environment and culture, wherein we still think that that type of separation and distinction is important and City University is not really challenging people to think beyond that.

FSL contributed to gender inequity on campus by upholding a strict gender binary and binary gender roles that provided fraternity men with privileges often denied to sorority women. To demonstrate this inequity, Arlene pointed to a Panhellenic rule that stipulated sorority houses must remain dry, or free of alcohol. Interfraternity Council (IFC) houses are not governed by this rule. Fraternity men are often allowed to serve alcohol at their parties and in their houses.[7] The rule allegedly exists because insurance rates are cheaper for organizations that do not allow alcohol on their premises than for those that do.[8] But this rule forces many women students to leave their homes, which is "home-field advantage," to engage in the campus social scene that is controlled by fraternity men and fraternity homes.[9]

Survivors elaborated on this gender inequity, demonstrating how fraternities and their members are privileged in specific ways that allowed men to dominate and control the campus social scene. Eliza declared that sexual violence occurs on campus for one main reason: "Fraternities and sororities. That's a big one. A huge one." Eliza later clarified that she was only speaking of "Panhellenic sororities and fraternities specifically. Because there are ones for Groups of Color. However, Panhellenic are the ones that have the houses. Those are the ones that have money. The frat houses are the ones where the parties are."

Eliza made a distinction between "Panhellenic sororities and fraternities" and "Groups of Color." The College Panhellenic Council (Panhellenic) includes 26 national and international women's only sororities and Greek letter organizations, while the IFC is made up of 58 national and international men's fraternities. Panhellenic and IFC organizations are historically and almost always predominantly white spaces that structure the historically white Greek system at many U.S. institutions of higher education.[10] The "Groups of Color" include the National Multicultural Greek Council (MGC) with ten affiliated Greek letter organizations and the National Pan-Hellenic Council (NPHC) with nine historically Black organizations.

The statuesque Greek houses that line the CU campus boundaries belong to either Panhellenic organizations or IFC organizations.[11]

Due to a history of racism and the exclusion of People of Color and their organizations from higher education writ large[12] and from the campus social scene,[13] MGC and NPHC organizations do not have official chapter houses close to campus. The institution does not publish demographic statistics for the student members of Panhellenic or IFC chapters, or for the students who live in these houses. However, photos from Panhellenic and IFC events and information on the organizations' websites suggest that most members, past and present, present as white.[14]

Only one of the 13 survivors I spoke with belonged to a CU Greek letter organization. Most Women of Color I spoke with perceived that sororities were made for, and only accepted, mostly white women students. Yet lack of membership in a sorority did not preclude survivors from feeling the influence of FSL and the gender and racial inequities it maintained for the campus community. Most Women of Color survivors I spoke with at CU relayed how, although excluded in many ways from participating in FSL, this exclusion did not prevent them from experiencing the consequences of and resulting vulnerabilities from these institutional structures.[15] Women of Color survivors demonstrated how these specific institutional structures contributed to "What's happening? What kind of discrimination is going on? What are the policies?"[16] Structures that upheld gendered and racialized inequities contaminated the environment for all students at CU, including many Women of Color survivors who were not directly involved with these organizations.

Above, Eliza claimed that Panhellenic and IFC organizations are "the ones that have the money." Historically white fraternities and sororities are often comprised of middle-to-upper-class white students who can pay thousands of dollars in membership fees every year.[17] Rich and powerful alumni are also a part of these historically white organizations. Forty-two percent of U.S. presidents are members of fraternities[18] and at least a quarter of CEOs from the Forbes Super 500 List of America's Largest Corporations are Greek affiliated.[19]

Eliza was also correct in suggesting that, due to a Panhellenic rule, "the frat houses are the ones where the parties are." Fraternity men, many of whom are white, often host the more popular and enticing parties *with* alcohol. The privilege to have parties with alcohol, particularly at a campus that shuts down on nights and weekends "leads to male dominance and control over the university party culture," which is "an important currency in the campus social scene."[20] Although most Women of Color at CU did not feel included within and/or engage with Panhellenic sororities on campus, many women did frequent events thrown by IFC members in their off-campus houses. For women who were not yet 21, fraternity parties were one of the few options to socialize and have the option of drinking alcohol.

Control over campus resources helps to facilitate and create a culture that reinforces attitudes that perpetuate power, dominance, and sexual control and coercion across campus. In a 2014 *TIME* article, journalist Jessica Bennet explained, "When it comes to campus social life, [fraternities] exert huge social control: providing the alcohol, hosting the parties, policing who may enter—based on whatever criteria they choose."[21]

What Bennet described in their article was happening at CU. Eliza shared:

> They'll have a group of girls and guys, and girls will want to go to a party. The guys will want to go too. And the girls will just casually be like, "You [guys] won't get in because you're not in a frat." It's not like, "Oh these [frat] guys want girls to be in the frat drinking. This is horrible. Let's go somewhere else." . . . We don't really sit back and think, "Oh my God this is so wrong."

At the end of their article, Bennet posed the question, "What do you expect to happen at a club where women are viewed as outsiders, or commodities, or worse, as prey, and where men make the rules?"[22]

Survivors often perceived that CU leadership condoned the control that fraternities held over the campus social scene; CU leadership was condoning gender inequity, white privilege, and campus rape culture. Clara, the one survivor who belonged to a sorority, stated outright that sexual violence happened on campus because of "City University's strong ties with the Greek system." She continued:

[It's CU's] refusal to crack down on their events. They basically let the fraternities run themselves. City University says, "Oh, we're monitoring them." But they're not. I've been in the fraternities a lot when I was dating a fraternity guy. I saw the way that they were basically their own government. They would still try to keep in mind of the rules. More so for their alumni. "What would the alumni think? They're the ones who are funding us." Not at all really keeping in mind the City University regulations. It was just basically, "The alumni have money, so we need to watch our backs or we at least need to be a little bit more coy about our alcohol or our drugs, or whatever." . . . I know I saw on the news recently that another assault happened and they banned alcohol. But I thought in my head, "Didn't they always . . . wasn't alcohol not allowed ever?" You know? . . . It's not changing anything. City has to lay down the law and actually start monitoring them.

With fraternity alumni as presidents, senators, and CEOs of fortune 500 companies, Clara's statement that "the alumni have money" and authority over current members may be accurate. At CU, IFC members often rely on alumni donors to fund scholarships, housing costs, and social events. For example, one CU fraternity chapter has nearly $400,000 in their capital campaign fund, the majority of which is from alumni donations. These funds are often used for large-scale, one-time projects, such as constructing a new fraternity home or providing updates to an existing home.

Clara is also somewhat correct in stating that fraternities "are their own government." Each fraternity is registered as a student organization with the CU Office of FSL, and staff members in the office advise and meet with each organization and council. Yet IFC fraternity houses, as well as Panhellenic sorority houses, are privately owned and controlled by the national chapter of each organization. CU does not have oversight over this property. Even if the institution kicked an organization off campus, or the organization disaffiliated from the institution, their house and their house parties might remain.[23]

Ann, a CU SVRC Advocate, shared how this quasi self-governance could often protect men in fraternities who perpetrated assault:

Greek life culture is really challenging to work with, because they can just do whatever they want. They're not really affiliated with the university. We just learned recently that IFC has their own reporting thing that you can do, that doesn't even go to City University. What's happening is a lot of students are reporting to Greek life, reporting to IFC. Who knows what database, who knows who's holding onto that material. You don't know! Students think that they're reporting to Title IX, but they're not. The university's not even aware of it. Greek life has always been, honestly on this campus, a really huge client caseload. Not to sound stereotypical, but that just hasn't really changed much. There's just so much freedom for them to be able to do whatever they want with the cases. They could just kick someone out if they wanted, or they could have them continue to live in the house. It's complicated because there's not enough oversight.

Student and alumni members of IFC had ranges of freedom to self-adjudicate and cover up sexual violence. Even if an IFC member did report the assault, they could seemingly bypass the Title IX Office and report to an unofficial source located within the IFC organization. What happened from there was up to the members of the organization.

Padma offered a direct example, at the student level, of how this self-adjudication showed up on campus. In her role as a Peer Health Coach, Padma became aware that a woman student in a CU sorority reported sexual violence, perpetrated by a member of a CU IFC organization, to the president of her sorority. This fraternity member was most likely a repeat perpetrator; he had allegedly assaulted other women on campus. When the fraternity was made aware of the most recent assault, they decided to punish the fraternity member. But, Padma sighed, "His punishment was not coming to a couple parties. And then afterwards his brothers would be watching him." Stunned, my mouth agape, I asked Padma, "This is a real scenario?" She looked me in the eyes and stated flatly, "This is a real scenario."

Several other survivors shared a recent high-profile case that demonstrates how CU did not, or perhaps could not, hold fraternities and their members accountable for assault. Above, Clara mentioned "that another assault happened," which influenced a ban on alcohol in CU fraternities. Clara was referring to a recent incident where a CU IFC member attempted to rape a CU woman student during a fraternity party. It was not the institution that imposed the ban. Instead, the IFC organization self-imposed an indefinite ban on "in house events" with alcohol. To be clear, the fraternity did not ban alcohol from their house. Rather, they did not allow alcohol at official house events.

Because IFC organizations controlled much of the campus social scene, I was not surprised that several other survivors mentioned this assault and resulting alcohol ban on campus. Rayn was extremely pessimistic about the ban and the implications it might have for perpetrators of sexual violence. Rayn stated, "I know recently fraternities were banned from serving alcohol at their parties . . . banning alcohol doesn't do anything. You're missing the whole point." The "point" being that sexual violence is not perpetrated because alcohol is present at parties. Sexual violence remains endemic because specific structures at CU foster gender inequity that allow men to control the social scene, providing them with freedom to do what they want within that social scene.

Faye's voice became shaky with anger as she discussed the recent ban on alcohol in fraternities, which lasted only six weeks:

> The president of Beta "fucking apple" Pi, he got arrested for sexual assault. . . . And the only thing this institution did was they suspended alcohol at frat parties for a couple weeks. . . . And now City University, as of like last week or whatever, the frats are back and everyone's having a good time again. You're going to forget the fact that this woman was violently assaulted in this exact room. It's not just something that goes away. And the school supports it.

Alcohol bans are a common response to the perpetration of sexual violence by fraternities and their members. After reports of drugging and sexual violence at fraternity parties surfaced at Cornell University, IFC, with the support of the institution, suspended fraternity-hosted parties and social events.[24] Approximately three months later, fraternities were allowed to resume their social events, but with procedures that aimed to amplify safety and heighten awareness on sexual violence prevention.[25] After Brock Turner, a Stanford student-athlete who we learn more about in Chapter 5, was found guilty of raping Jane Doe at a Stanford fraternity home in 2015, Stanford banned containers (750 mL and larger) of liquor, spirits, and hard alcohol on campus.[26] But, as many survivors suggested, these bans are often short lived and ineffective. Instead, the bans often "do little to prevent sexual assault and address the behavior of rapists, and instead emphasize telling potential victims, especially women, to change their own behavior in order to avoid being assaulted."[27]

So why might CU and other institutions continue to support fraternities, despite the damage they do? Revenue, prestige, and reputation. Although donor and revenue statistics for FSL at CU are not public, membership in a fraternity or sorority is highly correlated to alumni giving.[28] In *the Dark Power of Fraternities*, Caitlin Flanagan claims, "At least one study has affirmed what had long been assumed: that fraternity men tend to be generous to their alma maters."[29] Fraternities also provide institutions with a robust social life and party culture that may entice prospective students to apply and enroll in the institution. "Joe Jr.," a prospective student, may visit a campus and take "one look at the Fiji house and he gets the message: kids are getting laid here; kids are having fun. Maybe he ought to snuff out the joint and take a second look at that application."[30]

Sororities and fraternities, with their large off-campus houses, also allow the institution to admit more students without putting more money into expanding occupancy rates for on-campus housing.[31] Greek life is integral to the profitability and success of CU. Yet these organizations and their members can also be integral to the perpetration and perpetuation of gender inequity and campus rape culture. For CU, the benefits of IFC (revenue generation, higher enrollment, positive contributions to institutional reputation) might have outweighed the cost (short-lived negative media attention, sexual violence, perpetuation of rape culture on campus). When an institution values reputation over the safety of its members, "institutional betrayal may remain unchecked."[32]

Moments after Faye stated that the institution continues to support fraternities, despite the perpetration of sexual violence within these spaces, she added:

> You don't even just see [control of the social scene] in fraternities . . . the fact that it goes from fraternities and it impacts other parties, *it gives guys the permission to do everything else* [emphasis added]. . . . Institutionally, we are letting them and no one's stopping them from doing this. And they're able to do it and it doesn't end.

Control of the campus social scene by fraternity men upheld gender inequity. But this social control, and subsequent gender inequity, was not confined to fraternities. It seeped into other male-dominated organizations and spaces on campus and provided many men students with "the permission" to do—take control—as they pleased.

Several staff and survivors, for instance, demonstrated how gender inequity was maintained through the institutional treatment of specific men athletes. Some women survivors described a recent incident that occurred between CU men student athletes and the police. According to local and national accounts, top CU administrators helped to decrease the likelihood that several men athletes, who committed a high-profile crime, would be sentenced to jail. According to Leyla, CU was going to "bend bars and break bullets to get these players back and playing." Although the athletes were suspended from the team indefinitely, they were "back and playing" with their teammates the following season. According to a local news article, their tarnished reputations were redeemed because they were performing well, athletically, for the institution.

Institutions across the country often protect athletes who commit crimes, including sexual violence, all for the love (and the money and prestige) of the game. The Alabama basketball program was recently under scrutiny for allowing Brandon Miller, their star player, to continue the season despite his possible involvement in a fatal shooting.[33] On January 15, 2023, Darius Miles texted Miller, asking him to bring his gun, which was in Miller's car. When Miller arrived at Miles' location, Miles allegedly retrieved the gun from Miller's car. Moments later, Miles gave the gun to another man at the scene, and that man used the gun to shoot and kill Jamea Jonae Harris, a 23-year-old woman.[34] Alabama leadership immediately removed Miles from the team. Miller, however, played in his next game on January 17. In fact, Miller did not miss one game following the January 15 shooting. It was only made public on February 21, 2023, that Miller was present at the scene of the crime. The decision to allow Miller to continue playing for Alabama basketball was made in consultation with the university president, the Alabama basketball coach, and university legal counsel.[35] Miller was the No. 2 overall pick in the 2023 NBA draft and will make $49 million over four years with the Charlotte Hornets[36]

In 2013, a Baylor football player, Samuel Ukwuachu, raped a Baylor woman student.[37] The woman reported the incident to the institution and to police. Baylor's investigation was "shockingly brief" and "insufficient" and did not end in disciplinary action, although Ukwuachu was indicted by a grand jury on two counts of sexual assault in June 2014.[38] In June 2015, still under indictment, Baylor announced that Ukwuachu would return to the team that summer. Baylor remained startlingly silent as to why Ukwuachu had not played the previous season. In August 2015, Ukwuachu was found guilty of second-degree sexual assault.[39] He did not return to the football field, but he did graduate earlier, that May, from Baylor. After the gross mishandling of her case by the institution, the survivor transferred to another university in 2014.[40] The institutional messaging from Alabama, Baylor, CU, and many other institutions is clear: men athletes can perpetrate crimes with impunity. And the institution will often stand behind them.

"If you're an athlete on campus, it seems like you have a lot of different things that other folks don't have," Ann, a SVRC Advocate, observed. Ann quipped that this inequitable distribution of resources, such as state-of-the-art athletic training facilities, influenced student athletes' immense sense of entitlement on campus. She continued, "City University is very traditional in that aspect of, 'Athletics gives us money, so we're going to hold [athletes] high.'" NCAA Athletics is an integral part of CU's revenue stream and a feature of the CU social experience. Over the course of one recent year, CU Athletics generated over $105 million. Ticket sales alone generated $19 million for the institution. Donors, many of which are CU alumni, contributed over $16 million to CU Athletics. Out of all CU Athletics programs, the CU football program was gifted the most money in donations and brought in more than half of the athletic department's revenue. University athletics can also draw in more prospective students, charitable donations, and persuade state governments to act favorably towards the institution.[41]

As a gross display of gender inequity, the institution spent three times as much money funding men's sports than it did funding women's sports. In a recent fiscal year, the institution spent $1 million on the football team's equipment and supplies; this sum was more than the money spent on equipment and supplies for all women's sports combined for that same year. Because of the revenue and prestige that CU athletes—specifically football and men's basketball players—generate, the institution places these men athletes on a pedestal, often resulting in feelings of entitlement. According to Ann, this entitlement is "a big issue" for sexual violence because men begin to have the perception that they can do what they want with little fear of consequence. The entitlement is observable in Leyla's story outlined at the start of this chapter. Adam, and his teammates, could not fathom how any woman student on campus would not want to have (consensual) sex with them. He was, after all, a CU football player.

Ann did find it interesting, however, that all undergraduate students were required to participate in only one sexual violence awareness training during their entire time on campus. But student athletes and student members of FSL were required to complete sexual violence awareness trainings every year. "I just think that's interesting, that [CU leadership] hold them so high, but they also see them as very problematic enough to make that mandate," Ann pointed out. "It's probably risk reduction," she concluded. Ann perceived that the mandate for annual training was a way for CU to manage institutional risk. When members of these organizations perpetrated sexual violence, institutional leaders could point to the mandate and say, "See. We tried!" But if CU truly wanted to prevent sexual violence, they would address the gender inequity that was maintained through the institutional privileging of these men-centered organizations.

Reporting at City University: "White Man? Women of Color? Who's Gonna be Believed?"

"It was just because of him being a football player that was the issue," Leyla recalled about her decision to not report Adam to CU Title IX. Leyla perceived that if she did make a formal report, the institution would not protect her. Although the institution might believe Leyla's allegations, they would choose to protect their interest in athletes and athletics. "They're not going to do anything about [the allegation]. Instead, they would just switch up on me anyway even though they know what the truth is," Leyla stated with certainty. She clarified that this "switch" might involve the institution retaliating against her— expelling her, making her look like she was "crazy"—for daring to tarnish an athlete's reputation, and therefore the institution's reputation. Leyla believed that if she reported Adam, the institution would betray her. CU would respond inadequately to her report and may even retaliate against her for coming forward with allegations of rape by a football player.[42]

"There is no point. I'm one girl and there's the whole football team," Leyla sighed. "City University was not going to look out for one girl," she concluded. Smith and colleagues explained how "institutional betrayal often creates a sense of being a less valued member of an institution related to experiencing or reporting a traumatic event."[43] In both her experience with assault and her decision to not report her assault, Leyla perceived that women students were less valuable to the institution than men students, particularly men athletes. CU would not display institutional courage for one girl who held little value to the institution. Particularly because that "girl" was a Student of Color. Leyla confidently stated that CU leadership "doesn't do shit for Students of Color." She continued, "We're not supported here. We're not even seen." It was difficult for Leyla to believe that CU would do something to protect and provide justice to her, a Woman of Color.

"People never get punished by the institution. Never. Maybe punished isn't the word I'm looking for but, held accountable by the institution," Padma began to share her reasoning for not reporting her assault to the institution. She continued, "The system of accountability isn't really being accountable." Padma suggested that men who were found responsible for perpetrating sexual violence might be "punished" with a slap on the wrist, for example, they were required to write a paper on sexual harassment or they were given a warning. But these trivial sanctions often made men feel even more "entitled to things that you're not," such as women students' bodies.

In 2022, a *USA TODAY* investigation found that, across 56 large, well-known public institutions, students who perpetrated sexual misconduct were rarely suspended or expelled.[44] For cases that did not result in suspension or expulsion, the resulting sanctions were light, allowing perpetrators to continue at the institution with little interruption to their education.[45] At the University of Georgia, for instance, more than 80% of students found responsible were sanctioned with probation and/or training—sanctions that did not require them to miss class. This percentage includes students that perpetrated rape, intimate partner violence, stalking, and/or unwanted sexual contact once or multiple times.[46] This lack of accountability can dissuade many survivors from reporting their assault.

Padma did not report her assault to the institution. She, like Leyla, perceived that the institution would do very little to protect and provide adequate justice to Women of Color survivors, particularly because of her race and gender. Padma did not trust the institution to support her, a Woman of Color, over the white man and well-respected student leader who perpetrated the assault. She shared:

> Believability was really very present. Because there were multiple occasions when he was taking advantage [of me], and I could hear in my head the types of questions that I felt people would ask if I took it to more of an administrative thing. . . . A lot of concerns about: "What did you say? What did you do?" And just like, "Well, if you didn't [say anything] then how was he supposed to know?". . . I was just scared. I was, in that case, I was like, "White man? Women of Color?". . . Who's gonna be believed here?

Padma connected believability to her identity as a Woman of Color. Due to dominant conceptualizations of rape that are founded in racism and sexism, Padma perceived that CU administrators would not view her allegations of sexual violence as credible or believable. These dominant conceptualizations position Women of Color as inherently unrapeable[47] and, therefore, implausible in their allegations of rape. Asian women, for instance, are often socially constructed as exploitable because they are "sexually experienced whores"[48] and/or "passive, in need of domination, and eager to please."[49] Black women are often depicted as hyper-sexual, oversexed, immoral, and, therefore, responsible for their assault.[50] Indigenous women are framed as "dirty," and the rape of unclean bodies "simply does not count."[51] These dominant conceptions work to justify the rape of Women of Color, often perpetrated by white men, as a necessary tool for slavery/capitalism, genocide/colonialism, and orientalism/war.[52]

These historical conceptualizations of rape continue to influence racist and sexist understanding of Women of Color's bodies on the college campus.[53] Influenced by the stereotype that Black women are "sexual temptresses," white men students may view Black women survivors as more promiscuous than white women survivors, particularly when the perpetrator of assault is a white man.[54] Both Black and white students believe that rape is less serious when the victim is a Black woman than when the victim is a white woman; rape of Black women is less likely to be labeled as a crime and does not often rise to the level necessitated to report to authorities.[55] Latina and Asian women survivors often hesitate to disclose their assault to formal outlets for fear that racist myths may portray them as not believable.[56] Koo and colleagues, for example, found that Asian women students perceived that police would not believe their allegations because of stereotypes that paint Asian women as hypersexual, passive, and not "the white norm."[57] Padma was aware that she, a Woman of Color who was assaulted by a white man, would be viewed by her institution as a woman "who essentially got what they were asking for."[58]

Interestingly, these racist and sexist understandings also influenced two Women of Color survivors' decisions *to report* their assault to formal outlets. Both Clara and Eliza, two of the three CU survivors who formally reported their assault, were aware that their light/white phenotypes positioned them closer to whiteness and white privileges than if they had darker phenotypes, or, as Clara suggested, if she looked more like a Person of Color. These two women acknowledged that their proximity to whiteness, which was read on their bodies (e.g., light skin, straight hair) may have provided them with privileges throughout the reporting process.

As a transfer student, Clara arrived on the CU campus knowing exactly where she wanted to live, what she wanted to study, and the extracurriculars she hoped to take on. Once on campus, however, Clara was surprised by her growing interest in FSL. She suddenly had a desire to become better friends with several of the women in one specific, small, and somewhat "unpopular" sorority. Clara joined the sorority during her second semester on campus. That next semester, her second year at CU, she moved into the sorority house.

One fall night during her second year at CU, Clara, along with her sorority sister and roommate, Janelle, Janelle's boyfriend, and Janelle's boyfriend's friend decided to go to a bar in the city. Before that night, Clara had never met Janelle's boyfriend's friend, Patrick. Patrick was 27 and a CU staff member.

As Clara began to drink at the bar, she became increasingly uneasy with Patrick. He was clearly hitting on her. He was also plying her with drinks that she did not order. Clara grew more and more uncomfortable with the situation and told Janelle, "I just want to go home now. Can we just go home? I'm over this. Patrick is annoying and he's not respecting my wishes."

Eventually the four made their way out of the bar and back to Janelle's boyfriend's apartment. After Janelle and her boyfriend retreated to the back room of the apartment, Patrick raped Clara.

Clara woke up the next morning and hurriedly texted another friend in the sorority: "Hey, I think I may have just been raped." Her friend was out of town, but immediately asked another sorority sister to pick Clara up and take her home. Once home, Clara waited for her friend to drive back into the city and return to the sorority house. When she did, she took a quick look at Clara and stated, "I'm so sorry. You need to report this." Clara responded, confused, "I don't know how to do that. What does that mean, the reporting? Like calling the cops, or what?" Her friend answered, "No, I can go with you. We'll go to the hospital."

Clara, with the support of her friend, spent the day at the local Sexual Violence Crisis Center "being poked everywhere and checked everywhere." Shortly after, Clara moved forward with reporting the assault to CU Title IX. She also filed charges with the state. Clara did not think too deeply or for too long about whether to report the assault. For her, it was the next logical step.

Throughout our conversations, Clara was in the preliminary stages of the criminal case, but she had recently received a decision from CU Title IX. The institution found Patrick responsible for assaulting Clara. CU had terminated Patrick's employment contract shortly after Clara reported the allegations.

Clara knew that the outcome of her case was a unique privilege at CU. But she also had a theory for why the process was "smooth."

[I'm] very, very fortunate to have had a smooth process.... But I know it's not that way for everyone else and that's why it's really hard for me to kind of see that. I think I've had some sort of privilege that has allowed me to be, I don't even know, you know? I know other people aren't going to be as lucky.

Not wanting to break her train of thought, I quickly asked Clara to say more about her "privilege" in the reporting process:

I don't think that I'm treated like that much [a Person] of Color, just because I'm light-skinned. Sometimes I feel like I get the same privileges as if I was white. So that's why I'm really uncomfortable when I do get these results during this process. Because it makes me feel like, "Do I really deserve it?" But I am a Person of Color. I just happen to be lighter skinned.

Clara implied that many Students of Color may not be seen as deserving of a smooth reporting process within the CU environment. Clara may have benefitted from colorism, or "a form of discrimination based on skin tone that routinely privileges light-skinned people of color and penalizes darker-skinned people of color."[59] Margaret Hunter has written at length about how lighter-skinned Women of Color are framed in many societies as more beautiful, and more intelligent and respectable, than darker-skinned Women of Color.[60] Light skin can translate into a form of social capital that often provides light-skinned Women of Color with access to other forms of capital, such as economic and educational capital.[61] In general, Women of Color "who more closely resemble whites receive more rewards."[62] One such reward for whiteness/lightness, as Clara hinted, may be a "smooth" reporting process.[63]

In *Split Affinities: The Case of Interracial Rape*, Valerie Smith points to how the "differential value of women's bodies" results in differential levels of believability and significance when it comes to sexual violence.[64] While Women of Color's bodies have often been positioned as dirty, hyper-sexual, immoral, and, thus, unrapeable,[65] privileged white women's bodies have been constructed as virtuous, pious, morally superior, informing stereotypes of white women as sexually restrained, virginal, and interested in sex within the context of marriage and only for procreation.[66] Therefore, "crimes against less valuable women—women of color, working-class women, and lesbians, for example—mean less or mean differently than those against white women from the middle and upper classes."[67]

Smith makes an important distinction, clarifying some of Clara's assertions. Reporting sexual violence is not inherently accessible for *all* white women and inherently inaccessible for *all* Women of Color. White women with intersecting minoritized identities, for example, lesbian white women and working-class white women, can also be positioned as less valuable, important, or credible in their claims of violence. The reporting process can be dissuasive and damaging for *all* survivors.[68] What Clara perceived, however, was that institutional leaders at CU might respond to allegations of sexual violence according to the perceived identities and values of the parties involved; this is institutional betrayal.[69] Because Clara passed as light/white, her assault, perpetrated by a Man of Color, may have been viewed as more important or more credible than if she were a darker-skinned Woman of Color and/or if Patrick were a white man that held value with the institution.[70]

Where Does Intersectionality Take Us?

Several Women of Color survivors at CU insisted that the institution must focus on racial *and* gender inequity to effectively address campus sexual violence. Women of Color survivors often implored institutional leaders to support and include Women of Color students within the CU environment. This increased focus, support, and inclusion would allow Women of Color to feel empowered by their institution to report and heal from sexual violence. It would also demonstrate to the campus community that all students, not just certain men students, held equal amounts of power and prestige on the CU campus.

"Hire Women of Color to support Women of Color, because no one understands the experiences of Women of Color like Women of Color," Faye suggested. After recommending that the institution hire more Women of Color, Faye concluded, "Back up your values with money!" If the institution truly valued "diversity and inclusion" as it claimed, then institutional leaders must put money toward this espoused value and hire more faculty and staff who are Women of Color.

Faye perceived that Women of Color survivors would be more willing and able to report and disclose assault to other Women of Color faculty and staff. CU leadership, then, must hire more Women of Color to work with SVRC, Title IX, and other departments that concern campus sexual violence. The institution must also hire more Women of Color faculty and staff that work in roles outside of sexual violence. It is particularly important that these faculty and staff are knowledgeable about the ways that intersecting structures of oppression influence Women of Color's campus experiences.

While collecting data at CU, several survivors mentioned that our interviews were the first time they could fully process and unpack their experiences with violence. It was the first time that some women were provided a space to explore the ways that colonization, racism, sexism, family, culture, and much more, influenced their experiences with sexual violence. And they were able to sit in this space with another Woman of Color who was aware of these intersectional influences. Of course, there was one additional detail: I was not a mandatory reporter. Institutions must offer survivors the opportunity to speak with other Women of Color faculty and staff who can offer a safe, understanding space without fear that discussions and disclosures must be reported back to an institution that does not often feel safe for these women. The institution must challenge federal policies concerning mandatory reporting and designate other faculty and staff on campus (many of whom hold multiple minoritized identities), beyond just SVRC employees, as confidential reporters.

Leyla also felt that more diversity on campus would help to support Women of Color students. "They really do need to hire more people that make People of Color feel more comfortable. And I don't know, increase the amount of People of Color on this campus," she suggested. Leyla strongly believed that having more People of Color on campus would allow Women of Color to feel like they fit into the campus social scene. That they were not "weird" just because they were not white. With more racial diversity, Women of Color may feel an increased sense of belonging on campus, influencing their willingness to report violence. Leyla recommended that the institution divert the money they spend on new and unnecessary campus buildings toward scholarships for Students of Color and for hiring more Faculty and Staff of Color. Like Faye, Leyla hinted that the institution must invest their financial resources in their espoused valuing of diversity.

To better support Women of Color on campus, survivors also suggested that the institution highlight Women of Color students' unique experiences throughout sexual violence education. Clara, for instance, wanted "more culture specific, or inclusive workshops. . . . It's a different culture. It's a different way of approaching family members more so than say like, white people." Clara pleaded for education to account for the qualitatively different ways that Women of Color students can experience violence.

Mary also wanted CU to incorporate Women of Color's experiences into institutional resources, including sexual violence education. Mary suggested that this inclusion would send the following message to the CU community: "Oh, we see you. We know about you, Women of Color. We are considering you." Instead of just making Women of Color wonder like, "Oh, am I part of this too?" Approaching sexual violence education from an intersectional lens, CU might show the campus community that they value the experiences and the presence of Women of Color students.

To achieve this more inclusive sexual violence education, Erika wanted CU administrators to ask Women of Color alumni who are also survivors to speak with the campus community. She stated:

> I know that there are people who are willing to talk about their experiences and I'm definitely one of those people. And if it means coming back every year to talk about it, I definitely would . . . [a]nd be like, "These are all the things that happened to me. What can you take away from that?"

While attending CU, Erika never saw her story, as a Woman of Color, represented in the sexual violence education that existed on campus. Erika was itching to tell her story, especially if it helped other Women of Color students better understand sexual violence. The institution must evaluate their current approaches to sexual violence education—how does it include or exclude certain voices, stories, and populations? How does sexual violence education de/value and dis/empower Women of Color students? How is this education intersectional? (see Chapter 1 for tangible implications on how to approach sexual violence from an intersectional lens.)

Some women explored how the institutional response to sexual violence must account for the unique experiences and needs of Women of Color survivors. Serena first stated:

> [CU administrators] need to hear [Woman of Color student] voices and make sure action is taken. . . . People can talk all day, they can tell you their concerns, you can listen to them, but people will know if they've told you their story and nothing is being done.

For Serena, listening to and acting on Women of Color survivors' allegations of violence was particularly important given the questioning of believability and credibility that these women might encounter when reporting violence at CU. Serena suggested that administrators offer culturally specific resources for Women of Color, such as a Women of Color survivor support groups or academic courses that center race, gender, and sexual violence. If the institution listened to and believed Women of Color students' allegations of sexual violence, then, Serena believed, *all* students would feel "safe and secure" on campus.

Sometimes, intersectionality takes us toward unexpected terrain. When starting this research, I did not perceive that FSL would play much of a role in the stories of Women of Color survivors. Because Women of Color are often excluded from membership in FSL, I suspected that they would rarely speak about the connection between this structure and campus sexual violence.[71] My assumptions were misguided. Instead, women's stories from CU elucidated how FSL and athletics structured campus rape culture for students who did and did not formally belong to, and those who were informally excluded from, these institutional programs. Intersectionality, then, guides us to and through seemingly familiar terrain that concerns campus sexual violence toward deeper understandings of how exclusion and discrimination inform consequences and vulnerabilities for students with multiple minoritized identities.[72]

Five

"They Don't Care About Us"

REPORTING CAMPUS SEXUAL VIOLENCE

"I've only told my friends that are also Women of Color." Margaret took a breath and continued, "[Women of Color] have to just be a little more hidden about it. We have to just be a little more low key and deal with it ourselves."

A history of colonization, slavery, forced removal, cultural genocide, and continued violence against Communities of Color in the U.S. continues to influence Women of Color's experiences with reporting sexual violence.[1] For example, influenced by a history of police brutality against Communities of Color, some Women of Color students hesitate to report their assault to police.[2] Some Women of Color are expected to remain silent about issues of sexual violence that occur within their racial community to prevent the perpetuation of damaging racial stereotypes often attributed to Men of Color.[3] Unfortunately, these intersectional realities with reporting are not often accounted for in campus sexual violence research and practice.[4] Here, we account for these intersectional realities.

Through this chapter, the 34 Women of Color survivors explore their decisions to report their experiences with sexual violence to formal outlets, such as Title IX and campus police. Survivors also demonstrate how intersecting structures of domination influenced these decisions. Some survivors' stories of reporting are intertwined with disclosure, or "the act of discussing an experience of sexual assault with someone, regardless of whether it is officially recorded."[5] For instance, at Mountain University, survivors' disclosures to friends and their interactions with SVRC staff often influenced their willingness and ability to report their experiences. Therefore, the chapter focuses on survivors' decisions to formally report violence while also exploring survivors' stories of disclosure.

"A Stupid Brock Turner Sentence": Navigating the U.S. (In)Justice System

Lars Peter Jonsson and Carl Frederik Arndt observed the dwindling moments of the Saturday night college party scene as they rode their bikes through the Stanford University campus.[6] It was a relatively pleasant January evening in 2015 as the two Stanford graduate students biked their way toward a cluster of fraternity homes. Near one fraternity home, a sudden movement by a dumpster caught Jonsson's eye. Was that a man on top of a woman? The woman was not moving. Jonsson knew something was wrong.[7]

"Hey, she's fucking unconscious?" Jonsson shouted at the man from a distance.[8] The man looked up from the woman toward Jonsson and began to run. Arndt made his way to the woman by the dumpster to make sure she was still alive. Jonsson peeled off to chase after the unidentified man. Jonsson caught the stranger, pinning him to the ground. Arndt joined his friend to help restrain the man. Someone called 911. The woman was still unconscious when the police arrived.

The man that Jonsson and Arndt pinned to the ground was soon identified as Brock Turner, a Stanford student and swimmer/athlete. The woman's identity remained unknown. Court documents and journalists referred to her simply as Emily Doe. That same January morning, police arrested Turner, and Doe was taken to the hospital. Although Turner eventually admitted to engaging in sexual activity with

Doe, he claimed his actions were consensual.[9] Doe had no memory of providing Turner with consent. She did not remember the assault, nor Jonsson and Arndt's intervention.[10]

More than one year later, in March 2016, the trial against Turner (*The People of the State of California v. Brock Allen Turner*) began. Former teachers and coaches showed up to vouch for Turner's stellar character. Although Turner's abuse of drugs and alcohol were present in courtroom evidence, it was relatively absent from courtroom discourse.[11] The court was not so kind to Doe.[12] Doe's alcohol use was repeatedly questioned, as if to justify the rape. Doe would later write of the trial that it was as if she had "remained frozen, while Brock grew more and more multifaceted, his stories unfolding, a spectrum of life and memories opening up around him."[13]

Turner was eventually convicted of assault with intent to commit rape of an intoxicated person, sexually penetrating an intoxicated person with a foreign object, and sexually penetrating an unconscious person with a foreign object.[14] Judge Aaron Persky, a Stanford Alum and former Stanford Athlete, sentenced Turner to six months in jail with three years of probation. Prosecutors requested that Turner receive a harsher sentence of at least six years in jail. Persky was against this tougher sentence because it would have a "severe impact" on Turner, who had his whole (sports) career ahead of him.[15] When all was said and done, Turner served three months in the county jail.

People v. Turner was concluding with little attention from the media. At least compared to the media frenzy that was yet to come. On June 3, 2016, one day after Turner's sentencing hearing, *BuzzFeed News* published Doe's Victim Impact Statement.[16] The *BuzzFeed* publication quickly gained attention from the public. The site that housed Doe's statement received over 11 million views over the first four days.[17] Media outlets and sexual violence advocates began to lambast the extremely light sentence that Persky gifted Turner. Some pointed to how the "Stanford case shows why so many victims do not report their assaults to police or choose to testify in drawn-out trials that could end in sentences that, in this woman's case, are widely considered a slap on the wrist."[18]

The overwhelming criticism around Persky's preferential sentencing of Turner eventually resulted in his being recalled by voters of Santa Clara, California. Persky is the first judge in over 80 years to be recalled in the state of California.[19] And through it all, Doe remained anonymous.

But then, in September 2019, Doe released her powerful memoir, *Know My Name*. Through the book (and marketing for the book), Doe identified herself as Chanel Miller. Miller told her story nearly five years after the assault to counter the invisibility she experienced as an Asian American woman. "I had grown up without seeing people who looked like me in the public eye. I craved stories of Asian American women who embodied power and agency," Miller shared in a 2020 *TIME* article.[20] Through her memoir, Miller illuminated how the U.S. justice system tirelessly works to protect perpetrators of sexual violence and perpetually fails survivors. According to Miller, Women of Color survivors may be even more vulnerable—they are "used to being unseen, to never being fully known." But Miller was ready to be seen. She was ready for people to know her name.

Miller released her memoir as I concluded my interviews with survivors. But not one survivor mentioned Miller or her book. The name "Brock Turner," on the other hand, infiltrated many of my conversations. Felecia, for example, stated, "A lot of these stories get brushed under the rug actually. . . . I'm sure you've seen they're like, 'Oh! They didn't get convicted.' Or, 'Oh! Brock Turner got like two months for raping a student?' And they got a video of it."

Erika concisely connected her decision to not report her assault to her knowledge of the "Brock Turner case." Erika imagined that her perpetrator would be given "a stupid Brock Turner sentence." For Erika, this slap on the wrist sentence was not worth the pain, time, and money she would expend attempting to convince the institution and authorities of the assault. This now-public case, where a man student was caught raping a woman in front of witnesses but received a light sentence, weighed heavy on the minds of many women survivors who were deciding if they should formally report their experiences with violence.

The "Stanford case" also loomed over Serena's head as she made the decision to report her experience with sexual violence. One night during her first year at CU, Serena went out with friends to a party at a CU fraternity home. There, on the dance floor, a man zigzagged his way over to Serena as they began to dance to the latest hits. As Serena and the man danced, he suddenly and tightly grabbed Serena, swiftly lifted her skirt, and penetrated her with his fingers. Serena stopped cold. She was stunned. Her friends noticed what was happening and took over immediately. They snapped photos and a video of the perpetrator who Serena and her friends had never seen before. They ushered Serena, who was in shock, away from the perpetrator and off the dance floor.

Moments later, Serena's peers were already encouraging her to report the assault to the CU police. Serena was hesitant to report because she assumed the justice system might "turn it around" on her. I probed Serena a bit, asking her to say more about from where this low-bar belief about the justice system stemmed. Serena responded quickly: "You remember the Stanford case about Brock Turner or something about how it's been an ongoing thing?" I nodded in affirmation as my mouth upturned in a knowing expression. Having talked to several survivors before Serena, I suspected where she was about to take us. Serena read my nonverbal affirmation and continued:

> I think it was within the last year or two that [Turner] actually got a punishment and it was bare minimum. And that girl had to fight constantly for that to happen. And people basically made jokes out of it. They basically said, "Oh, this is what happens when you let women drink," and all of that. And it's basically humiliating for that woman's identity for a while, even though she's anonymous. But it's still humiliating to hear how some people talk about women. And they basically call most women liars . . . that they're just making scenes and all of that. And I get worried. I don't want that. What if that reputation gets around or everyone thinks that I'm a liar?

The Turner case functioned as a warning for Serena. Sara Ahmed has written about how "a warning about 'what would happen' can be predicated on what has happened."[21] Ahmed explained further, "The past is used like an arrow that points to what will happen. You are being told the likely consequences of complaint before you proceed, as if what will happen to you will be the same thing as what happened to others before you."[22] The outcome of the Turner case warned Serena that, if she were to file a report, she would be humiliated, made fun of, and cast as a liar. The best outcome she could expect would be for the perpetrator to receive a "bare minimum" sentence after a drawn-out process. Warnings work to stop complaints, to stop survivors from reporting assault.[23]

Wrapped up in this warning was Serena's awareness of U.S. rape myths that might position her at fault for the assault. The U.S. justice system has supported this myth with laws that force women survivors to demonstrate how they resisted their rape to prove victimhood.[24] These laws allowed judges and juries to scrutinize whether women "were innocent victims or women who essentially got what they were asking for."[25] Another myth, that many women "cry rape" is also present in U.S. society. Yet only 2–10% of rape allegations are found to be false.[26] These myths paint a colorful narrative about sexual violence in the U.S. that silences women survivors—sexual violence is not a real occurrence, and if it is, women are often at fault. And let's not gloss over context: Serena experienced sexual violence while attending CU, an environment where many Women of Color were made to question their believability and credibility, because of their race and gender, when deciding to report violence.

The morning after the interaction on the fraternity dance floor, Serena visited the CU police station to report the assault. Although culpability and believability remained in Serena's mind, she decided to report because she felt that she had sufficient evidence. Serena was one of three women at CU who did report their assault. (She was also the one that reported because she had proof, not necessarily because of her proximity to whiteness.) After exploring her skepticism of the U.S. justice system via the case of Brock Turner, Serena smiled slightly and stated, "But then I remember I have eight to nine witnesses and someone who was literally right next to me." She also had the photos and video that her friends captured of the perpetrator. With this evidence, Serena hoped that the police would be more likely to believe that she was in fact assaulted and that the assault was not her fault.

"Who Would Believe Me?"

Unlike Serena, most survivors I spoke with did not perceive themselves to have reliable evidence or proof of their assault. Without evidence, women survivors questioned if they should even bother to report to their institutions. Who would believe them without proof? Christine asked me this question directly as she recalled her decision to not report her assault:

> If I do report, how do they believe me? There's no actual evidence. And then usually the hospital will do the little [rape] kit and stuff and I didn't know that. It's been two or three days, it's not going to be the same. If I did report, who would believe me?

After experiencing sexual violence during her first Halloween weekend on the RU campus, Christine had no clue what to do or who to turn to make sense of what happened. She felt underprepared to respond to the violence. Her institution, RU, was not very forthcoming with where survivors could or should turn for help. A few days after the assault, Christine learned that one of her options in that moment was to visit the local hospital and complete a sexual violence forensic exam, or a rape kit. But, in her understanding, it was now several days too late to collect this evidence. And without this evidence, Christine was not open to reporting her assault. Who would believe her?

Women of Color survivors who did not have "actual evidence" often perceived that it would be strenuous and tenuous to attain justice from institutional and state justice systems. The day after Jasmine was raped on the MU campus, her good friend convinced her to visit the local Planned Parenthood. She walked into Planned Parenthood with the one goal of receiving medicine that would mitigate the transmission of STIs and prevent pregnancy. But once in the examination room, Jasmine disclosed to the Planned Parenthood nurse that a man raped her the previous night—she wanted medication and nothing more. "They were being really forceful. They were like, 'You should [file a report]. You should really do it.' And the nurse was like. 'I would do it if I was you,'" Jasmine recalled of the nurse's response to her disclosure. Jasmine responded to the nurse succinctly. "Okay. Well I don't want to." The reason Jasmine hesitated to file a report was because she did not have proof of the assault:

> I remember thinking that I didn't have any proof. It had been a while and [I] had washed all my clothes. All the stuff they tell you to not do, I had already done. I was like, "Okay, it's kinda late for that." And it's like, "If I don't have any proof, they're never going to take up the case." It was too far out of reach getting any sort of justice for it.

Jasmine added, "I feel like if I told anybody at MU, 'Hey, this guy did this to me.' Everybody would believe me. But other than that, nobody would [believe me]." Jasmine did disclose her assault to peers at MU, who offered support after her disclosure, i.e., "Hey, let's get you to Planned Parenthood." But formally reporting to the institution or to police was a different context. Without proof, Jasmine was not willing to file a report. Without proof, she feared reporting would become a long, drawn-out process.

"Where do you get that messaging from, [that] you need proof to take up a case?" I asked Jasmine. "I see all this stuff on Twitter. People go to the Supreme Court, and they still don't believe them," Jasmine responded emphatically. She leaned back in her chair and gave a slight shrug while saying, "So, I'm just like . . . you know?" Jasmine was referencing the recent confirmation hearings for now Supreme Court Justice Bret Kavanaugh. Like the name "Brock Turner," the name "Kavanaugh" weighed heavy on the minds of some women survivors. The confirmation hearing, like the coverage of the case against Turner, functioned as a warning for several Women of Color survivors.[27]

"Men can really just get away with a lot of things. Especially, again, white men. Like Kavanaugh," Margaret sighed. She continued, "I know that the justice system is innocent until proven guilty, but I think [sexual violence] is something really hard to prove." Margaret wondered how the U.S. justice system expected Christine Blasey

Ford to provide tangible proof that U.S. circuit judge Bret Kavanaugh assaulted her 35 years prior. At the time of our interview, Ford, a white woman, and Professor of Psychology, had just testified in front of the Senate Judiciary Committee that Kavanaugh, a Supreme Court Justice nominee, sexually assaulted her while the two attended high school in Maryland.[28] Ford provided some evidence to support her testimony—therapeutic records from 2012 and results from a lie detector test.[29] Yet, for Margaret, the expectation that Ford and other women provide evidence was "strange." There was no way Ford could adequately "prove" her assault and, therefore, there was no way she would receive justice.

What's more is that Ford is a "credible" white woman—a "credible" white woman who was often discredited and disbelieved by U.S. media and the U.S. government.[30] If society did not value and believe this credible white woman's claim of sexual violence, would they believe Women of Color? In writing about Ford's testimony, Anne Helen Petersen named "the incredibly high bar of believability" that her story reinforced:

> Ford is white, upper-middle class, married, and highly educated. She is calm but demure. She is visibly shaken yet steady. She could afford the therapy that helped document her psychological past. She has a support system and the means to hire a lawyer. Imagine if you lack even one of these qualities. Imagine if your behavior, or your voice, or your face, or the life you've lived doesn't perfectly match what is demanded of the ideal victim. Would you be believed?[31]

For Women of Color survivors, "Would I be believed?" was often a rhetorical question. Many survivors understood that because they do not "perfectly match" that of the ideal victim—a credible, privileged cisgender heterosexual white woman—there was little hope for justice, particularly without substantial proof.[32]

Although some people may claim, "Oh, the justice system's broken," Margaret was sure that the justice system "was designed that way. Especially for People of Color. It just wasn't made for us. [It was] made to work against us." These intersectional failures and the way they

silence and isolate Women of Color influenced Margaret's decision to
not report her assault:

> I think it's just different for Women of Color because we're always dis-
> counted. Especially with the white feminist movement going on. They
> don't care about us. We're like double marginalized I would say. And,
> just reporting, if you do it, I don't really think anything's gonna come of
> it, because they don't seem to take it seriously.... Especially Women of
> Color, we just don't really have an outlet for it to be taken seriously....
> I don't really think legal help, it's very farfetched. I don't think that it
> ever really works. Justice doesn't really work.

Women of Color who make allegations of assault are often less likely
to be believed than white women who make similar allegations.[33] And
violence against Women of Color often results in less prosecutions and
convictions, and shorter prison sentencing than violence against white
women.[34] To be clear, the U.S. legal system's treatment of sexual violence discredits *most* women, but the intersections of racism and sexism
often result in the attribution of less credibility to Women of Color—
and credibility is key in the eyes of the court.[35]

Unfortunately, as Margaret suggested, feminist movements do not
often account for "the cultural narratives that undermine the credibility of Black women" and other Women of Color in rape reform and ju-
dicial justice.[36] Feminist movements, such as the #MeToo movement,
almost always focus on what justice looks like for privileged, cisgender
heterosexual white women while discounting the rights and needs of
many Women of Color.

Feminism and the #MeToo Movement

On October 15, 2017, actress Alyssa Milano tweeted, "If you've been
sexually harassed or assaulted write 'me too' as a reply to this tweet."[37]
Within moments, the tweet went viral. As I write this book, the tweet
has received over 60,000 comments, 38,000 retweets, and 46,000 likes.
Many of the comments represent survivors responding simply, "me

too." Other survivors included descriptions of their experiences with sexual violence, followed by the hashtag #MeToo.

#MeToo swiftly morphed into a global movement where sexual violence, and perpetrators of sexual violence, were critiqued on a public stage. *TIME* Magazine dedicated their 2017 Person of the Year Award to the Silence Breakers—the many individuals who broke their silence by publicly claiming "me too."[38] Several actors dressed in all black at the 2018 Golden Globe awards to protest and bring awareness to the sexual violence that is often condoned in Hollywood.[39] The #MeToo movement inspired a television series, *The Morning Show*, starring actresses Jennifer Aniston and Reese Witherspoon.[40] And all the while, survivors continued to post "me too."

The movement made it difficult to continue to deny the pervasiveness of sexual violence and the abuses of power that occurred in Hollywood and elsewhere, including sports and politics. Some men in positions of power were suddenly reckoning with #MeToo: U.S. gymnastics doctor Larry Nassar, comedian Louis C.K., film producer Harvey Weinstein, actor and comedian Aziz Ansari, news anchor Matt Lauer, and New York Governor Andrew Cuomo were accused of abusing their power and perpetrating sexual violence.[41] The movement began to reverberate outside the walls of Hollywood, sports, and politics and seeped into our universities, workplaces, and homes. As the 2017 *TIME* article suggested, "When a movie star says #MeToo, it becomes easier to believe the cook who's been quietly enduring for years."[42] Suddenly, the pervasiveness and perpetration of sexual violence was a topic open for public conversation, and people were ready to discuss.

Prior to Milano's tweet going viral, Tessa had already started the Title IX reporting process at MU. During the reporting process, Tessa began to see #MeToo on her social media and hear "me too" in campus conversations. "#MeToo is just more validation, and it makes me feel so reassured and validated by things that other women are saying," Tessa described her initial thoughts about the movement. #MeToo compelled Tessa to ask herself, "Why can't I be one of those women who works to reassure and validate other women who maybe aren't speaking out?"

Seeing other women speak out about their assault encouraged Tessa to be "more open and vocal" about her experience with violence.

Tessa used Twitter to disclose her assault and to educate and support others on the pervasiveness of sexual violence. The movement, however, was not what compelled Tessa to visit SVRC and report her assault to MU Title IX. As we observed in Chapter 3, the MU peer environment influenced Tessa's decision to use SVRC and eventually report her perpetrator to MU Title IX. But #MeToo did allow Tessa to be more "constructive" while processing her assault, which influenced her willingness to disclose more often and publicly about her experience.

Although she was initially hesitant of the movement, #MeToo eventually inspired Samantha to disclose her assault. During her first year at MU, Samantha took a gender and sexuality course. This was the same semester that a man student sexually assaulted her. For the gender and sexuality course, Samantha was required to present on an assigned topic—the #MeToo movement. Prior to receiving her topic, Samantha had never heard of the movement. Her first search for "me too" was instantly triggering. Samantha had just experienced sexual violence. How could she read thousands of survivors' stories and disclosures? Samantha quickly closed her search tab and decided, "Oh my God. I'm not doing this right now."

Knowing that her grade depended on the project, a few days later Samantha forced herself to look at several posts on Twitter with the hashtag, #MeToo. Slowly, Samantha's feelings about the movement changed. "I'm not alone," she realized as she scanned Twitter. She quickly found that she could not stop reading posts. Each tweet let her know, "'You're not alone and other people understand.' It's crazy that just those two words could make such a big difference." And those two words—me too—did make a difference in Samantha's decision to disclose her assault. Before presenting her project in class she tweeted "#MeToo" for the first time. She hoped that other survivors might see her tweet and think, "I'm not alone."

#MeToo, however, was not always inspiring. The movement was also met with intense backlash and scrutiny. Many journalists, politicians, and actors scrutinized the movement for blowing sexual harassment out of proportion. Some called it a "witch hunt," others, a "vindictive plot against men."[43] In writing about the allegations we first read about in Chapter 3 against actor and comedian Aziz Ansari, Caitlin Flanagan wrote that the #MeToo movement "is starting to sweep up all sorts of people into its conflagration: the monstrous, the cruel, and the simply unlucky."[44] A movement meant to center survivors was starting to center perpetrators who were almost always men, "unlucky" men who were egregiously under attack.

Influenced by the backlash against the movement, some Women of Color survivors found it even more difficult to talk about, let alone report, their assault. Rayn perceived #MeToo as a "witch hunt" that influenced others to play "devil's advocate" on behalf of some alleged perpetrators. As a result of the backlash against the movement, Rayn decided to remain silent about her assault because she no longer felt the same possibilities for validation and support that she felt prior to #MeToo.

Christine observed how within the #MeToo movement, "No one ever wants to believe the [survivors]. They always want to stand up for the male. They are always like, "No this didn't happen. We need proof. We need evidence." Survivors sometimes connected their perceptions of the movement to their concerns about proving their assault with evidence. Kavanaugh's confirmation hearings took place amid #MeToo. When protestors took to the streets to protest Kavanaugh's appointment to the Supreme Court, some signs were adorned with, "Me Too." #MeToo was one influential factor in encouraging Chanel Miller to leave behind her anonymity and share her story. But Miller's memoir, and the courage of Blasey Ford, were also unsettling reminders of how unjust justice could be—particularly in the court of public opinion.

"We Don't Fit the Role of a Survivor"

"The founder for me too is a Black woman," Samantha stated as she excitedly shared the information she gathered to complete her class presentation. Samantha's love for #MeToo grew even more when she learned that Tarana Burke, a Black woman, was the founder of me too.

For Samantha, Burke "is representing other Women of Color" who experience sexual violence.

Eleven years before Milano tweeted "me too" into the Twitter universe, Tarana Burke founded the "me too" movement™ and organization.[45] The main purpose of the organization is to support survivors with resources for and healing from experiences with sexual violence. Me too (not to be confused with #MeToo) and Burke are committed to interrupting "sexual violence and other systemic issues disproportionately impacting marginalized people—particularly Black women and girls."[46] But Burke's original, race-conscious vision for me too as an organization became somewhat lost within #MeToo.

In conversation with Elizabeth Adetiba, an editorial intern for *The Nation*, Burke explored how #MeToo often lacked an intersectional understanding of sexual violence:

> It defeats the purpose to not have those folks centered—I'm talking black and brown girls, queer folks. There's no conversation in this whole thing about transgender folks and sexual violence. There's no conversation in this about people with disabilities and sexual violence. We need to talk about Native Americans, who have the highest rate of sexual violence in this country.[47]

Privileged, cisgender heterosexual white women, however, were often the face of #MeToo: Alyssa Milano, Rose McGowan, Ashley Judd, Lady Gaga, Taylor Swift, and yes, Christine Blasey Ford. The movement rarely accounts for the intersections of minoritized identities and works to silence trans* women, queer women, women with disabilities, working-class women, and Women of Color.[48] Women of Color were being erased and excluded from their own movement.

"Yeah. This movement is not intersectional," Maribel stated as she observed how Women of Color were absent from #MeToo. Maribel was one of several women survivors who did not see themselves reflected in the movement. Queenie was another. Although #MeToo was important for Queenie because "it captured mainstream attention," she also pointed out how the movement was "missing different stories" and that white women's stories of violence "wasn't really my narrative."

During the height of the movement, Padma's professors brought up #MeToo and sexual violence as a topic for classroom conversation. But Padma questioned her professors, "Why are you talking about this without making sure that students can leave if they want to, before you even start talking about it?" Padma was also "triggered" by the intersectional failure of these classroom conversations and of the overall movement:

> That movement is really triggering because it was created by a Woman of Color and then kind of co-opted by white women. And really doesn't center Women of Color at all. Like, super white feminist. Talking about [#MeToo] as "This is what change looks like." It's like, "No. This is what exclusion looks like." This is what it's always been. This doesn't feel like change to me. This feels like whenever we talk about feminism in class, all the white girls have something to talk about, but I don't feel like I can talk about race. Because they don't think that's feminist. I believe that feminism is more than just gender.

Padma did not see herself represented in #MeToo. And the movement did not inspire her to speak up about sexual violence. In fact, she felt the opposite—silenced. Padma's experiences with sexual violence were racialized *and* gendered. But #MeToo, a feminist movement, often honored stories of *only* gender, which equated to stories of white womanhood. Due to this centering of whiteness, Padma refused to discuss sexual violence in class, and she was not open to disclosing her assault on social media. What exactly was the point of sharing her intersectional story in a movement permeated by intersectional failure?

The intersectional failure of the movement reinforced the image of who was a typical survivor—white cisgender women. The movement often (re)positioned Women of Color as "bad women within cultural narratives about good women who can be raped and bad women who cannot."[49] By packaging privileged, cisgender heterosexual white women as good women who can be raped, and are, therefore, survivors, feminist movements often further the implausibility that Women of Color experience violence and may need to report this violence. The movement pushed further from our minds the possibility of Women of Color as survivors.

Organizers "always miss the mark," Monae claimed as she began to share her thoughts about #MeToo. She continued:

[Feminist movements and organizations] trying to spread awareness, they always focus on who is acceptable to be a survivor, who is allowed to be a victim. I think it's always going to be a white woman. And if you're anything else, you can't be a survivor. So, we can't help you because you're never going to be a victim because you're not. You don't fit into that category. So I think, "Okay, that's cool that you're helping them, but what about us?"

"We're Mexican. We don't fit the role of a survivor. So, we're harder to believe because of that," Monae added. Unlike several women survivors at MU, Monae did not report her assault to MU Title IX or use MU SVRC. Her understanding that she did not "fit what a victim is supposed to be" due to her intersecting identities may have been more influential in her reporting decision than the peer environment at MU.

Women of Color survivors were often silenced by feminist movements that center heterosexual cisgender, privileged white women and do not account for white supremacy and racism. But many of these same Women of Color survivors found little visibility within antiracist movements that center Men of Color and do not account for patriarchy and sexism. Feminism and antiracism often contend in ways that limit Women of Color's ability to find representation and justice within these competing discourses of resistance.[50]

"He's Not a White Male": Antiracism and Protecting Men of Color Perpetrators

"I don't want to press charges against this person because they have a career. They're going to be doing things. I don't want to be the one to stop them from living their life," Faye explained of her decision to not report her perpetrator, a Black and Filipino man student. Several Women of Color survivors, such as Faye, hoped to protect their perpetrator by not reporting the assault. What if the perpetrator goes to jail? Do I really want to ruin his life? Will my community shut me out for throwing this man under the bus? What if police become involved and they harm, or worse, murder the perpetrator? Women of Color survivors only asked these questions when their perpetrators were Men of Color. The survivors I spoke with who were assaulted by white men did not ruminate on these questions.

Within Communities of Color, Women of Color are often expected, if not forced to remain silent about issues of violence to preserve the image of the community and to prevent the perpetuation of deleterious racial stereotypes attributed to Men of Color.[51] Jennifer Gómez and colleagues suggests that this protection relates to (intra)cultural trust, or a collective sense of racial loyalty and responsibility within minoritized communities.[52] Gómez and Gobin explain, "(intra)cultural trust is engendered by needs for psychological protection from societal trauma, including racial trauma, perpetrated by individuals, institutions, systems, and policies of the dominant culture."[53] When Women of Color experience intra-racial violence, this trust is violated, influencing cultural betrayal trauma. But this (intra)cultural trust simultaneously influences (intra)cultural pressure, or when Women of Color feel overt or covert pressure to remain silent about intra-racial trauma and cultural betrayal to protect an entire minority group.[54] This may influence why Women of Color are hesitant to report to police and other governmental entities, systems that are perpetually racist toward Communities of Color and particularly hostile toward Men of Color.[55] Title IX policies, for example, "operate with carceral logic in a way that individualizes harm and focuses on punishment rather than restoration."[56] Ivonne, the MU SVRC Director acknowledged this reality in her work with survivors, stating, "A lot of the perpetrators are Men of Color. And that's the other pieces to think about how [Women of Color] don't want to involve another Person of Color in the system. And I have to respect that."

The case between Aziz Ansari and Grace detailed in Chapter 3 connects to how some South Asian women survivors were hesitant to throw Men of Color "under the bus." Immediately after relaying how she would not report her assault because she did not want to ruin the professional or life chances of her perpetrator, Faye explained why protecting Men of Color perpetrators, such as Aziz Ansari, is complex:

> In light of what's going on with Aziz Ansari in the past couple days, me
> being South Asian, I've followed it pretty closely and have seen what
> my community's response has been, and a lot of it was, "I hope this girl
> wasn't brown, because you can't throw your own people under the bus
> like that." And this idea that we are expected to swallow our own pain
> to move our community forward and to do it for our people.

Rayn also pointed to Ansari to explore the complexity between being a South Asian woman survivor and needing to protect South Asian men. Rayn was hesitant to "critique" Ansari because she, as a South Asian woman, needed "to defend all the men of my community" to "protect our culture and our community in an incredibly xenophobic environment." Protecting Men of Color from the violent manifestations of white supremacy, including xenophobia, antiblackness, and racist nativism was a priority for many women survivors.

"No part of me wants to care that anything should happen to him to get punished" Naomi stated as she described why she did not feel compelled to report her assault. Earlier that year, Naomi was having the summer of her life. She felt wildly happy, independent, balanced, and mentally strong. Near the end of the summer, Naomi's parents went out of town for the weekend. As soon as she learned that her parents would be gone for several days, Naomi invited some friends from RU over for a small gathering. Almost all of Naomi's friends flaked on her party. But Andrew, a man student she had met that summer, showed up with a bottle of alcohol. That night, Andrew sexually assaulted Naomi.

The next morning, Naomi woke up in confusion. Andrew stirred in bed next to her. He reached for his phone to see the time: 6am. Andrew shot out of bed and announced, "I'm on the soccer team here. I'm going to be late!" In a blur, he gathered the few things he had brought with him and hurried out of the house. Naomi got up after Andrew to lock the front door. She shuffled back to her bedroom, climbed into bed, and tried to collect her thoughts. She continued to be confused about what happened the night before.

Naomi must have drifted in and out of sleep because a FaceTime from her good friend woke her up hours later. "What did you do last night?" the friend asked Naomi with an accusatory tone. Naomi was unsure how to answer the question. "What did you do?" The friend asked again. Naomi provided vague details. "Well, I hung out with Andrew." Her friend began to laugh. She told Naomi that she had just received a Snapchat from Andrew's friend that said something to the effect of, "Why did I just hear the funny story about how Andrew fucked Naomi?" This is how Naomi learned she was raped. Through Snapchat.

Naomi was adamant to her friend, and later to Andrew, that she did not provide consent; she was too incapacitated to have sex or consent to have sex. When Naomi confronted Andrew with her anger he replied plainly, "Well, no more Tequila Sunrises. LOL!"

Like all women survivors I spoke with at RU, Naomi did not report her assault. And, like many women survivors at RU, she attributed her hesitancy to report to the "modest" nature of the institution. At RU, sexual violence was normalized, not a big issue. Naomi minimized her assault so that she could believe, "It doesn't feel so huge. It just feels like something that happened." Naomi was one of the last women I talked to at RU, so I was not surprised that she minimized her assault and therefore did not report the violence. I assumed this was the only contributing factor to why she did not report and quickly moved on to another question. But I assumed wrong. At the end of our first conversation, I asked Naomi, "Do you have anything else to say that's on the record for today?"

"Well, I was gonna say another reason why I think I haven't reported it," she replied. I nodded my head for her to continue. Naomi did not want to "punish" Andrew. Andrew was attending RU on a sports scholarship, and she did not want to compromise his scholarship or his academic career by reporting the assault. Naomi was aware of the racial dynamics that might come into play if she reported Andrew, a Man of Color and an international student. She relayed, "He's not a white male. I don't know how it is here, but I feel like it'd be easy for them to kind of boot him out ... he's a big minority in that sense." If Andrew were a white man, he would have the protection of white supremacy and white privilege. There would be no need for Naomi to protect Andrew—the institution, U.S. society, the justice system—would protect him. But Andrew is not a white man. He is not protected by white supremacy. So, it fell on Naomi, a Woman of Color, to protect Andrew.

"The Machismo Culture" and Antiracism

On their third date together, Terri and Kevin—a Mexican man and a student at MU—went out to the local bars where they met up with several of their mutual friends. After spending a few hours at the bars, they all decided to go back to one of Terri's friend's apartments to keep the party going. Terri stated that Kevin was quite drunk upon returning to the apartment.

At one point in the night, Kevin stormed out of the small apartment where they landed after returning from the bars. Terri was concerned by Kevin's sudden and somewhat angry exit. She stepped outside to look for Kevin but could not find him anywhere. Kevin finally answered one of Terri's frantic phone calls. He let her know he was in his car, alone. Terri's worry spiked. "Obviously, red light, red flag because I'm like, 'Well, you're really drunk. You're evidently drunk. I'm not going to let you drive,'" Terri recalled. Terri finally found Kevin in his car and recognized that his mental head space was a bit off. "I'm not a good person," Kevin repeated several times when Terri joined him in his car. Terri was aware that there was "a lot of stuff" going on in Kevin's life, but she was not sure what that "stuff" was.

There was no way that Terri was going to let Kevin drive home. Terri invited Kevin back to her apartment so that he could wait to drive home until he was sober. Once the pair arrived at Terri's apartment they began to kiss. In those initial moments, Terri thought, "Okay. Yeah. I want to do this. I trust this person. It's been a couple dates." But once Kevin became more aggressive with his kissing, Terri's body froze, and her mind shifted. She no longer wanted to be intimate with Kevin.

She told Kevin to stop. Kevin did not stop and became more forceful. After what felt like a lifetime for Terri, Kevin finally stopped.

Terri immediately told him to leave her apartment. Kevin thought she was joking. She became more forceful. "LEAVE!" she yelled. After a moment, which felt like another lifetime to Terri, Kevin left.

Terri did not remember if she slept that night, but she did remember getting out of bed the next morning knowing she was not okay. That same morning, she disclosed the rape to a few of her close friends who were also students at MU. As was often typical in the MU environment, Terri's friends reacted in helpful and supportive manners to her disclosure. One of Terri's friends encouraged her to visit the MU SVRC for additional help. Terri was also aware of her option to report the assault to MU Title IX. Yet Terri did not visit SVRC or Title IX.

For Terri, there were many reasons why she did not report the rape. She was busy with homework and graduate school essays. She did not want her family to find out about her experience. Terri, however, continuously came back to one "main" reason for not reporting. She did not want to harm Kevin. She did not want to compromise his reputation or his life chances. Kevin planned to enroll in law school after graduation and Terri refused to do anything to jeopardize his future. Instead, Terri justified Kevin's actions to excuse his behavior. If she could excuse his behavior, she would not need to report, and Kevin could head off to law school:

> I wasn't even placing the blame on him. I felt like the intentions weren't malice. I felt that the intentions were ignorance. He didn't know better and he wasn't taught better. Men aren't taught what "No" really means. Maybe it is [because] he's Mexican. He was into all of the Mariachi stuff, and all that, which was a first for me. I know in that culture you're taught differently and its very machismo.... I feel like that plays a huge role in not reporting.

Machismo "vaguely refers to a standard of behavior exhibited by men" in Latinx culture.[57] Behaviors of machismo often revolve around male dominance of women, hyper-masculinity, sexism, and aggression.[58] Recently, however, scholars have argued for an expanded definition of machismo that accounts for more positive aspects of the construct, such as hard work, protection of one's family, and honor.[59] While toxic masculinity is one way to perform being a man, machismo is one way to perform being a Latino man.

Terri's justification for the assault was that Kevin, as a Mexican man, was socialized into a culture of machismo. Kevin was not at fault for his violent behavior that night; it was society, it was the culture of machismo, Mexican culture, Terri's culture, that was at fault. As I listened to Terri talk about machismo and forgiving Kevin for his actions, I observed her cultural understandings of marianismo. Marianismo is connected to machismo and dictates acceptable standards of behavior for Latina women, including familismo, or acting as a pillar for one's family, remaining subordinate to men, and simpatía, or the silencing of self to maintain harmony.[60] At one point in our conversations, Terri subtly referenced these concepts of marianismo:

> Women are taught that we're there to please men. . . . It's definitely deeply ingrained in society. Especially in cultures like the Hispanic culture, where you're taught the specific roles where women are supposed to be serving their husbands their plate of food.

In justifying Kevin's behaviors, Terri exhibited simpatía, a cultural script of marianismo that "dictates behaviors that maintain harmony in relationships such as being patient and forgiving of others, not talking about controversial subjects such as sex and birth control, and not being critical of others."[61]

Terri acknowledged that she had "more leniency with a Man of Color" because she is a Woman of Color. She explained that her ex-boyfriend is white and if he had assaulted her, she would think, "Well, you're even more a male of privilege." There was no need to protect a white male perpetrator because he was already protected by his white privilege. Men of Color, such as Kevin, did not have this societal protection. Because society would not protect Kevin, it was Terri's duty to protect him. Communities and Women of Color must protect Men of Color and their homes, which "function as a safe haven from the indignities of life in a racist society."[62]

Machismo culture influenced several other Latina women's decisions to report their assault. During her second year at RU, Daisy attended an off-campus house party. The men who lived in the house were all Latino and belonged to a Latino-based fraternity. Daisy belonged to the Latino fraternity's "sister sorority," which was centered on the empowerment of Latina women. The night of the party, Barry, one of the fraternity members, was giving Daisy "bad vibes." Barry launched several lewd comments at Daisy. He later grabbed Daisy's butt. And then, on the make-shift dance floor, Barry stuck his hand down Daisy's pants.

Daisy purposefully did not react to Barry' behavior. She refused to bring attention to the situation. She explained:

> I didn't want anyone to know about the situation. I didn't want to cause a bad image for me, or him, or just the organizations in general. I knew especially how these kinds of things could affect an organization. . . . I didn't want to draw attention to it.

Daisy continued:

> Something [my sorority] tries to combat a lot is the machismo culture. I think that's an issue in Latino culture in general, and that's something that we try to diminish as an organization. As Women of Color, we are very aware of these stereotypes and the backgrounds people come from. . . . That's something we say we try to diminish, that we say our generation is changing, but I always think that [machismo] background is there. People are brought up like this.

It was unclear if Daisy was attempting to "diminish" the racist stereotypes of Latino men as macho and/or if she was attempting to dismantle the actual culture of machismo. Yet it was clear that Daisy remained silent about her assault to prevent the perpetuation of racist stereotypes attributed to Latino men and to preserve the image of the Latino organization.[63] Daisy, like Terri, exhibited understandings of marianisma. She was acutely aware that she would disrupt the harmony of the community by reporting the assault.

Women of Color survivors often felt a need to protect perpetrators who were Men of Color. And some Latina women further demonstrated how the concept of machismo, as well as marianisma, influenced their feelings of protection for Latino men who perpetrate assault. Women of Color often remained silent to shield Men of Color from racist structures and systems that pose a threat to these men and to Communities of Color. Unfortunately, this silence, which is conditioned and condoned by societal structures, did little to diminish racism, sexism, and violence within these communities. This is because the antiracist priority to protect Men of Color perpetrators and their communities "tends to be interpreted as obliging women not to scream rather than obliging men not to hit."[64]

Where Does Intersectionality Take Us?

Women of Color survivors' stories demonstrate how the U.S. justice system and institutional reporting processes are riddled with intersectional failures that often influence their decisions to report assault. In critiquing higher education's fascination with Title IX and compliance, Xhercis Méndez agrees that "the deep imbrication between university goals, policies, and practices and settler-colonial and carceral logics has fundamentally structured responses that consistently fail and will continue to fail to address racialized gender-based violence at any level."[65] The federal government and institutions of higher education expect survivors to trust in and use "justice" systems that are rooted in slavery and settler-colonialism and center on the criminalization, surveillance, and policing of People of Color's bodies.[66] This is intersectional failure.

Transformative justice challenges these intersectional failures. In an article detailing the criminal case of Larry Nassar, the former team doctor for USA Gymnastics who abused hundreds of women and girls, Kelly Hayes and Miriam Kaba explain what transformative justice is and what it can do:

> Transformative justice is not a flowery phrase for a court proceeding that delivers an outcome we like. It is a community process developed by anti-violence activists of color, in particular, who wanted to create responses to violence that do what criminal punishment systems fail to do: build support and more safety for the person harmed, figure out how the broader context was set up for this harm to happen, and

how that context can be changed so that this harm is less likely to happen again.[67]

Although some higher education institutions have adopted restorative justice practices,[68] transformative justice is different from restorative justice. The two share several similar principles, but restorative justice is ancillary to the criminal justice system while transformative justice seeks to abolish this system.[69] In writing about the two approaches to justice, Angela P. Harris states, "Given the embeddedness of gender violence in both civil society and the state, true security lies not in 'restoration,' but in transformation."[70]

Grounded in the work of Activists of Color and critical race feminism, transformative justice challenges the feminist anti-violence movement's tough-on-crime approach to sexual violence.[71] It challenges carceral feminism's reliance on police, criminal courts, surveillance, and incarceration—structures that often further oppress and silence Communities of Color—as the answer to addressing gendered violence.[72] Transformative justice identifies "the complicated ways in which race, gender, and other modes of domination are mutually entwined" and how "each incident of personal violence should be understood in a larger context of structural violence."[73] Central to transformative justice is an understanding of how intersecting systems of domination are embedded throughout this context.[74]

If institutions started from a place of transformative justice, there would be less barriers for Women of Color specifically, and all survivors broadly, to seek justice and heal from sexual violence. This is because transformative justice is concerned with survivors' safety, healing, and agency rather than policy and compliance.[75] Survivors' interests, needs, and their definition of justice are central to sexual violence intervention and prevention.[76] With transformative justice, survivors' allegations of sexual violence are immediately believed and acted upon; collusion, cover-ups, and institutional betrayal are less likely to occur.[77] Evidence or proof would not be a necessary precursor to the pursuit of justice. What is more, transformative justice does not operate on the assumption that there exists a typical survivor, that is, white privileged women.

With transformative justice, Women of Color may not question if their reports of harm would be believed or if they would receive justice.

Women of Color may also be encouraged to report violence, particularly when perpetrated by Men of Color, through a transformative justice process because these systems do not equate to punitive justice.[78] With transformative justice, the community enables "the person who caused harm"[79] to take accountability for the harm they caused. This accountability occurs through community strategies, not through criminal punishment.[80] The person who caused the harm must first acknowledge the harm and its impact on others and then make reparations for the harm. Survivors can decide what these reparations and interventions might look like, but reparations almost always work toward transforming attitudes, behaviors, and social conditions that encourage liberation and prevent future violence.[81]

People cause harm because they are "given permission by the inequitable practices and arrangements of power within the society in which we live."[82] Therefore, transformative justice also holds accountable the institutions, organizations, and contexts that allow individuals to perpetrate violence, sometimes repeatedly. This accountability guides transformation. It interrogates and aims to eliminate the inequitable practices that allowed for the harm to occur in the first place. Justice, then, resembles transformation for the survivor, the person who caused harm, and for the context in which the harm occurred.[83]

Currently, federal policies allow institutions to adopt "informal resolution options," which can include restorative justice processes.[84] Institutions must look beyond restorative justice toward transformative justice. We cannot expect these informal resolutions and transformative justice to be effective within our existing system of compliance and carceral logics. I am aware that, for many, the implication to implement transformative justice might read as "science fiction."[85] But transformative justice is where intersectionality has brought us. It is where we must go if we aim to address campus sexual violence, repair intersectional failures, and provide healing for individuals and communities.

Six

"We Heal Differently"

HEALING FROM CAMPUS SEXUAL VIOLENCE

"We heal differently," Coraline stated about Women of Color survivors' healing processes. Rayn expressed a similar sentiment, relaying that "healing looks so different" for her, a Woman of Color survivor. The Women of Color survivors I spent time with often preferred to heal through cultural connections and within Communities of Color. Queenie, for example, was healing through her exploration of Asian witchcraft. Between our first and second conversation, Queenie attended an "interesting convening of Asian witches." The convention brought together Asian American artists and healers. The convening involved meditation, healing practices, and other "weird shit," as Queenie put it. But it was not Queenie who thought witchcraft was "weird shit." Rather, she knew it was an odd practice to outsiders—to white society—who could not conceptualize witchcraft, let alone Asian witchcraft, as a valid form for healing. Witchcraft is "outside of what is normally thought of [as] healing," Queenie acknowledged.

Queenie went on to describe how "normal," or mainstream options for healing involved talking to friends, family, or licensed professionals about assault. But for many Women of Color, such as Queenie, healing through talking about assault was not something she desired. Women of Color survivors did not often find healing through these dominant healing practices such as talk therapy and disclosure.[1] In fact, for Queenie, the most healing component of the convention was that she did not need to talk about her assault. Instead, she was able to focus on a cultural practice with others who shared her interest without needing "to perform how broken you are."

Raquel also mentioned not feeling connected to dominant approaches to healing, specifically talk therapy. She explored healing practices that originated from within Communities of Color. Raquel's visit to a sweat lodge became an integral part of her healing journey. She had several friends who were studying Anthropology at MU. These friends developed a close relationship with an MU faculty member who taught in the Anthropology department, is Native American, and hosted a sweat on her land once a month. With encouragement from her friends, Raquel decided to attend one of the monthly sweats. She passionately described how this experience offered her healing:

> You have to come very early. You have to clean the land. You have to do all the maintenance and get everything ready [for] the sweat and bring a lot of tobacco, bring a homemade meal to contribute. And we would spend the day cleaning and working together. And it was super-hot. It was not fun, but it was still fun because you're doing it with these people. And then we would sit in a circle with a talking stick, and every single person listened to why they were there. And everyone had a reason why they were there. And then we would all go into the sweat, and we would sing together and mourn and grieve for our reasons together as a community. And we would come out and that was community healing.

For Raquel, it was critical that there were members from Native American tribes at the sweat and that the MU students who attended came from many different cultural backgrounds. It was also important that the group spend the day together, working and healing alongside one another. "It's having that diversity and having that culture, [it] strengthens connections. And having those strong connections is what heals people from these things. And that's what saves people," Raquel reflected.

Queenie, Raquel, and several other Women of Color demonstrated how they were healing through collective approaches that centered culture and agency as a core component of their well-being, also known as healing-centered engagement.[2] Introduced by Shaun P. Ginwright, healing-centered engagement counters deficit-based psychological models that are often centered on individuality. Instead, healing-centered engagement centers community, shared experiences, and identity as necessary components in healing.[3] Raquel, for instance, was drawn to sweats and talking circles, Indigenous healing practices that allowed her to develop a heightened sense of belonging within a specific cultural community. Queenie engaged in witchcraft with other Asian Americans to build community and explore her identity.

Healing-centered engagement offered some survivors an opportunity to develop identity. And not just any identity; a cultural identity rooted in race and ethnicity. This was particularly important for many survivors who felt a shift of, or a loss of identity after experiencing assault. There is "this loss of identity," Noelle explained about the shift in her South Asian identity post-assault. Noelle believed that if she disclosed to her family, they would blame her for the violence and reject her. Noelle's inability to tell her family influenced feelings of disconnection from her South Asian community and her South Asian identity.

After her assault, Tessa also felt a loss of identity. She felt compelled to seek out healing modalities and resources that would help her explore her cultural identity. "For myself [I] did something a little different than I would expect other people to do. I got a lot more cultural," Tessa explained. She continued to describe her healing journey, "I used my family and the traditions that we have and just my culture. And I started expressing it ten times more than I did before. Because at that time, I just feel like I was looking for an identity again."

Tessa described a plethora of ways that she reconnected to her South Asian culture. She had recently celebrated Diwali, an Indian holiday often referred to as the "festival of lights." Prior to her assault, Diwali was not important to Tessa. She did not go home for the holiday, and she never engaged in any celebrations on or near the MU campus. But after experiencing assault, Tessa relayed, "I actually did everything that I could do. I went out and I bought the stuff. I cleaned the entire apartment because it's our New Year. I lit oil lamps and I put them on our balcony." Re-connecting to Indian traditions helped Tessa re-gain a sense of identity that had shifted after experiencing assault. Women survivors gravitated toward these cultural healing practices because they encouraged them to connect to others, but also, to re-connect to one's identity.[4]

For Women of Color survivors, connecting to (their) culture, their communities, and their identities offered opportunities for healing. Survivors made these connections through various modes and manners. Queenie, for instance, was drawn to witchcraft in the Asian American community and Tessa began to celebrate Diwali. "Cultural and indigenous practices" such as drumming circles, dance, sweat lodges, and "contemplative practices" such as mindfulness and meditation also provided healing opportunities for many Women of Color survivors.[5]

Although survivors engaged in various opportunities for healing, the 34 women survivors often explored three main healing modalities—yoga, therapy, and activism. Throughout this chapter, I explore survivors' relationships with these three modalities, how they dis/connected to culture, and, subsequently, how these modalities encouraged, and sometimes discouraged, Women of Color survivors' healing journeys.

"We Were There to go into Ourselves": Healing with Yoga

After Leyla experienced rape perpetrated by Adam, a football player at CU, she never found the time or the energy to heal from the assault. A few months after the rape, Leyla's estranged family member reached out to her. They wanted a relationship with her for the first time in Leyla's life. Then, there was a death in Leyla's family. Leyla also discovered that she had to stay on campus for the summer to complete several core requirements for her major. All the while, Leyla was attempting to navigate academic and social life on campus while simultaneously avoiding

Adam and his teammates. "I couldn't do anything. It was awful," Leyla said of her first and second years at CU.

While Leyla described these two difficult years, I sensed positivity in her voice and observed the bright smile on her face. Was Leyla coping? Compartmentalizing? Was she healing? As if sensing my internal questioning, Leyla freely shared, "Now I'm in my third year and things have gotten a lot better because I've come to terms with a lot of what's happened. And the Healing with Yoga class helped me change my whole perspective."

Earlier that year, while in summer school, Leyla woke up one morning and decided, "I am sick of being sad. My next year, my third year, needs to be a different year." That week, she signed up for a free week of yoga at an exercise studio near campus. Leyla had previously seen advertisements for the studio, but her sudden urge for change encouraged her to take the plunge.

A few days into her free week, Leyla mentioned to her friend and CU student that she was falling in love with yoga. The friend, knowing that Leyla had experienced campus sexual violence, told Leyla about the CU Healing with Yoga program. Leyla instantly looked up the program, which invites students who have experienced trauma to come together and practice yoga while exploring their bodies, their experiences, and their identities.

Right then and there, she applied to join the next yoga program cohort. Leyla participated in the semester-long program that fall and fell even more in love with yoga. She finally felt like she was healing from her experiences with violence because, as Leyla described, the yoga space was "such a safe space and I had not been in a safe space in so long. It was addicting to be in that safe space."

Leyla had been navigating an unsafe campus for almost two years, but with the help of the yoga program she was able to identify some spaces on campus as "safe." With sheer joy, Leyla described further why the yoga program felt safe:

> It's probably the instructor telling us that we can do whatever we want to do when we come into the room. We can take a nap, we can talk,

we could not talk. We participate, we cannot participate. We can do all
the poses or if a pose is uncomfortable you can stop. It's like someone
telling us we have the freedom to not go along. . . . And it was a unity in
silence thing because no one wants to talk about it because we weren't
there to talk about it. We were there to go into ourselves. It wasn't supposed to be a therapy session. I really liked that.

Leyla's yoga instructor was also a Woman of Color. She encouraged
participants to explore their bodies at their own pace. Each yoga class
aimed to show survivors that they were in control of their yoga practice and of their bodies, encouraging program participants to (re)gain a
sense of bodily awareness and strength, both physical and mental.

Leyla was emphatic that she did not have to talk during yoga. This
silence was different from her previous experiences with talk therapy.
Prior to finding yoga, Leyla saw a psychiatrist and a psychologist. "That
shit did not help," Leyla summed up her journey with talk therapy. She
continued:

Talking about it wasn't going to help me. When I realized that talking
about it just made me more upset, when I realized that wasn't working,
I told my psychiatrist, "Counseling doesn't work, this is ridiculous."
And that's when I tried yoga.

Yoga, not talk therapy, was the modality that allowed Leyla to begin to
heal and feel safer in some campus spaces.

All three institutions involved in the research ran some form of
a Healing with Yoga program. The three different programs were
grounded in a curriculum that was created by a Woman of Color survivor and yoga practitioner. The creator of this curriculum crafted the
program with the intention of honoring the intersections of survivors'
race, gender, and trauma in healing. SVRC coordinated and housed the
program at each institution. But survivors' knowledge of and engagement in the program differed between the three institutions.

Although several survivors at RU were aware that SVRC offered
the yoga program, no survivors I spoke with participated in it. This
low/no enrollment may map back to the duffel bag environment of

the campus—students were not always around to participate in the program. It may also connect to the institutional and individual minimization occurring at RU. Students did not participate in the yoga program because they perceived that their experiences with sexual violence were not serious enough to warrant healing through a formal program.

At MU, almost all Women of Color survivors were aware of the yoga program. This may be because many of the survivors at MU used SVRC post-assault and SVRC informed clients about their options for healing, which included the yoga program. Additionally, aligning with the community-oriented peer culture at MU, peers who had completed the program and found it integral to their healing often encouraged other survivors to sign up for it. Six Women of Color survivors at MU practiced yoga with the intention of healing from violence.

Women at CU, such as Leyla, often happened upon the program—a friend told a friend, someone saw a flyer, it was mentioned in a training—but once they learned about Healing with Yoga, survivors were often interested in joining. Four Women of Color survivors enrolled in the CU yoga program, but only three of these four women completed the program.[6]

Yoga, Women of Color, and "Coming into that Identity"

"Body-based work is important, I think, in terms of healing," Mary explained why she was drawn to practice yoga post-assault. Body-based practices, sometimes referred to as somatic practices, are centered on bodily awareness and the body's connection to the mind.[7] Some of these body-based practices are rooted in the knowledges of Communities of Color. Yoga, specifically, is an ancient practice originating from India.[8] Communities of Color have been using yoga to heal from trauma for decades. For instance, in 1975, *EBONY* magazine published the article, "Yoga: Something for Everyone." The article demonstrated how Black Americans, such as Angela Davis, turned toward yoga for healing from the daily inequities of navigating U.S. society in a Black body.[9]

"A lot of the coping skills, like yoga or body-based stuff, I've learned from other Women of Color and not from therapy with white therapists.

You know?" Mary continued. The fact that Women of Color have practiced and taught yoga for decades was important to some Women
of Color survivors. But therapy, unlike yoga, was rooted in western
culture, whiteness, and often involved white therapists.[10] For many
Women of Color survivors, yoga was more aligned with their cultures,
communities, and their values.

Women of Color's role in the creation and use of body-based healing practices often inspired survivors to explore these modalities. "A lot
of healing practices that are used widely in the west now were created
by People of Color," said Padma, explaining why she felt compelled to
practice yoga. She continued:

> My relationship to different healing practices, but also just my under-
> standing of the roots of those practices—even if they aren't from my
> culture, being these are ancient and were often created by Women of
> Color—[I feel] some sort of affinity to those healing practices.

Padma was drawn to Women of Color's roots in these healing practices,
but she also acknowledged that white western culture has "appropri-
ated" many of these practices. Although yoga originated in India, yoga
today, in a U.S. context, is often associated with being "skinny, white,
and even upper class."[11] Because of this perceived cooptation, Padma
had a complex relationship with practicing yoga in the west as a South
Asian woman. She was particularly upset that she had only ever taken
one yoga class (outside of the healing program) that was taught by a
South Asian teacher.

Regardless of this complexity, or perhaps, because of this complexity, Padma believed in the power of yoga to help Women of Color heal
from trauma. She described the CU Healing with Yoga program as
"Amazing! [A] really, really incredible resource!" Yoga offered Padma
an opportunity to explore her racialized and gendered identity, which
was crucial to her healing journey:

> Part of my healing journey has been exploring my identity as a Woman
> of Color. Women of Color is a political identity. . . . I think for me,
> coming into that identity has been part of my healing process in a way

that just wouldn't make sense for a white woman because it's not her identity.

While healing, Padma asked herself the question, "What does healing need to look like for me based on maybe what it looked like for [my mom], or maybe what it didn't look like for her?" Padma suspected the answer to this question was complex for Women of Color survivors who must navigate historical, intergenerational, and individual-level traumas. The answer to Padma's question involved reconnecting with her community, particularly her Indian mother, reading Hindu texts, and practicing yoga, which connects to the Hindu religion. Through these practices, she gained a stronger sense of her South Asian identity, felt more connected to her South Asian community, and began to discover a new identity as a survivor of sexual violence.

Yoga, identity, and culture were also intertwined throughout Ananya's healing journey. Ananya's parents are both South Asian-Indian. When they moved to the U.S., her parents attempted to expose Ananya and her siblings "to a lot of different cultural activities to feel that connection that a lot of other Indians had." The family went to the temple every weekend, participated in cultural activities with their Indian community, and Ananya grew up practicing Indian classical music.

For as long as Ananya could remember, her mother taught "very authentic yoga." The yoga that involved "meditation practices and these things that date back thousands, and thousands, and thousands of years." Because she grew up with yoga and meditation, Ananya also expressed growing "up with that feeling that therapy wasn't for our culture or wasn't for us." Yoga and meditation were therapy.

As Ananya applied to colleges, it was important for her to attend a college with a racially diverse student body that included a large population of South Asian students, specifically, Indian students. Ananya believed that MU would meet her needs for diversity and connection to her culture. "I was excited that there was a big [Indian] population. There were a lot of clubs for Indian people, like dancing and things like that, that I was really excited about," Ananya recalled her expectations prior to her first year on campus. But Ananya would never fully feel comfortable within the MU Indian community.

Ananya had several experiences her first year of college that made her feel excluded and ostracized from the Indian community. But one specific experience stood out. During the fall semester of her first year at MU, Ananya met an Indian man, Shaq, at an off-campus party. Shaq was clearly flirting with Ananya. For the next few weeks, Shaq and Ananya texted one another non-stop. One night, several weeks after meeting, Shaq sent Ananya a text. "Hey. Want to come to this house party this weekend?" Ananya jumped at the invitation. "Yes!"

That weekend, Ananya went to the party. Before she told me more about that night, Ananya stressed that she does not drink. She went on to relay that she only had a few sips of a drink that night. There was no reason for her to have blacked out. Ananya was adamant that someone—perhaps Shaq—put something in her drink. She did not remember much from that night, but she did remember Shaq taking advantage of her.

Ananya did not say anything to anyone about the assault until one year later. During her sophomore year, Ananya became close with another woman student and disclosed the assault to this new friend. As many peers at MU tended to do, Ananya's friend immediately responded to her disclosure with, "You need to tell someone!"

With her friend's encouragement in mind, Ananya decided to visit the MU Title IX Office to learn more about her options for reporting the assault, particularly because Shaq was not an MU student.[12] The Title IX staff told Ananya, "It'll be difficult to pursue a case against him, because he's not an MU student." Title IX did offer to investigate the MU fraternity to which Shaq was seemingly connected. Ananya walked away from the meeting knowing that it was pointless to pursue a case against Shaq because he was not enrolled at MU. And there was no way she was going to pursue a case against "a very Indian frat." She did not want to become even more of a social outcast from MU's Indian community for throwing Indian men under the bus. In the end, Ananya did not file a report with Title IX.

After her visit with Title IX, Ananya visited SVRC. But after meeting with a SVRC Advocate she still did not find much relief—talking about the assault was not helpful for her healing journey. "I felt that I needed to get it out some other way," Ananya realized. During her conversation with the SVRC Advocate, however, Ananya learned about the MU Healing with Yoga program. She decided to enroll. After completing Healing with Yoga, Ananya had positive things to say about the program and about her healing journey:

> It was really relieving. It gave me something to do. It gave me a chance to be in a room with a lot of people, and it wasn't necessary that we had to share our stories. And no one did. And I liked that. I liked that we didn't have to sit and talk.... [I liked being] in a room with a lot of other women who have gone through something similar and just know, silently, that you're not alone.... That helped a lot.

Ananya, who was raised with the understanding that "[talk] therapy was not for our culture" needed other avenues, beyond talking, to pursue healing. Yoga became one of those therapies. The yoga program allowed Ananya to reconnect to an identity. Because her assault occurred within the Indian community at MU, the community she so badly wanted to be a part of throughout her college experience, she found herself pulling away from her Indian friends and family post-assault. "At first, that process was very difficult. I was very distant with my friends and family. Being connected to my culture was the last thing I wanted," Ananya sighed. But then, "With yoga, it really helped me reconnect." Yoga helped Ananya reconnect to her community, her culture, and her identity. And more specifically, it allowed her to reconnect to her mother, the yoga teacher, who had encouraged her to practice yoga and meditation from a young age.

Therapy: "It's Not a Thing"

"Have you done therapy before? Talk therapy?" I asked Coraline during our second interview. "No. It's not something in my culture. It's not a thing," Coraline replied. When she was younger, one of Coraline's family members saw a therapist. But there was a lot of tension and negativity toward this family member because they went to therapy.

Coraline's family did not look kindly on therapy. In fact, Coraline's grandmother once said of therapy, "You don't need that. You're fine." Leading Coraline to believe that trauma is "just something that you deal with."

"Why do you say, 'It's not a thing'? What is it about culture?" I pushed Coraline to tell me more about her perceptions of culture and therapy. She answered quickly:

> You handle your business. You don't air your dirty laundry. Stuff like that. It's like, "No, we don't talk about this.". . . It's just something about keeping things private. It's like we're just not taught. Because it also has to do with, at least Latinos and especially Latinos who come from migrant families, or they are a migrant family. It's like we don't bring up anything. . . . It's just better to stay under the radar.

Coraline's mother immigrated from Mexico at a young age. She was a single mother who worked tirelessly for the success of her family. Coraline did not want to draw attention to her community, or to her mother, by airing her "dirty laundry" to a therapist. What if she told the therapist something that could be reported to authorities? Could she really talk freely about the inner workings of her community to someone who was not from her community? Coraline believed she was protecting her family and her community by not seeking therapy.[13]

Given the racist history of psychology and mental healthcare in the U.S. I was unsurprised that some Women of Color survivors suspected that therapy and therapists could cause more harm than help for them and their communities.[14] In 2021, the American Psychological Association, the largest scientific and professional organization of psychologists in the U.S., apologized for how psychology has "through acts of commission and omission, contributed to the dispossession, displacement, and exploitation of communities of color."[15] Although some psychological organizations and individual psychologists are attempting to practice more inclusive or multicultural care, the field remains "rooted in oppressive psychological science to protect Whiteness, White people, and White epistemologies."[16] The racist history of the profession is currently reflected in the 86% of psychologist in the U.S. who identify as white.[17] And due to these past and present racist realities, many People of Color continue to hold "cultural mistrust" of mental healthcare in the U.S.[18]

The use of psychology to harm Communities of Color may have contributed to Women of Color survivors' understandings that, as Margaret put it, "counseling wasn't a thing." Like Coraline's family, Margaret's family did not believe in mental health care. Telling white therapists information concerning People and Communities of Color was not something that should be done. Margaret described her thoughts on therapy:

> I just feel like [Women of Color] have to be a little more quiet about it. We're just a little more like, it stays within our small communities.... This year someone finally told me, "You should go to counseling and stuff." I was like, "No.".... Coming from Indian and Mexican [cultures], I just couldn't bring it to light.

For several survivors, therapy was not an option if they desired to protect their "small communities." Women of Color survivors did not often grow up with the messaging that talk therapy was a viable option for healing. It was not something that People of Color engaged in, especially if they wanted to protect their communities, families, and themselves from white society and white supremacy. Yet some survivors *did* engage in talk therapy—or entertained engaging in talk therapy—often because they believed the benefits of therapy might outweigh the risks.

"A Whole System of Shenanigans": Policies and Procedures for Counseling and Therapeutic Services

As a psychology major, Monae had no misgivings about visiting the MU Counseling Center after experiencing sexual violence. With the support of her MU therapist, Monae discovered that she had PTSD, general anxiety, and depression. In the following months, Monae continued to see her MU-appointed therapist, started a therapeutic relationship with an off-campus psychiatrist, and began to take medication for her mental health. Within weeks of her first visit to the Counseling Center, Monae noticed a drastic improvement in her mental health and well-being.

I was excited to hear more from Monae, a survivor who was healing through therapeutic processes. "I'm really interested in the therapy aspects. Are you still in therapy?" I eagerly asked. "No, I'm not," Monae responded quietly. My heart slumped. "Was there any reason why you stopped going?" Monae responded with a twinge of regret:

> I was in therapy here, but they have rules. After [a certain number] of sessions, they send you off campus. And I don't have a car. So, getting off-campus help is really hard. And if you miss appointments with off-campus providers, they have really high fees. And then if you would like to go see them once you have a fee. . . . And I'm a college student. I can't afford their $200 fees.

After eight sessions at the MU Counseling Center, Monae was forced to find a new, off-campus therapist. Although the Counseling Center provided Monae with a link to help in her off-campus search, the website was "a mess." And the fees and transportation were even more of a nightmare to navigate. So, Monae decided not to navigate the mess. She stopped seeing her therapist and, eventually, she stopped seeing her psychologist. "Getting healthier is kind of hard," Monae concluded.[19]

What was this rule that Monae referenced? Why would a student only have eight sessions with their on-campus therapist and then be sent off-campus? I became even more intrigued by this rule when other women survivors, across the three campuses, mentioned that they were allowed only *three* sessions at the campus counseling center before being sent to an off-campus provider. Still other women relayed that they did not seek out institutional counseling because they did not have insurance through the institution.[20] Institutional policies and procedures surrounding therapeutic services were becoming confusing for me, and for the Women of Color survivors, to navigate.

I browsed the institutional websites and the insurance policies to gain clarity on the number of sessions students were allowed to have with the institutional counseling centers. And I attempted to better understand the role institutional insurance played in deciding these numbers. But I was never able to locate information about the length of therapeutic care for students, with or without insurance. My mounting confusion fueled my excitement to talk with Deanna, the Director of the CU Counseling Center.

As a Woman of Color, and as the supervisor for the CU SVRC Office, Deanna held insight into how therapeutic services helped and hindered healing for Women of Color survivors at CU. But before diving into her intersectional knowledge, Deanna provided clarity on why students might find the policies and procedures surrounding the Counseling Center challenging.

Deanna took a long sigh before launching into her explanation of who can access the Counseling Center and for how many sessions. Because the Center is partly funded through student fees, CU is required to allow all students access to the Counseling Center. But, according to Deanna, it would not be equitable if the Center provided the same amount of access for all students. CU students who bought into the institutional health insurance plan were paying several thousand dollars more a year to the institution than students who did not have the plan. That additional payment, theoretically, should provide students *with* institutional insurance more amenities and access to the Center than students *without* institutional insurance. To secure these resources for students *with* insurance, students *without* institutional insurance were provided up to three sessions at the Counseling Center and then referred off campus. This policy, however, did not guarantee that students with institutional insurance could permanently access the Counseling Center.

"I'm supposed to provide them with ongoing treatment. . . . Guess what? There's just more trauma than treatment in CU—all around the world," Deanna exhaled. Approximately 30 CU therapists for 45,000 CU students was not working well. Higher education institutions are experiencing a mental health crisis—demand from students is outpacing institutional mental health resources.[21] Even students with institutional insurance could not be served by the Counseling Center forever. They too were eventually referred off campus. "I have to make some decisions about who gets seen and how long they get seen," Deanna stated. She summed up the mental health policies and procedures at CU as "a whole system of shenanigans."

Most students, regardless of insurance policy and institution, were eventually referred off campus. And accessing off-campus therapy was often complex for Women of Color students who, as Serena said, "don't have the exact time or exact social economic capabilities to be spending money on weekly therapy sessions or having the same resources [as upper-class white women students]." Serena, who had institutional insurance, was open to seeking therapy with the CU Counseling Center, but she quickly learned that she would have to wait one or two months for her first appointment. Serena refused to wait. She investigated off-campus, out-of-network therapists. Again, she met with disappointment. The cost for each off-campus session ranged from $150–$200. Too expensive for Serena. She could not ask her parents for money to see a therapist. Her parents would ask, "Why do you need to see a therapist?" Serena was not willing to disclose her assault to her family. Serena was convinced that her Asian parents would not be willing to put their income toward therapy, a healing modality that was taboo within their culture and among family members.

"I Need Access to Care That's Culturally Competent"

Survivors were also weary of therapy because clinicians often lacked cultural competence and knowledge of historical and intergenerational trauma. Deanna, the Director of the CU Counseling Center, acknowledged this issue within her own Center:

> For a Woman of Color who's coming in with a history of chronic trauma, and a recent trauma, is the Counseling Center going to really serve you? And I can't guarantee the cultural competence of everybody. Because guess what? The field of psychology is predominantly, the narrative is about, if you think about it, from the very beginning, it's about white people deciding what's normal and what's pathological.

Deanna offered her clinicians professional development workshops to increase their cultural competence. At the time of our conversation, she was working with the most racially diverse staff she had ever worked with at CU. But, as Deanna explained, many clinicians remained unaware of how "oppression has intergenerationally produced this level of trauma" for Women of Color. White clinicians, specifically, struggled with understanding oppression and intergenerational trauma because "their culture is so situated in individualism. They can't feel it," Deanna stated. Several Women of Color survivors were aware of how intergenerational trauma influenced their experiences with violence. And many Women of Color were seeking mental health care that would account for this trauma throughout their healing journey.

After experiencing rape, Faye did not think to use the CU Counseling Center. She did not have institutional insurance. The Counseling Center staff notified her that, without insurance, she would have to wait a month for an appointment. Even then, she'd be sent off campus after a few sessions. "My mental health can't wait for a month," Faye realized after hearing she would need to wait for therapy. But even if Faye had been able to schedule an earlier appointment with the Counseling Center, she remained concerned that her therapist would lack cultural competence and an understanding of intergenerational trauma. Faye described why this competence in therapy was vital to her healing:

> I need access to care that's culturally competent. I need people to understand what domestic violence looks like, what sexual violence looks like in an immigrant household, and why that happens. And the anxieties and stressors of being in a house like that. What immigration does to you. Intergenerational trauma is so big, you need to understand that when I talk about sexual violence . . . I carry that pain. It doesn't go away. I can't have that overlooked if I want to heal. You know what I mean?

Without a culturally competent therapist—without someone who understood intergenerational trauma—Faye believed she would "get nowhere" with healing through therapy. Mirroring my conversation with Deanna, Faye was particularly hesitant about white women therapists who often "choose their whiteness over their womanhood." A white woman therapist might center gender and womanhood but fall short in connecting these concepts to race and racism. "My healing process and my understanding of what happened, is very, very, very connected to my culture" Faye concluded. If her therapist was unable to make the connection between Faye's culture and her experiences with sexual violence, therapy would not be helpful for healing.

"It's probably the biggest thing that has to do with my mental health," Jane said of intergenerational trauma. Jane's parents are Vietnamese refugees who escaped Vietnam following the end of the Vietnam War. Jane knew that her parents continued to carry this trauma with them. It influenced their "inability to be healthy people and healthy parents," which influenced Jane's in/ability to be a healthy person.

Jane first learned about intergenerational trauma in one of her first-year college seminars. After hearing the term, she contemplated, "What does that even look like?" After searching the internet for more information on intergenerational trauma, Jane had an epiphany, "Oh shit! That actually happens. I see it in my own life and I don't even realize it." Jane began to connect her parents' trauma to how she was raised. Perhaps, she thought, intergenerational trauma was one of the reasons she was not healing from her experiences with intimate partner violence.

During her second year at RU, Jane ended an abusive relationship in which she consistently experienced violence. Once she left the relationship, Jane was concerned because she did not immediately feel "liberated" from the trauma of the relationship. Jane asked herself, "What do I do now? How do I reclaim myself or my sense of self again?"

Jane turned to therapy to help her answer some of these questions. But she had a very specific goal with therapy—to unpack her family dynamics and explore intergenerational trauma. For Jane, healing from sexual violence was intertwined with healing from intergenerational oppression, from the Vietnam War, from being forced to escape one's country. Her therapist's ability to help Jane explore intergenerational trauma was critical to her healing journey:

> It's definitely intergenerational trauma, how I navigate the world as all these different identities and how I just feel like such a heavy weight on my shoulders just being sometimes. I know [my therapist] understands because I told her from the very first session. I was like, "I need

a therapist who will understand my political ties. My mental health is not separate from my political ties." And she understood that from the beginning.

Jane was one of the last survivors that I interviewed. I spoke with over 30 Women of Color before her, many of whom did not pursue therapy or had poor experiences with culturally unconscious therapists. I felt relief, and a bit of disbelief, when Jane explained that therapy "definitely helped" in her healing journey. Jane's therapist addressed systemic oppression and "understands cultural competency too, because she's a South Asian woman." Jane clarified that she did not need her therapist to be South Asian, but she *did* need someone who was culturally competent.

Jane had been seeing her therapist, who worked at the RU Counseling Center, every week for about four months. I quickly did the math. Jane had already attended 16 therapy sessions with her RU therapist. Knowing other survivors' experiences with the limit on sessions, I asked Jane, "Are there any limits here on how many therapy sessions you can go to or there's no limits?" Jane responded, "See that's what I thought at first!" Prior to seeing her therapist for the first time, Jane heard from other students and RU staff that the Counseling Center was committed to "short-term care." Students were allowed four to eight counseling sessions and then referred off campus.

This policy was "really stupid," Jane stated. Despite warnings about "short-term care," Jane pursued therapy at the RU Counseling Center. Once in therapy, Jane asked her therapist how many sessions she could have before she would need to find an off-campus therapist. "I don't like giving numbers, because everyone's different, so however long you need," Jane's therapist replied. Jane had no plans to look for an off-campus therapist. Why would she? She had found a culturally competent and affordable therapist on campus. It was unclear why Jane might be able to access long-term care at RU when other students at RU, CU, and MU could not. It was clear, however, that affordable, accessible, and culturally competent mental healthcare could be integral to Women of Color's healing journeys.

"Being an Advocate Was my Healing": Healing through Advocacy and Education

During her first year at RU, an RU student who was a friend assaulted Carrie while she was watching YouTube in the friend's residence hall room. Immediately after the assault, Carrie returned to her room in the same residence hall. She was extremely confused about what happened. Aligning with the pattern I observed at RU, Carrie did not label her experience as "assault." It was not stranger rape, and it was not violent. Carrie concluded that she was overreacting to the interaction. She did not tell anyone about the experience. But Carrie's decision to remain silent changed a few weeks later when she participated in a student-led retreat.

A month before her assault, Carrie auditioned to be an actress in the RU Vagina Monologues. She could not recall the reason for auditioning. At that time, she did not even know what the play was about. But soon after her audition, Carrie was cast in the play that aims to address "women's sexuality and the social stigma surrounding rape and abuse."[22] Carrie experienced assault between the time of her audition for the Vagina Monologues and the Vagina Monologues retreat.

At the retreat, student organizers educated Carrie and her fellow actors about V-Day, an organization and activist movement that aims to end violence against women, through education. One of the most well-known educational components of V-Day is the Vagina Monologues.[23] As student participants began to learn more about the mission of V-Day and the purpose of the Vagina Monologues, they began to talk more about their experiences with sexual violence. As others discussed, Carrie remained decidedly quiet. But inside, her mind was racing:

> I didn't really know that I was one of those people until after we started discussing other people in the group's stories at the retreat. And I was like, "Wow. That sounds kind of like what happened with me." That was kind of the moment when I was like, "Wow, why didn't anyone tell me that this happened and everything?"

As she continued to participate in the retreat, Carrie processed for the first time that she was a survivor of sexual violence. She realized, "Wow. Maybe something did happen and I just didn't realize it. Maybe that's why I felt so gross."

After the retreat, Carrie began to label her experience that first year at RU as sexual violence. Yet Carrie remained steadfast in her decision not to report the assault to the institution. It was not serious enough and she did not want to ruin the perpetrator's life chances. Carrie, however, grew increasingly passionate about sex education and sexual violence prevention on campus. She did not want other RU students to lack the knowledge that she had lacked about sexual violence. Carrie also wanted to support other survivors of sexual violence. "I just kind of went into advocacy because that was the first thing I thought. 'I don't want this to happen to someone else,'" she explained.

Eventually, Carrie became a peer educator with RU SVRC. SVRC Peer Educators are students who educate the campus and surrounding community on sexual violence, including rape culture, healthy relationships, and bystander intervention. As a peer educator, Carrie joined a small cohort of RU women students, many of whom were survivors, that advocated for more sexual violence education and survivor support on campus. While involved in the peer education program, Carrie learned more about campus and community sexual violence resources that she did not know existed prior to her experience with violence. Invigorated by what she was learning, Carrie made it her goal to share these resources with her peers at RU.

"What's been helpful in healing or coping?" I asked Carrie near the end of one interview. "Working in the SVRC office," Carrie replied confidently. She added, "Being an advocate was my healing." For Carrie, advocacy was a critical component in healing from sexual violence.[24] Some women survivors, such as Carrie, found healing through advocating for more and better education around sex, sexual violence, and health more broadly.

Healing through advocacy looked different for different survivors. Carrie, for instance, worked directly with RU SVRC to educate the campus community about sexual violence and to support other survivors of sexual violence. Like Carrie, Padma found healing through a peer education program on campus, but the program was not directly connected to sexual violence advocacy and education.

As a CU Peer Health Coach, Padma educated other CU students on various topics that concerned health, including managing stress, sexual health, nutrition, social well-being, and digital harm reduction. Padma described that her job was to push her peers "toward prioritizing themselves, self-care, emotional intelligence, understanding their patterns, and really, resilience building." Through the Peer Health program, Padma aimed to support and educate other Students of Color at CU. She explained why she found this goal important:

> In terms of wanting to be a support for other people, a lot of that just stems from not feeling like I had a lot of support previously. . . . And I think everyone deserves that chance to heal . . . especially People of Color, we hold onto generations of trauma. And to allow ourselves to heal is to create a new generation of more healed people. And that's really what I want to see for People of Color.

After experiencing sexual violence, Padma did not feel supported by her institution. She also found that there were not many spaces for her, a Woman of Color survivor, to process intergenerational trauma post-assault. The lack of support encouraged Padma to advocate for and institute some of this culturally competent care on campus.

While Padma educated her peers, she was also learning from her work as a Peer Health Coach. She learned more about cognitive behavioral therapy, self-talk, schemas, mindfulness, and managing stress. Learning these concepts were vital to Padma's healing. After completing her first year as a coach, Padma was astounded by the difference in her mental state. "I swear to god, if I hadn't had this program, I don't know where I would be," she exclaimed. The education that Padma received through the program was empowering and healing. And she found even more healing by sharing her new knowledge with peers. She found healing in supporting others' healing.

Healing through advocacy work, however, did not always connect to formal institutional peer education programs. After experiencing sexual violence at CU, Anika's healing process "wasn't good, it wasn't positive." Anika noticed a "weird" relationship with herself, and she felt uncomfortable in her own skin. Anika's friends at CU did not offer her much support. When disclosing her assault to a few women friends, Anika was met with unsupportive and negative reactions. Anika felt lost. And depressed. She decided to take a self-proclaimed "healing semester" off from college and explore different modes and methods for healing.

During this semester, Anika journaled, read, and spent a great deal of time outside and with nature. Anika also saw a therapist at the CU Counseling Center. But the white therapist did not understand Black culture. "Something was missing in that connection," Anika stated about her therapy sessions. After her allotted three sessions (Anika did not have institutional insurance), she stopped seeing her therapist.

Throughout her healing journey, Anika continued to be disappointed in her friends' lack of support for her needs. She was also underwhelmed by the institutional resources that CU offered for healing. It was only during the last semester of her final year at CU that she learned about the yoga program for survivors. "I would have loved that at that time. That would have been great," Anika lamented upon learning, too late, about Healing with Yoga.

After she experienced assault, Anika longed for a campus program or a "big sister" with whom she could process sexual violence. But Anika was never able to locate this resource on campus. So, through her role as a Resident Assistant, she became this resource for other students and student survivors. Anika explained how she advocated for and supported survivors as a Resident Assistant:

> That's one of the things that was important about me being a Resident Assistant. If I ever have to deal with a situation, I'm so ready for it. I want that. I want you to tell me exactly how you're feeling. And I want to be there for someone like that. . . . I made a point to tell my residents at the very beginning, "I am a survivor, if you ever go through anything please, please don't hesitate to knock down my door. I will be there."

Although her role as a Resident Assistant did not require her to talk about sexual violence, or disclose her identity as a survivor, Anika

found these discussions important. Disclosing to her residents that she
was a survivor and that she would be there for them if they experience
violence was yet another moment for Anika to explore healing.

Although Anika healed through disclosing her identity as a survivor, disclosure was not necessary to engage in advocacy work or to heal
from sexual violence. Carrie, for example, did not disclose her assault
to student program participants or to her fellow peer educators. More-
over, women embarked on advocacy through different roles and forms.
Some were directly involved with sexual violence advocacy, for example as SVRC peer educators, while others engaged in advocacy through
broader campus roles, for example as Resident Assistants. A through-
line, however, of women's campus advocacy was that they aimed to
provide peers with the resources, education, and paths for healing that
were not often available to them after experiencing violence.

"Healing while I'm Also Watching Other People Heal"

Some women survivors healed through advocacy work that did not
involve educating or supporting peers on campus. Instead, survivors
worked with community organizations that were connected to anti-
sexual violence advocacy. In working with these organizations, Women
of Color survivors often interacted with other survivors that the organizations were advocating for and supporting. Interactions with
other survivors positively influenced several student survivors' healing
journeys.

Ananya, a public policy major at MU, volunteered with a law firm
that was located near campus. The law firm helped to clear the criminal
records of women survivors of human trafficking and sex trafficking.
While working with the firm, Ananya heard countless stories of violence and survival from clients/survivors. Ananya described her reaction to the survivors' stories:

> Working at the firm that I work at has helped me a lot, because I hear
> stories. It's crazy, because there are women who are like 30 years old,
> or 40 years old and they're talking about that length of time being traf-
> ficked. It has helped me. Because I see that they're coming forward with

a very difficult story, and they're finding healing. . . . It's just very empowering to see that process from beginning to end.

In speaking about the influence that her work with the law firm had on her healing, Ananya concluded, "It was really empowering to be able to be healing while I'm also watching other people heal." Hearing other survivors' stories of healing after trauma empowered Ananya's healing journey. Being surrounded by other women survivors also reminded Ananya that she was not alone in experiencing and healing from violence.

Rayn found support for healing while interning for a local community center that supported Asian Pacific Islander women and children who experience domestic violence. The center worked closely with another local advocacy organization that focused specifically on domestic violence for the South Asian community. In her work with the center, Rayn participated in an intern training program that covered issues related to domestic and sexual violence in the Asian Pacific Islander and South Asian community—Rayn's community. Her gratitude for this training was palpable.

"Sitting in training last summer, and hearing South Asian women talk about violence specific to our community was the first time I've had that kind of space," she recalled. Spaces where South Asian women might talk openly about violence were often "so far away" for Rayn and for her community. And these spaces did not exist on the CU campus. According to Rayn, CU leadership is "willing to slap token Students of Color on their brochures to advertise the university, but they do nothing to actually take care of Students of Color."

Rayn found healing through her work with the community center. She described this healing:

I've been working with a lot of children who experienced domestic and sexual violence. And watching them heal has kind of helped me tap into emotions and memories that I need to process in order to heal. So they're kind of demonstrating what I can do to support myself. And seeing them open up and be more vulnerable has encouraged me to do the same.

Rayn had recently begun to process how her experiences with domestic violence in childhood connected to her experiences with campus sexual violence. Hearing stories of violence and healing from members of her community was integral to Rayn's healing. She found it particularly influential that the survivors in the center were South Asian women and children. "I don't wanna invalidate white woman's experience with domestic violence, but just the way it manifests, and the way it's normalized is so different compared to Communities of Color," Rayn concluded.

For some women survivors, such as Ananya and Rayn, advocacy work was about learning from and listening to other survivors. I observed that most women survivors who healed with community advocacy organizations attended MU. Women survivors at CU and RU were seemingly more focused on advocacy efforts that educated and supported their peers on campus. These differences aligned with my observations of the campus environments at each institution. The peer climate at MU may have influenced the expectation that all students were already educating and supporting their peers. Women survivors at MU may have felt more able to focus their advocacy efforts outside the institution, while women at CU and RU were drawn to first advocate for change on campus.

Where Does Intersectionality Take Us?

Many higher education institutions focus on therapeutic and counseling services when responding to survivors' needs for healing.[25] Yet Women of Color survivors faced several challenges to using these services, including issues with insurance, financial barriers, months-long wait times, stigma, and a lack of culturally competent providers.

In both this chapter and in Chapter 1, survivors demonstrated how intergenerational trauma was intertwined with experiences of violence. This trauma must be accounted for within survivors' healing journeys. Institutional leaders, specifically those working with campus counseling and psychiatric services, must hire only culturally responsive counselors. This does not mean that campus leaders hire only Therapists of

Color. Rather, counselors must understand and account for how intersecting systems of oppression influence the experiences of survivors with multiple minoritized identities. It is imperative that Women of Color survivors be able to talk with their therapists about intergenerational trauma and intra-racial politics. These identity-specific aspects are central to students' healing.

Recently, the American Psychological Association (APA) committed to reimagining the "graduate training curriculum to promote epistemological justice by centering diverse, non-western cultural perspectives in U.S. based training programs."[26] In acting on this commitment, counseling graduate programs must center the development of cultural responsiveness throughout program curricula. Programs might include a curricular focus on intergenerational trauma, intersectionality, and more diverse, culturally responsive approaches to therapy, such as somatic therapy or eye movement desensitization and reprocessing therapy. APA and other psychological and counseling-based organizations must support graduate programs to achieve this epistemological justice with money, trainings, and additional resources.

Women of Color survivors also demonstrated how insurance policies, finances, and wait times to see a therapist made healing with therapy inaccessible. Institutional leaders must provide free therapy to all students, regardless of their insurance status. You may read this implication and ask, "With what money?" Méndez explained that institutions spend an "exorbitant amount of resources" to address institutional "liability as opposed to providing resources for survivors and addressing the conditions that enabled the harm in the first place."[27] The money will come from redirecting resources away from offenders and institutional compliance toward counseling services and transformative justice.[28]

I hesitate to encourage institutions to dispel the stigma around therapeutic services that exist within many Communities of Color. Psychological interventions are often rooted in whiteness and do not connect to Women of Color's cultures and communities.[29] It is imperative that institutions think beyond psychological approaches to healing and consider other ways that culture, connection, and identity can be centered in programs and processes meant to support survivors' healing.

Trauma-informed yoga was integral to Women of Color survivors' healing from sexual violence. Yoga should not be the only alternate option for therapy. Several other modalities for healing can allow survivors to connect to community, culture, and identity. These modalities might include drum circles, dance, writing, photography, hiking, sweat lodges, mindfulness and meditation, and healing circles, where individuals sit in a circle and share, one by one, their thoughts on a problem or question.[30] When instituting these modalities, institutions must foreground the important aspects survivors identified about the Healing with Yoga program, including the silent nature of the activity, being in a community with other (Women of Color) survivors, exploring agency, and healing through practices that are rooted in Communities of Color.

To implement multiple and various options for healing, many campuses will need to re-structure their services. Some survivors named how SVRC was one of few offices, if not the only office, that offered avenues for healing outside of the counseling center and talk therapy. Multiple divisions and departments, beyond just SVRC, must implement healing initiatives. For instance, the campus writing program might host a writing for healing workshop, while ethnic studies can offer healing circles, and the office of religious and spiritual life institutes a healing through hiking program. These healing programs must take a community and collaborative approach because sexual violence, and healing from sexual violence, is a community issue. It can no longer fall to just one or two offices to address students' healing.

Women of Color also expressed that working alongside and hearing stories from other survivors, particularly Survivors of Color, offered opportunities for healing. We need more stories from People and Women of Color about survival and healing. We need more spaces where these stories are welcomed, embraced, and valued. Some of these spaces already exist outside the institution, within Communities and Organizations of Color. The question, then, is how do institutions provide survivors with more knowledge of and access to these spaces? The institution could offer a program that matches students with advocacy organizations that relate to the students' interests. The institution might offer academic credit to students who engage in this advocacy work. And the institutions could provide free and accessible transportation for students to access these off-campus sites.

Women of Color also healed through advocacy work that allowed them to educate their campus community about sex, sexual violence, and healing. Although a powerful healing modality, survivors' need to educate peers makes me think back to Chapter 1; if postsecondary institutions instituted comprehensive sex education, survivors may not find it necessary to seek out and share this information with peers post-assault.

Conclusion

Where Has Intersectionality Brought Us?

We continue to fight today's battle against campus sexual violence because of the intersectional failures from yesterday.[1] The stories from the
34 Women of Color survivors demonstrate many of these intersectional
failures and how they manifest in postsecondary contexts. Yet I refuse
to conclude this book by focusing on these failures. We must hear survivors' stories and use them to move toward intersectional repair. The
34 Women of Color survivors' stories help us "see the things we need to
see" to "get us to where we need to go."[2] So, where do we go? We move
toward action.

On Policy and Practice

Intersectional repair through sexual violence policies and practices
accounts for the many realties that the 34 Women of Color explored
throughout this book. This includes a trauma-informed and empowerment approach to institutional response and reporting, focusing on
healing-centered engagement, accounting for intergenerational and historical trauma in survivors' experiences with violence, acknowledging

the influence of racist and sexist stereotypes in the lives of these women, and hiring more Women of Color staff and faculty members that might support Women of Color survivors on campus.

For example, policies and practices that focus on intersectional repair and survivors' reporting of violence would move away from punitive justice toward transformative justice. Reporting procedures would account for how antiracist discourse often socializes Women of Color to remain silent about violence to protect their community and how feminism continues to support the social construction of who can be a believable or typical survivor.[3] Intersectional policies and practices recognize that many survivors experience intergenerational and historical trauma, both of which must be centered throughout healing processes. Specifically, institutional counseling and therapeutic services must account for the intersections of race, gender, and class in survivors' experiences with violence.

Intersectional repair through policy and practice is not focused on institutional liability and compliance—it is centered on students, on survivors, and on the community. There are several models and concepts, many of which the Women of Color survivors mentioned, that guide us toward more effective policies and procedures which are relevant to students' identity-specific needs and experiences. A trauma-informed lens, for example, "recognizes the ongoing impact of past and current trauma on survivor needs," such as historical and intergenerational trauma, and includes principles of safety and support.[4] Transformative justice also focuses on support and safety, but specifically throughout the justice process; it centers on the person harmed, the broader context in which the harm occurred, and how that context must change to reduce future harm.[5]

I am particularly interested in how empathy and empowerment, two concepts that seemed to make a difference in sexual violence response at MU, can become a foundation for campus sexual violence policies and procedures. Weaving these concepts—trauma-informed services, empowerment models, avenues for transformative justice— throughout existing policies and practices will not get us to where we need to go. We must throw out the policies and procedures we have used throughout this long battle and move toward new understandings of policy and practice that are framed by intersectionality.

I encourage readers to visit the section, "Where Does Intersectionality Take Us?" at the end of each of the preceding chapters. These previous sections explore targeted and tangible implications for moving toward intersectional repair through sexual violence policies and practices. In Chapter 1, for example, I explore how policies that dictate K-12 sex education curriculum and campus prevention education must expand to become more comprehensive and informative for young adults. Chapter 5 encourages the use of transformative justice, rather than punitive or restorative justice, to offer healing, safety, and agency to survivors and their communities. In the final chapter on healing, I suggest several ways that institutions might infuse healing-centered engagement, or collective approaches to healing that center culture and agency as a core component of survivors' well-being, into survivors' opportunities for healing.[6]

On Institutional Context

The 34 Women of Color's stories demonstrated how context matters. The context of an institution is critical in understanding and exploring students' experiences with campus sexual violence. Institutional context is integral in preventing and responding to violence at specific institutions with individual climates. For instance, at Mountain University, I was skeptical of the focus that institutional leaders gave to bystander intervention. But after spending time on campus, I observed how the community-oriented campus environment perceived bystander intervention to be a useful, if not expected, intervention strategy. Therefore, prevention and intervention strategies may have different impacts at various institutions, which have differing characteristics and, ultimately, differing cultures for sexual violence.

Although the government, scholars, and institutions of higher education have started to focus more on the campus context for sexual violence, this focus often falls short in understanding and operationalizing campus climate.[7] For example, sexual violence climate assessments often focus on the behavioral and psychological dimensions of climate, missing an opportunity to explore how institutional and societal factors influence violence. Most surveys assess prevalence of victimization and students' individual perceptions of the campus, but few assess students' sense of belonging, institutional structures, and the history of the institution in relation to violence.[8] Moylan and colleagues explained the influence of these shortcomings on sexual violence prevention and response: "Without a comprehensive definition of climate and a clear conceptualization of the connection between climate and experiences of sexual violence, we may miss opportunities to identify relevant risk factors, design effective preventive interventions, and appropriately respond to sexual assault."[9]

Furthermore, although campus climate surveys were originally used to explore the campus racial climate,[10] existing research and assessment that explore institutional context and campus sexual violence often gloss over students' racialized realities with climate and violence. These surveys rarely assess issues related to race and racism, let alone diversity, equity, and inclusion.[11] These assessments do not often capture how institutional values around whiteness may dissuade some Women of Color students from reporting their assault, or how a racially diverse peer climate may encourage Women of Color to seek help after violence. Current conceptualizations of institutional context and climate do not account for intergenerational trauma, racialized and gendered stereotypes, and competing discourses of resistance. "As a result of this siloing, institutions of higher education possess a limited ability to notice and address patterns of injustice and inequity that cut across campus climate domains."[12]

We must account for institutional context in future work on campus sexual violence. And we must position students' stories within these contexts. Moving forward, however, we must use comprehensive definitions of climate that account for racism, sexism, and intersecting systems of domination. Recently, in 2021, Moylan and colleagues proposed a multidimensional definition of climate that would allow the sexual violence field to better define, assess, and address sexual violence.[13] To conceptualize their framework, the scholars drew heavily from Hurtado and colleagues' foundational work on the campus racial climate, which accounts for how race and racism influence students' experiences in the *historical, compositional, behavioral, psychological,* and *organizational* dimensions of a campus.[14] These climate frameworks allow for a comprehensive definition of climate and account for how campus sexual violence is intertwined with the campus racial climate. Moving forward, I urge scholars, practitioners, and policymakers to use Moylan and colleagues' multidimensional framework, as well as Hurtado and colleagues' campus racial climate framework, to account for intersectionality, campus sexual violence, and institutional context.

We must also continue to explore institutional betrayal and institutional courage as it relates to campus context and sexual violence. The 34 survivors' stories led me to think deeply about the connections between institutional betrayal, intersectional failure, institutional courage, and intersectional repair. At MU, for instance, I observed how individual and institutional courage could work toward intersectional repair, as well as mitigate institutional betrayal and intersectional failures related to Title IX. Across institutions, survivors' experiences with the yoga program influenced intersectional repair and could also be connected to institutional courage and the mitigation of institutional betrayal.

Although some scholars have begun to conceptualize the ways that institutional betrayal impacts minoritized students' experiences, more scholarship, polices, and procedures must connect institutional courage to intersectional repair.[15] We must center how institutional courage looks and feels when approached from an intersectional lens. We must interrogate how we courageously structure intersectional repair throughout our institutions. Survivors' stories provide a foundation for better understanding these connections through their explorations of counseling and intergenerational trauma, yoga and healing-centered engagement, the influence of diverse institutional environments, and more.

We can no longer divorce the institutional from the intersectional; we know this through theory, and the 34 Women of Color survivors' stories show us this in practice.[16]

On Intersectionality

After spending several years with the 34 Women of Color survivors and their stories, I have gained even more respect and reverence for intersectionality. Intersectionality has allowed me, and now us, to examine "what we haven't been able to see, what's not remembered, the stories that are not told."[17] Intersectionality pushes us to hear these stories, to learn from these stories, and to act on these stories.

I will continue to use intersectionality to ask questions of campus sexual violence, but I will also explore what it means for intersectionality to frame these questions. For example, while writing the institution-specific chapters, I continually questioned whether centering the stories of the Women of Color survivors was intersectional-enough. In the three institution-specific chapters, I worried that I did not do enough to explicitly connect survivors' stories to intersectional concepts, such as antiracist discourse or cultural representations. But I *was* focusing on Women of Color survivors' experiences within institutional and societal contexts. My thinking led me to ask myself, "Is intersectionality only intersectionality when it is explicitly tied to the three forms of intersectionality?" and "When is an intersectional analysis 'enough' to warrant claims of using intersectionality?" I concluded, with the help of survivors' stories, that intersectionality does not need to be explicit to have an impact or to claim "intersectionality." Yet I continue to mull over these and other questions to remain attentive to the power and uses of intersectionality as a framework and as a movement.

I encourage others who aim to explore "the interactive effects of multiple forms of discrimination" as it relates to sexual violence to take up intersectionality in their work.[18] In fact, I urge all those who have an interest in "seeing and telling different kinds of stories" and for sensing what may be wrong with specific policies and procedures to take an interest in intersectionality.[19] Although intersectionality (as a term) has existed for more than 35 years and intersectionality (as a concept) has been around for many more, there is still much more to do with and learn from the framework.[20]

We must use intersectionality to expand on its possibilities for repair in the midst of "the intersectionality wars," in which politicians, educators, and others dispute "nearly everything about intersectionality," including "its histories and origins, its methodologies, its efficacy, its politics, its relationship to identity and identity politics, its central metaphor, its juridical orientations, its relationship to 'black woman' and to black feminism."[21] Instead of theoretically musing about what intersectionality can and cannot do, we will learn a great deal more about the possibilities of the theory through its use in our research and practice. Crenshaw agreed, "I've consistently learned more from what scholars and activists have done with intersectionality than from what others have speculated about its appeal."[22]

Throughout this research, I learned a great deal through intersectionality. It often took me to places that I did not expect to go. Theoretically, I knew that the framework would help us work toward intersectional repair, but I did not foresee how it would offer immediate, tangible repair for both survivors and for myself.

Spending time with 34 Women of Color survivors and immersing myself in their stories for several years was one of the most transformative experiences of my life. These women taught me immense amounts about sisterhood, survival, and the power Women of Color hold. Their stories and our conversations allowed me to heal and grow in ways I did not know were possible.

Many Women of Color survivors felt similarly about our time together. Survivors often explored how our interviews offered repair from the intersectional failures they had experienced within their institutions.

In our conversation about healing, Faye stated, "How am I healing? Honestly, I feel like this conversation has been the most healing thing, these past two interviews." At the end of our final conversation together, Leyla offered her gratitude, "Thank you for having this [interview]. Seriously. No. It's really important. Because even this process has been healing. Talking about things that I don't necessarily think about all the time or even just talking about it [openly]." Rayn also offered her gratitude, "I really appreciate you working with [this] space. Because like we've talked about, these spaces are just nonexistent. I really appreciate you're putting energy into this."

These survivors, and others, went on to suggest that the space we co-created through our conversations was the first time they could think and talk about the ways that racism, sexism, classism, and other systems of domination influenced their experiences with violence. Our conversations encouraged them to process their experiences with violence alongside their identities as Women of Color, which included their experiences with intra-racial violence, intergenerational and historical trauma, punitive justice systems, feminism, and racialized and gendered stereotypes.

When survivors offered their gratitude, I was humbled. But I also thought, "All I did was account for intersectionality!" These women were sharing their stories, and often finding healing through sharing, because I acknowledged how intersecting systems of domination influenced their experiences with violence. Intersectional failure was so normalized for many Women of Color that incorporating intersectionality into just two, 90-minute conversations influenced remarkable moments of intersectional repair.

My hope is that these Women of Color and their stories motivate us to work toward additional moments of intersectional repair. My hope is that these stories continually "inspire us to get shit done."[23]

Appendix

Methods and Institutional Context

While speaking at the 2016 Women of the World Festival, Dr. Kimberlé Crenshaw encouraged us to use intersectionality to explore how "structures make certain identities the consequence of and the vehicle for vulnerability ... you've got to look at the context."[1] With this suggestion in mind, I use intersectionality to frame institutional context. Specifically, in Chapters 2, 3, and 4, the stories and perceptions of survivors and staff demonstrate how key aspects of the campus context influence various experiences with campus sexual violence.

This Appendix contains additional details and descriptions of each institution's context, including student body demographics, institutional resources, institutional mission, and built environment. The three institutions and their environments should not be compared to one another. Instead, institutional descriptions are meant to provide background and further meaning for participants' stories within each institutional environment. The three institutions were chosen due to their similarities (e.g., large, public) and due to the presence of my existing networks at each institution—gaining access to these institutions may have been easier than gaining access to institutions where I had no pre-existing connections.

At each institution I used my pre-existing professional networks to recruit Women of Color undergraduate students who experienced campus sexual violence. Student affairs professionals, chairs of academic departments, and relevant student groups disseminated recruitment messages via listservs, social media, and posting flyers on campus. Recruitment messages included a link to the study website, which interested participants could browse to gain detailed information about the study. Interested participants were asked to fill out a Qualtrics survey, which allowed me to gauge if they met the criteria for participation: that is, that they be 18 years old or older, self-identify as a woman, self-identify with a racially minoritized population, and have experienced sexual violence while an undergraduate student at one of the three research sites. Across the three institutions, 56 women expressed interest in the research. However, some women did not meet one or more of the research criteria, several women did not answer my initial email to set up an interview, and few did not show up for their scheduled interview. Thirty-four cisgender Women of Color students participated in the research process. Although I hoped to include stories from Women of Color survivors who identified as non-binary and/or trans*, all 34 women participants identified as cisgender women. Survivors self-reported their racial, ethnic, gender, and intersecting social identities. I use survivors' self-reported identities throughout the book.

River University: "It's Not a Huge Party School"

RU is nestled into an urban city that is known for its low crime rate and extremely safe community. Throughout the city, in all directions, you can observe peaceful suburban-feeling neighborhoods that are populated by model-homes, families with small children walking their dogs, and tranquility. The RU campus benefits from the surrounding city's utopian reputation, reassuring prospective students and their families that the campus is one of the safest around.

The RU campus is positioned around a sprawling green space, complete with trees, flowers, benches, and picnic tables. Several ordinary academic buildings surround this greenery, forcing students to walk through lush grass and tall trees to reach any given side of campus. To the west of the greenery and academic buildings sits a decent-sized parking lot and the football field, athletes' gym, and basketball stadium. The athletic "zone" is somewhat removed from campus, as if it were an afterthought of inclusion to the landscape. Several more parking lots line the south and east sides of campus. Two large clusters of residence hall buildings tower over the parking lots. The campus residence halls house nearly half of the undergraduate student body.

To the north of the sprawling lawn and academic buildings, students congregate around the spaces and places that encompass their extracurricular lives, including the Student Union, the Multicultural Center, several cafes, eateries, and a good-sized convenience store. I rarely observed students taking advantage of the green space in the center of campus. Rather, students often gathered in and around the cafes by the Student Union. On some afternoons, the path leading to and from the Union was full of students tabling for their respective student organizations, hoping to recruit new members, fundraise, or publicize an upcoming event. On other days, this area was merely a tranquil path for students to scurry from one obligation to the next.

RU enrolls approximately 30,000 undergraduate students and admits about 30% of its applicants. Approximately 50% of undergraduates are first-generation college students and nearly 75% of students receive some form of financial aid. RU holds national honors for being a supportive institution for low-income students in both affordability and likelihood of graduation. Administrators at the university consistently mentioned the high number of first-generation students and low-income students that they served. The Dean of Students believed these student characteristics created a specific campus environment:

> It's fairly academically focused. It's not a huge party school in that sense.
> We certainly have parties. We're not immune to it. But we're not a big

football school. It's not like that. A lot of first-generation students. I think
actually that creates a healthier climate for our student body academi-
cally, because our students are here [for the education]. I'm very proud
of our students, always. Students are amazing, and they're here for a lot
of the right reasons.... They're not here to just party and goof around.

Both students and staff noted how RU is not a party school. While athletics are present at the institution, it is not the central focus. And students did not describe a strong "party" or alcohol culture on campus.
Both athletics and a culture of drinking can influence sexual violence
perpetration in the campus environment.[2] But at RU, academics are a
focus. Sloane, a survivor at RU, agreed, "It's not run by athletics, not
really, because athletics sucks. Nobody really knows about RU's athletics. And when it comes to academics, you work hard."

Fraternity and Sorority Life was also present on campus. Less
than 6% of undergraduate students were members of the 40 RU recognized Greek letter organizations, which included several Black
Greek letter organizations and organizations from the Multicultural
Greek Council. Some student participants mentioned that fraternities and sororities held parties, but that these parties were often by
invite-only and reserved for the small percentage of students who
wore Greek letters.

The lack of focus on athletics and on fraternities and sororities were
not the only reasons that students and staff labeled RU as "not a party
school." Many RU students go home during the weekends. Jennifer,
the Interim Director of Fraternity and Sorority Life, stated that the
high population of first-generation students influenced RU's status as
a "duffel bag" campus. "We have students that live on campus during
the week, but then they pack a duffel bag to go home on the weekends,"
Jennifer explained.

Asian American students make up more than 40% of the undergraduate student body at RU. Latinx students represent 25% of the
student population. White students represent 12% of the student population, while international students comprise a slightly higher percentage (15%). Native American students represent less than 1% of

the student body, and Black students make up 3% of the undergraduate student population. RU does not report back demographic information for students who identify with more than one racial heritage.
Female-identified and male-identified students attend the institution
at similar rates. The institution did not report back demographic information beyond this binary.

Students at RU perceived that their institution was racially diverse,
often exploring how Asian American and Asian International students
represented most students on campus. For example, Anastasia stated,
"I feel like there's a lot of Asian students here. It's like Asian and then
Hispanics. I feel like I don't see the Hispanics. It's a lot of Asians." Although several women survivors perceived that RU was "diverse-ish,"
with Asian students making up most of the student body, many survivors also perceived the RU student body to self-segregate into ethnic
enclaves or "cliques." Daisy described:

> I feel like there's always those cliques of cultures. It's hard to break
> those cliques. You see a lot of international students always together or
> a lot of the Latino students always together. Because they come from
> the same background, because they go through similar experiences,
> similar obstacles, you see them sticking more to these cultural niches.

At RU, students were often hyper-focused on their studies and tended
to, as Carrie put it, have academic "tunnel vision" and concentrate on
school, not friendship. This resulted in some students never connecting
with a group or organization on campus. But usually, students found
one organization or "clique" they felt comfortable within and rarely
branched out from there. In fact, many of the women survivors at RU,
such as Felecia from Chapter 2, expressed their own journey of feeling
out of place on campus and then finding their "home" within one of the
600 student organizations on campus.

Mirroring the student body, the RU administration did not often describe intermingling or collaborating with one another. This, however,
may have been due to the high staff turnover rate at the institution.
While I collected data at RU, there were multiple job openings for staff,
including Vice Presidents, Directors, and Coordinators. Many interim

staff members occupied these open positions. Jennifer, the Interim Director of Fraternity and Sorority Life, occupied one such position and relayed that there were several senior leadership positions that were currently filled by interim roles. "We were like River University Interim ... which caused a lot of issues for us. Because all of us were interim, some of the institutional changes and things that we would want, we had to wait a lot, a long time for," Jennifer explained. Communication and collaboration were different, if not difficult, during the academic year because several offices were under-staffed. Jennifer also suggested that, although students may not know about "Interim University," they may feel the effects of the turnover, such as a lack of clear and consistent communication from institutional leaders.

Although Jennifer noted that this turnover may be specific to the academic year, other staff perceived that the consistent turnover within SVRC, across several years, precluded them from fully collaborating with that specific campus unit. RU was the only institution in this research that had a stand-alone Women's Center *and* a stand-alone Multicultural Center. Staff in these two Centers did not often collaborate with SVRC. Mollie, the Director of the Women's Center, shared her thoughts on the constant turnover in SVRC and how this influenced the development of relationships between campus units.

> These SVRC Advocates keep leaving. In the nine months that I've been there, one advocate left, another advocate left, another advocate just announced that they're leaving in the fall. Every time I think I'm going to be able to establish a connection with someone in that office, they leave.... All the people I would feel 100% confident in sending my students to in the SVRC have left.

Mollie perceived that the turnover in SVRC existed because sexual violence advocacy requires staff to constantly interface with trauma. Subsequently, "the burnout can be high," Mollie stated.

While there was continued turnover in SVRC, it was an integral unit at RU. Founded prior to most advocacy units at neighboring institutions, RU SVRC employed at least seven full-time employees, including more than two Prevention Coordinators, multiple Advocates, and a Director and Assistant Director. RU's Title IX Office was also well-resourced. The Title IX Coordinator explained, "We have a ton of resources that we put toward sexual violence.... I have seven investigators, which is pretty unusual and shows the institutional commitment." According to Robin, one of the RU SVRC Advocates, "mutual respect" existed between Title IX and SVRC. The SVRC Director also appreciated Title IX because they "understand that we are not the same" and they do "not try to take over our role." Although SVRC and Title IX had a collaborative relationship, the SVRC Director was aware that the Center's relationship with some Identity Based Centers, such as the Women's Center, waxed and waned depending on who oversaw those spaces.

Mountain University: "They're Very Community Minded"

Although MU is in an urban city, life on campus moves at a slow pace. Rows of campus-affiliated and non-campus affiliated three-story apartments, painted a lackluster beige, stand in a dotted line and border north campus. A few convenience stores and gas stations are scattered every few blocks and disrupt the homogeneity of the beige apartment complexes. In juxtaposition to the unvaried north end of campus, a freeway acts as a natural eastern border. Several fast-food restaurants, coffee shops, local eateries, gas stations, and a supermarket exist to the west of the freeway. It's a short yet packed one-mile strip of land that offers quick conveniences to students before merging with an urban downtown area boasting taller buildings and more foot and car traffic.

Majestic trees, tall grass, and sprawling flat land hugs the southeast and eastern borders of the campus. This seeming nature reserve reminds the onlooker that MU was once a research station for agricultural development. MU only added to its academic specialties once it earned university status years after its founding. Still, the land to the southeast and east of campus remains relatively untouched—according to the institution, the land is reserved for future development.

The MU campus is practical, not overstated. The athletic facilities include a track stadium, football field, and athletic complex. This athletic space is somewhat removed from the campus and does not draw attention away from central campus. Survivors very rarely spoke about MU Athletics.

During the day, student life was concentrated in or around the Student Union, located at the center of campus. The Union sits between academic buildings to the south, student support services to the north, and student residence halls to the east (30% of undergraduate students live on campus). The Union has a food court, study spaces, game rentals, and a small convenience store. On any given afternoon, the Student Union and its outdoor patios are populated with students; it seemed a popular space to stop and congregate as they navigate their campus lives.

MU's institutional admission rate is close to 60%. Over half of the 20,000 undergraduates are first-generation college students and nearly 90% of students receive some form of financial aid. At MU, Latinx students (40%) and Asian American students (35%) represent nearly 75% of the undergraduate student body. Native American students represent less than 1% of the student body. Black students make up 3% of the undergraduate student population. And 6% of students identify with more than one racial heritage. Only 10% of the undergraduate population at MU identify as white and 3% are international students. Female-identified students make up 10% more of the student body than male-identified students. The institution did not report back demographic information beyond this binary.

Mountain University holds accolades for being the "best" environment for Hispanic students, providing students with generous financial aid, offering social mobility to its students, and being affordable. MU also boasts a reputation for being one of the more racially diverse institutions in the U.S., which serves a large percentage of first-generation Students of Color. While many institutions that claim to focus on racial diversity often fall short in achieving these goals,[3] MU is seemingly following through on its espoused commitments. At first, Samantha, a survivor and student at MU, was skeptical of MU's commitment to diversity. She thought that the institutional valuing of diversity was "kind of B.S." But after spending three years in the campus environment, Samantha declared, "Okay, it's actually just true though. It's just a fact. We are just diverse."

Institutional campaigns, the mission statement, and the university website are saturated with the theme of community: campus community, local community, peer community, global community. Joy, the SVRC Prevention Educator, described how the diversity of the student body influenced a tight-knit, community-oriented campus environment:

> As a result [of diversity] . . . it's an incredible group of students that are very community based. They really want to get involved with community programs, peer programs. They're very active and appreciative of a lot of the services and resources on our campus. They really take advantage of them. They're very community minded. On our campus, the culture is a lot of socially engaged students who are involved in multiple programs.

Students felt similarly about the community-oriented and diverse nature of MU. Terri was "deeply rooted" in the MU environment. She was involved in multiple organizations and marveled at the diversity of interactions and opportunities on campus. Terri explained, "I think because people intermingle and intermix they have different types of friendships and relationships that you're more likely to step out and try something that isn't within your comfort zone of your culture." Because Terri transferred to MU from a small predominantly white institution where she felt uncomfortable and lacked a sense of belonging, she reveled in MU's diversity. At one point in our first interview, she exclaimed, "I love this campus! I love this school!"

MU students were socially engaged and "intermingled" throughout campus. Women survivors were often involved in more than one of MU's 500 student groups and organizations, including sororities, Black Student Union, Business Fraternities, and dance teams. The institution recognized over 30 national fraternities and sororities, 20 of which are cultural, for example, Black Greek letter Organizations. Less than

10% of the student body were involved in Fraternity and Sorority Life. While MU did not have a Multicultural Center, some students were involved with the Cultural Programs Office, which hosted racial and ethnic student programs that provided a "constructive" environment for Students of Color. MU also had a Women's Center, which some survivors visited or were involved with on occasion.

The Title IX Office at MU was comprised of a six-member staff, including a Title IX Officer and Assistant Title IX Officer. During most of the time I spent at MU, interim staff members occupied several positions in the Title IX Office. MU SVRC was founded when students demanded that the institution address sexual violence more seriously; this was only a few years prior to my starting the research at MU. Prior to its founding, there was no confidential advocacy or resource option for MU students. For most of its life on the MU campus, only two staff positions—a Director and an Assistant Director—were dedicated to SVRC. More recently, the institution allocated funds for SVRC to hire a Sexual Violence Prevention Educator.

SVRC and Title IX had a working relationship. Ivonne, the SVRC Director, however, found it difficult to fully believe in Title IX because it can be a long and dehumanizing process for survivors. Yet Ivonne knew that her main "job is to make sure that the student gets all their questions answered" and to "edify the process for them" so that they might have closure. Because students were their number one priority, SVRC staff made it a point to remain in regular contact with Title IX. SVRC staff also maintained contact with MU Campus Police, the Women's Center, the Counseling Center, and other relevant offices and resources on and off campus.

The collaborative relationship between SVRC and Title IX was not a unique relationship at MU. At first, I was skeptical of the collaborative spirit at MU. It was only after all interviews at MU were complete that I finally accepted that MU staff were collaborative and, for the most part, fiercely student-centered. Staff members and MU Offices often worked together to ensure the success of the student body. In our conversation, the Vice President for Student Affairs explained one reason why collaboration was a foundational value at MU.

We believe that our students deserve the absolute best that we have to offer them. And collaboration and the collaborative spirit allows us to band our resources together to give them the very best that we possibly can, given the resources that we are allocated.

Moments later, the Vice President acknowledged that MU is an "institution where you're not receiving the level of resources that you should be receiving, and we don't want that for our students." Collaboration between offices was a way to ensure students' well-being, particularly while attending an under-funded university.

City University: "I Feel Like There's a Lot of Privilege in Just the Name"

CU is in an energetic, diverse, and sprawling city. But CU's bustling geographical location might slip your memory as you walk around campus. A quiet, upper-class, majority white neighborhood hugs one side of campus. The well-manicured lawns of mansion-style homes in the neighborhood seamlessly melt into the grassy knolls that mark the northern border of CU. The sight of several towering residential halls, which house nearly 50% of CU undergraduate students, is one sign that signals you have crossed over from the private-owned properties onto campus.

To the east of campus, sorority houses stand resolute. To the west, the colossal fraternity houses. Approximately 13% of the CU student body are active in Fraternity and Sorority Life. Due to wealthy donors' stipulations, the women's sorority homes remain geographically separated from the men's fraternity homes. The sorority homes to the east of CU's borders appear sleepy, almost unoccupied. But the fraternity homes to the west display telling signs of (over)use and enjoyment. Soiled banners emblazoned with national sports teams' logos and ripped state flags hang from balconies, windows are missing their screens, and front lawns are littered with tattered sofas, abandoned shopping carts, and lawn chairs. On any given day or night, you might observe CU students on the front lawns of the fraternity houses, engaging in a rousing game of beer pong or lounging in Adirondack chairs with red solo cups in hand.

Grocery stores, coffee shops, and restaurants create the southern boundaries of campus. This small strip of commerce mimics a small college town. "CU" decals decorate storefront windows and throngs of students, often wearing CU paraphernalia, rotate in and out of restaurants and shops. Although the area to the south of CU serves the immediate needs of students with its grocery stores, pharmacies, post offices, and restaurants, students' social lives often take place outside of this tiny strip of life. Some students, particularly those with cars, venture off campus to experience the bustling city's art, food, events, dance clubs, and bars. However, most students' social lives revolve around CU residence halls and off-campus house parties, including the fraternity houses. Taryn, the Director of CU Fraternity and Sorority Life, described social life at CU:

> The social environment is in apartments, in chapter houses, in dorm rooms. There's not this like, "We're just going to go to the bowling alley and hang out." Or, "We're going to go to the park and hang out." Or, "We're going to go to the whatever it is." It's not there. It's not supported. It's 6:00[pm] the university basically closes up shop. And it's like well, the students are living after 6:00[pm].

The CU Student Union is not known for student engagement and entertainment. The few restaurants in the building did indeed close around 6pm every day. There are no other full-service restaurants on campus dedicated to the CU student body. After the Union closes at 6pm, there is not much for students to do on campus that does not revolve around the residence halls, apartments, and/or fraternity houses.

Although the Student Union sits squarely in the center of campus, its presence is eclipsed by several neighboring buildings dedicated to athletic life at CU. At the center of campus sits a state-of-the-art gym specifically for student athletes, an older gym for all students, faculty, staff, and community members, an expansive basketball arena, coaches' offices, a sports museum, tennis courts, multiple football and soccer fields, and a track.

City University enrolls over 30,000 undergraduate students and admits less than 15% of their applicants each year. Student athletes undergo a separate admissions process than prospective students who are not athletes. According to a recent CU admissions report, admitted student athletes have, on average, lower grade points than admitted students who are not athletes.

Several administrators were quick to point out that the institution is an "elite public institution." This elite status is showcased by the multiple awards, recognitions, and accomplishments gained by the institution and its faculty, staff, and students. While walking around campus there is no shortage of reminders that the institution has produced multiple Nobel Laureates, received billion-dollar grants for research, and holds top tier titles in multiple nationally ranked and recognized academic and athletic categories. The elite status of the institution permeates the student body. Anika stated that CU's elitism made many students think, "You've made it! You can have the world. The world is yours. City University. I feel like there's a lot of privilege in just the name."

Although white students comprised less than a third of the student body, several participants perceived that white students "dominate" the campus environment. Eliza claimed:

> The amount of [Students of Color] with the exception of Asian, is significantly lower than the amount of white people. People of Color are fetishized. I think whites are actually second to the Asian population, but I feel like them still being dominant [sic]."

Eliza later added that many Students of Color who attend CU "are aware that the institution doesn't do a lot [for them]." According to many Women of Color survivors at CU, the institution did not seem particularly concerned with Students of Colors' academic or social well-being.

Eliza was spot on about the demographic statistics of the institution. White students (30%) and Asian American students (30%) comprise most of the undergraduate student body at CU. Native American students represent less than 1% of the student body, and Black students make up 3% of the undergraduate student population. Six percent of the

student body identify with more than one racial heritage, while Latinx
students represent slightly more than 20% of the student body. International students represent the final 12% of the undergraduate population. Female-identified students make up 20% more of the student
body than male-identified students. The institution does not report
back demographic information beyond this binary. Approximately
30% of undergraduate students are first-generation college students
and slightly more than half of the undergraduate student body receives
some form of financial aid.

Women survivors' perceptions that the institution did not care
about Students of Color or that the institution was predominantly
white was unsurprising. Most CU tenured and tenure track faculty
are white. There is more racial diversity amongst CU staff. But as one
climbs up the organizational ladder, this diversity evaporates. And,
like clockwork, almost every year, if not every semester, a CU student
or CU student organization perpetrates a racist incident. A search
through the CU student newspaper offers detailed information on several student-sponsored racist themed parties, as well as racist photos,
videos, and posters that involved CU students. Within the newspaper
articles, CU Students of Color often cite how institutional leaders respond to these racist campus incidents with inaction or neutrality.

Several survivors also explored how the institution often mistreated
and silenced Women of Color students. "The institution has made it
really hard to be a Woman of Color here," Padma lamented. Leyla perceived, "[Students of Color] are very invisible here. It's like we don't
even go here, and it's so weird." Some Women of Color survivors did
perceive that CU was racially diverse and supportive of People of Color.
At the same time, these survivors acknowledged that their positive perceptions were influenced by their upbringing in racially homogenous,
predominantly white environments. They acknowledged that their
perceptions of CU as racially diverse were not shared by most other
Peers of Color.

CU does not have a Women's Center or a Multicultural Center.
The campus is lacking in formal units that might support Women of
Color specifically, which may contribute to the invisibility they feel on

campus. Yet most women students in this research belonged to one or more of the over 1,000 student clubs and organizations at CU. Women's membership in these clubs often revolved around their racial and ethnic identities, including the Black Student Union, South Asian Acapella Club, Indian Dance Team, and the Multiracial Student Alliance.

CU staff members also shared some gripes about the institution, most of which related to the organizational structure. Amy, a SVRC Advocate, noted, "Campus is pretty disjointed in terms of their efforts.... Because the campus is so [big], there's a lot of people that work here and a lot of people who have different ideas on how to help students." Arlene, the Director of SVRC, explained this fragmentation further: "It feels like there have been intentionally created silos. It was not an accident that all these services happened separately. And I think that that really serves to quiet everything, because we can't be a united voice." The large population of students and staff, the physical grandness of the campus, and a top-down organizational structure may have influenced a lack of collaboration across many CU units.

CU has a Title IX Office with multiple staff members, including a Director, Assistant Director, and four Investigators. The Director of the Counseling Center oversees SVRC, but the Counseling Center and SVRC remain two separate units. Prior to the Dear Colleague Letter, one counselor at the CU Counseling Center was dedicated to sexual violence advocacy. But a few years after the publication of the Dear Colleague Letter, CU dedicated institutional resources to hiring a full-time Director for SVRC. SVRC grew over several years to include one Director, two Advocates, and a Program Coordinator. The two SVRC Advocates see over 800 clients annually, which, according to the SVRC Director, "is a fraction of the number of people who are actually referred to us." SVRC's client load influences a breakdown between SVRC and Title IX. The SVRC Director explained, "[Title IX] is buried, we're buried. There is not enough people to have a seamless relationship. So, we're all just up in the air!"

TABLE A.1. *Institutional Context**

Institution	Control	Under-graduate Enrollment	Enrollment by Gender	Enrollment by Racial Identity	Number of Survivors Interviewed	Staff Participants
River University	Public	30,000	50% women / 50% men	40% Asian American and Pacific Islander (AAPI); 25% Hispanic; 3% Black; <1% Native American; 12% White	10	Title IX Coordinator; Dean of Students; Director of SVRC; Advocate for SVRC; Director of the Multicultural Center; Interim Director of Fraternity and Sorority Life; Director of the Women's Center
Mountain University	Public	20,000	55% women / 45% men	35% AAPI; 40% Hispanic; 6% Multiracial; 3% Black; <1% Native American; 10% White	11	Dean of Students; Director of SVRC; Advocate for SVRC; Prevention Educator for SVRC; Director of the Women's Center; Dean of Students for Diversity
City University	Public	30,000	60% women / 40% men	30% AAPI; 22% Hispanic; 6% Multiracial; 3% Black; <1% Native American; 30% White	13	Title IX Special Assistant; Dean of Students; Vice President of Student Affairs; Director of SVRC; 2 Advocates for SVRC; Director of Counseling Center; Interim Director of Fraternity and Sorority Life; Director of Community Crisis Center; Campus Police Chief

*Each institution collected students' gender identities in binary manners. Racial identity was also recorded via static, socially constructed categories.

TABLE A.2. *Survivor Demographics for River University*

Name	Self-Reported Racial & Ethnic Identity	Self-Reported Salient Identities*	Age	Student Standing	Experiences with Violence	Did they report to a formal outlet? e.g., Title IX	Did they use the RU SVRC?
Daisy	Hispanic	Latinx, first-generation student, low income	20	Junior	Unwanted sexual contact perpetrated by a man student acquaintance during her second year at RU	No	No
Margaret	Mexican / South Asian (Indian)		20	Sophomore	Rape perpetrated by an RU student acquaintance during her first year at RU	No	No
Coraline	Latinx white	Pansexual	20	Junior	Intimate partner violence perpetrated by ex-partner on campus during second year at RU	No	No
Anastasia	Hispanic (Mexican)		20	Sophomore	Unwanted sexual contact perpetrated by an acquaintance during her first year at RU	No	No
Felecia	Mexican/ Hispanic		21	Senior	Three different instances of sexual violence perpetrated by three different men students on three separate occasions during her first year at RU; first two assaults involved unwanted groping and touching; the third was rape	No	No

(continued)

TABLE A.2. (continued)

Name	Self-Reported Racial & Ethnic Identity	Self-Reported Salient Identities*	Age	Student Standing	Experiences with Violence	Did they report to a formal outlet? e.g., Title IX	Did they use the RU SVRC?
Sloane	Vietnamese American		19	Sophomore	Unwanted sexual contact perpetrated by a man student acquaintance during her first year at RU	No	Yes
Carrie	Black / African American	Bisexual; Black-woman-queer	21	Senior	Unwanted sexual contact perpetrated by a man student acquaintance during her first year at RU	No	No
Naomi	Half Mexican / half white		20	Junior	Rape perpetrated by an RU student acquaintance during the summer between her second and third years at RU	No	No
Christine	Black	Religious identity (Christian); the intersectionality of being both Black and female	22	Senior	Unwanted sexual contact perpetrated by a man student acquaintance during her first year at RU	No	No
Jane	Asian	Low SES family, daughter of Vietnamese refugee parents, queer	20	Junior	Intimate partner violence perpetrated by man student during second year at RU	No	No

Although I hoped to include stories from Women of Color survivors who identified as non-binary and/or trans, all 34 women participants identified as cisgender women.

TABLE A.3. *Survivor Demographics for Mountain University*

Name	Self-Reported Racial & Ethnic Identity	Self-Reported Salient Identities	Age	Student Standing	Experiences with Violence	Did they report to a formal outlet? e.g., Title IX	Did they use the MU SVRC?
Melanie	African American / white	I don't really have any	20	Sophomore	Unwanted touching and sexual harassment perpetrated by MU employee during her first year at MU	Yes; Title IX and police	Yes
Tessa	South Asian (Indian)	First generation born in the U.S.	20	Junior	Unwanted sexual contact perpetrated by a man student acquaintance during her first year at MU	Yes; Title IX and police	Yes
Veronica	Asian	First generation born in the U.S.	22	Senior	Unwanted touching and physical violence perpetrated by a man student acquaintance during her second year at MU	No	No
Katrina	Black / African American	Pansexual, adopted	19	Sophomore	Unwanted touching perpetrated by a man student during her first year; Intimate partner violence during second year at MU	Yes; Title IX and police	Yes
Terri	Latina	Student	24	Senior	Rape perpetrated by a man student during her senior year at MU	No	No
Raquel	North African	Woman	25	Alumna	Rape perpetrated by a man student acquaintance during her senior year at MU	Yes; Title IX	Yes

(continued)

TABLE A.3. (continued)

Name	Self-Reported Racial & Ethnic Identity	Self-Reported Salient Identities	Age	Student Standing	Experiences with Violence	Did they report to a formal outlet? e.g., Title IX	Did they use the MU SVRC?
Samantha	Mexican/ Vietnamese	Race and gender	20	Junior	Unwanted touching perpetrated by a man student during first year at MU	Yes; Title IX	Yes
Monae	Latina	Christian	22	Junior	Intimate partner violence perpetrated by man student during first year at MU; unwanted touching perpetrated by a man student acquaintance during first year at MU	No	No
Noelle	South Asian (Indian)		21	Junior	Rape perpetrated by a man student acquaintance during her second year at MU	No	Yes
Jasmine	Mexican	Sister, daughter	20	Junior	Rape perpetrated by a man student acquaintance during her first year at MU	No	Yes
Ananya	South Asian (Indian)		21	Senior	Rape perpetrated by an acquaintance, who said he was an MU student, during her first year at MU	No	Yes

TABLE A.4. *Survivor Demographics for City University*

Name	Self-Reported Racial & Ethnic Identity	Self-Reported Salient Identities	Age	Student Standing	Experiences with Violence	Did they report to a formal outlet? e.g., Title IX	Did they use the CU SVRC?
Alice	Vietnamese		20	Junior	Intimate partner violence perpetrated by man during first and second years at CU	No	No
Padma	South Asian (Indian)	Daughter of immigrants, domestic violence household, survivor	21	Senior	Unwanted touching perpetrated by a stranger during first year at CU; unwanted touching perpetrated by a man student acquaintance during second year at CU	No	No
Clara	Latino		23	Alumna	Rape perpetrated by a CU employee during second year at CU	Yes; Title IX and police	No
Queenie	Asian / Vietnamese	Queer, disabled	25	Alumna	Intimate partner violence perpetrated by a man during first and second year at CU; unwanted touching perpetrated by a stranger during second year at CU	No	No
Maribel	Latina and Native American	Recently Chicana	22	Senior	Unwanted touching perpetrated by multiple men students in a shared Uber ride during her third year at CU	No	No

(continued)

TABLE A.4. (continued)

Name	Self-Reported Racial & Ethnic Identity	Self-Reported Salient Identities	Age	Student Standing	Experiences with Violence	Did they report to a formal outlet? e.g., Title IX	Did they use the CU SVRC?
Rayn	Asian / South Asian	Immigrant, neurodivergent	21	Senior	Intimate partner violence perpetrated by man student during first year at CU	No	No
Erika	South Asian (Indian)	Daughter, girlfriend, first generation American-born	21	Senior	Unwanted touching perpetrated by a man student acquaintance during her first year at CU	No	No
Anika	Black	I don't think about them individually, but they are all important to who I am	21	Senior	Rape perpetrated by an acquaintance, who she believed was a CU student, during her first year at CU	No	No
Faye	South Asian (Indian)	Survivor, Womxn of Color, South Asian American, daughter of immigrants	19	Sophomore	Rape perpetrated by an acquaintance during her first year at CU	No	No

Name	Self-Reported Racial & Ethnic Identity	Self-Reported Salient Identities	Age	Student Standing	Experiences with Violence	Did they report to a formal outlet? e.g., Title IX	Did they use the CU SVRC?
Leyla	Half Black / Half Pakistani	Sister, daughter, friend, dyslexic student	20	Junior	Rape perpetrated by a man student acquaintance during her first year at CU	No	No
Serena	Asian	LGBT, disabled	20	Junior	Unwanted touching perpetrated by a stranger during her first year at CU	Yes; campus police	Yes
Mary	Black / white	LGBT	21	Senior	Intimate partner violence perpetrated by man student during first year at CU	No	Yes
Eliza	Multiracial		22	Senior	Unwanted touching perpetrated by a man student acquaintance during senior year at CU	Yes; Board of the housing co-op	Yes

Acknowledgments

This book was born into existence through the conversations I had with the 34 Women of Color student survivors. My professional goals never included writing a book. In the field of education, writing a book, especially prior to tenure, is often frowned upon. But then, one by one, I heard the stories of the 34 Women of Color survivors. I was captivated by each woman and their story—by their vulnerability, their power, and their insight into the world. I wrote a few articles about the stories I heard, but these articles never felt complete. I was doing a disservice to women's beautiful lives and stories by dissecting them into various 30-page, double spaced, word documents. The solution was obvious. I was going to write a book.

Thank you to the 34 Women of Color survivors who inspired me to write this book. I am eternally grateful for the stories they shared with me and now, the stories they have shared with you. This book would not exist without these women. These acknowledgements can't begin to capture my gratitude for the 34 women and the time they spent with me. But my hope is that this book, and the way I have told women's stories, acts as a tangible, more meaningful "thank you" than just this acknowledgements section.

I am also grateful for the Women of Color scholars who have provided a foundation for my thinking around this book. Gloria Anzaldua,

Audre Lorde, the Combahee River Collective, Kimberlé Crenshaw, Patricia Hill Collins, my aunts, my grandmother, my mentors, and many more—thank you for your knowledge and for sharing this knowledge with others. To Nadeeka Karunaratne, thank you for helping to make this research project a reality through the interviews and analysis you completed and the wisdom you contributed.

I am indebted to the staff members at each institution who participated in the research and provided more information on the context of each university. Staff members' narratives added context and depth to survivors' stories. Yet I recognize that it was not always easy for staff to speak about campus sexual violence at their institution, especially as it relates to institutional betrayal and institutional courage.

I hold immense gratitude toward the Spencer Foundation and the National Academy of Education for helping to fund my research and resulting book.

To Eddie Cole, who supported and guided me throughout this entire process—start to finish—thank you for reading chapter drafts, answering voice memos, and for reminding me that I am capable. To Ananda Marin, Giovan Alonzi, and the many other colleagues who supported me while writing, thank you for listening to my musings and offering your opinions and solutions. To my amazing friends and family, some of my biggest champions, thank you for pushing me to persist, for your consistent check-ins, and for your constant support.

And finally, to my partner, Jian. Thank you for everything throughout this process: the morning coffees, the encouragement, the support, the walks, the talks, and above all, the laughs.

Notes

Introduction

1. Women of the World Festival 2016. "Kimberlé Crenshaw—On Intersectionality—Keynote—WOW 2016," YouTube Video, 1:19, March 14, 2016, https://www.youtube.com/watch?v=-DW4HLgYPlA&t=245s.

2. "Sexual violence" is a non-legal term often used by individuals and U.S. organizations to reference violence on a global scale and includes sexual assault, rape, incest, intimate partner sexual violence, and stalking (see RAINN.org [Rape, Abuse & Incest National Network] for more information). In 1957, Kilpatrick and Kanin published one of the first studies that focused on campus sexual violence, finding that over 50% of the women students surveyed had experienced "erotic aggressiveness" while in college; Clifford Kilpatrick and Eugene Kanin, "Male Sex Aggression on a University Campus," *American Sociological Review* 22, no. 1 (1957): 53. In the 1970s, the height of the feminist anti-rape movement helped to establish several community rape crisis centers that partnered with nearby colleges and universities to serve student survivors of violence; Jody Jessup-Anger et al., "History of Sexual Violence in Higher Education," *New Directions for Student Services* vol. 2018, no. 161 (2018): 9–19. In 1990, what is now known as the Clery Act was signed into law. Clery required campuses to record and disclose all campus crime that happens on or near campus; The Clery Center "The Jeanne Cleary Act: Summary, Reporting Requirements, and Clery Center Resources," 2022, https://clerycenter.org/policy/the-clery-act.

3. Title IX, Education Amendments of 1972, 20 U.S.C. 1681–1688; "Dear Colleague Letter: Office of the Assistant Secretary," 2011, https://www2.ed.gov/about/offices/list/ocr/letters/colleague-201104.html.

4. U.S. Department of Education, "Dear Colleague Letter: Office of the Assistant Secretary," para. 1. In 2020, U.S. Secretary of Education, Betsy DeVos, and the Department of Education released regulations that rolled back Obama era guidelines on Title IX. The new regulations institute a narrower view of sexual harassment, hold schools less accountable for responding to sexual violence, particularly those occurring off campus, narrow reporting requirements, and shift the evidentiary standard; U.S. Department of Education, "Summary of Major Provisions of the Department of Education's Title IX Final Rule," 2020, https://www2.ed.gov/about/offices/list/ocr/docs/titleix-summary.pdf. As I write this introduction, we await the Biden Administration's "dramatic overhaul" to Title IX; Collin Binkley, "Biden Administration Proposed New Title IX Protections for Campus Sexual Assault," PBS News Hour, 2022, https://www.pbs.org/newshour/politics/biden-administration-proposed-new-title-ix-protections-for-campus-sexual-assault. My interviews with survivors, however, were completed prior to fall 2020. Therefore, participants' understandings of Title IX and other federal and institutional policies often related to the Obama era guidelines.

5. RAINN. "Campus SaVE Act," 2023, https://www.rainn.org/articles/campus-save-act.

6. Sexual assault refers to any unwanted sexual contact. Sexual violence is a more encompassing term that refers to sexual assault, stalking, and intimate partner violence. Through this book, I focus on sexual violence, but I use specific, narrower terms of violence, for example, sexual assault, when referring to documents that use these terms and/or when study participants reference these specific forms of violence; White House Task Force to Protect Students from Sexual Assault, "Not Alone: The First Report of the White House Task Force to Protect Students from Sexual Assault," April 2014, https://www.justice.gov/ovw/page/file/905942/dl.

7. U.S. Department of Education, "Dear Colleague Letter"; Jacquelyn D. Wiersma-Mosley and James DiLoreto, "The Role of the Title IX Coordinators on College and University Campuses," *Behavioral Sciences* 8, no. 38 (2018): 1–14.

8. Tara N. Richards, "An Updated Review of Institutions of Higher Education's Responses to Sexual Assault: Results from a Nationally Representative Sample," *Journal of Interpersonal Violence* 34, no. 10 (2019): 1983–2012.

9. Richards, "An Updated Review of Institutions of Higher Education's Responses to Sexual Assault."

10. White House Task Force to Protect Students from Sexual Assault, "Not Alone," 16.

11. Jessica C. Harris et al., "Reimagining the Study of Campus Sexual Assault," *Higher Education: Handbook of Theory and Research* 35 (2020): 1–47; Jessica C. Harris and Chris Linder, "Introduction," in *Sexual Violence and its Intersections on Campus: Centering Minoritized Students' Voices*, ed. Jessica C. Harris and Chris Linder (Sterling, VA: Stylus, 2017), 1–22; Chris Linder et al., "What Do We Know about Campus Sexual Violence? A Content Analysis of 10 Years of Research," *Review of Higher Education* 43, no. 4 (2020): 1017–1040; Sarah McMahon et al., "Campus Sexual Assault: Future Directions for Research," *Sex Abuse* 31, no. 3 (2019): 270–295.

12. Laura Ly, "Dartmouth Cancels Classes After Student Protest, Online Threats," *CNN*, April 25, 2013, https://www.cnn.com/2013/04/24/us/dartmouth-cancels-classes-protest/index.html; Ishani Premaratne, "Sexual Assault Protest Cancels Dartmouth Classes," *USA TODAY*, April 27, 2013, https://www.usatoday.com/story/news/nation/2013/04/27/dartmouth-sexual-assault-protest-cancels-classes/2117159/.

13. Allie Grasgreen, "Enforcement for the Enforcers," *Inside Higher Ed*, July 15, 2013, https://www.insidehighered.com/news/2013/07/16/sexual-assault-activists-protest-level-federal-title-ix-enforcement.

14. Sara Lipka, "An Arc of Outrage," *The Chronicle of Higher Education*, April 13, 2015, https://www.chronicle.com/article/an-arc-of-outrage/; Libby Sander, "4 More Colleges are Targets of Students' Complaints Over Sexual Assault," *The Chronicle of Higher Education*, May 23, 2013, https://www.chronicle.com/article/4-more-colleges-are-targets-of-students-complaints-over-sexual-assault/.

15. David Cantor et al., "Report on the AAU Campus Climate Survey on Sexual Assault and Sexual Misconduct"; Jessup-Anger et al., "History of Sexual Violence in Higher Education"; Lipka, "An Arc of Outrage."

16. Lipka, "An Arc of Outrage," para 7.

17. Cantor et al., "Report on the AAU Campus Climate Survey on Sexual Assault and Sexual Misconduct"; Kolby Cameron and Jason Wollschleger, "Examining the Institutional Features Influencing Sexual Assault at Small Colleges and Universities," *Sociological Inquiry* 91, no. 1 (2021): 162–180; Carrie A. Moylan and McKenzie Javorka, "Widening the Lens: An Ecological Review of Campus Sexual Assault," *Trauma, Violence, & Abuse* 21, no. 1 (2020): 179–192.

18. Scott Neuman, "55 Colleges, Universities Under Investigation for Abuse Claims," *NPR*, May 1, 2014, https://www.npr.org/sections/thetwo-way/2014/05/01/308702112/55-colleges-universities-under-investigation-for-abuse-claims; Jennifer Steinhauer and David S. Joachim, "55 Colleges Named in Federal Inquiry into Handling of Sexual Assault Cases," *The New York Times*, May 1, 2014, https://www.nytimes.com/2014/05/02/us/politics/us-lists-colleges-under-inquiry-over-sex-assault-cases.html; Office of Civil Rights, "Pending Cases Currently Under Investigation at Elementary-Secondary and Post-Secondary Schools as of May 8, 2023 7:30am Search," U.S. Department of Education, May 8, 2023, https://www2.ed.gov/about/offices/list/ocr/docs/investigations/open-investigations/tix.html.

19. The Chronicle of Higher Education, "Title IX: Tracking Sexual Assault Allegations," *The Chronicle of Higher Education*, June 6, 2023, http://projects.chronicle.com/titleix/#overview.

20. Women of the World Festival 2016. "Kimberlé Crenshaw—On Intersectionality—Keynote—WOW 2016."

21. Women of the World Festival 2016. "Kimberlé Crenshaw—On Intersectionality—Keynote—WOW 2016."

22. In the 1970s, the term *Woman of Color* grew out of a movement of resistance and a need for solidarity among a group of racially minoritized women who shared a similar position in a U.S. hierarchy of oppression. *Women of Color* is a "solidarity definition, a commitment to work in collaboration with other oppressed Women of Color who have been 'minoritized.'" Western States Center. "The Origin of the Phrase 'Women of Color,'" YouTube Video, 1:30, February 15, 2011, https://www.youtube.com/watch?v=82vl34mi4Iw. At times, the term is used as a biological reference rather than a solely political one, which risks placing Women of Color into a monolithic group of people who share the exact same experiences; Western States Center, "The Origin of the Phrase 'Women of Color.'" Throughout this book, I foreground how "the existence of the group as the unit of analysis neither means that all individuals within the group have the same experiences nor that they interpret them in the same way"; Patricia Hill Collins, "Comment on Hekman's 'Truth and Method: Feminist Standpoint Theory Revisited': Where's the Power?," *Signs: Journal of Women in Culture and Society* 22, no. 2 (1997): 377. I note how the 34 Women of Color survivors have similar group experiences, but I also draw out dissimilarities within group experiences. I use the term "Women of Color" to center the experiences of these women as a political, not biological, group that often shares a history of power and oppression. Centering Women of Color as a political

group acknowledges the "social, cultural, and historical specificity of one's location and embodied knowledge as crucial in developing and mobilizing effective strategies to end violence against women and their communities"; Shireen M. Roshanravan, "Passing-as-if: Model-Minority Subjectivity and Women of Color Identification," *Meridians: Feminism, Race, Transnationalism* 10, no. 1 (2010): 6.

23. Uma Narayan, "The Project of Feminist Epistemology: Perspectives from a Nonwestern feminist," in *The Feminist Standpoint Theory Reader: Intellectual and Political Controversies*, ed. Sandra Harding (New York: Routledge, 2004), 213–224; Jennifer C. Nash, "Re-Thinking Intersectionality," *Feminist Review*, no. 89 (2008): 1–15.

24. Nash, "Re-Thinking Intersectionality," 3.

25. Subini Ancy Annamma et al., "Conceptualizing Color-Evasiveness: Using Dis/Ability Critical Race Theory to Expand a Color-Blind Racial Ideology in Education and Society," *Race, Ethnicity, and Education* 20, no. 2 (2017): 147–162.

26. Valerie Lundy-Wagner and Rachelle Winkle-Wagner, "A Harassing Climate? Sexual Harassment and Campus Racial Climate Research," *Journal of Diversity in Higher Education* 6, no. 1 (2013): 59.

27. Kimberlé Crenshaw et al., "What Does Intersectionality Mean?" March 29, 2021, in *1A*, produced by *NPR*, podcast 43:15, https://www.npr.org/2021/03/29/982357959/what-does-intersectionality-mean.

28. MAKERS. "Kimberlé Crenshaw. The 2020 MAKERS Conference," YouTube Video, 13:45, February 14, 2020, https://www.youtube.com/watch?v=cSTf89pLclo.

29. MAKERS. "Kimberlé Crenshaw. The 2020 MAKERS Conference," 1:48.

30. MAKERS. "Kimberlé Crenshaw. The 2020 MAKERS Conference," 11:10.

31. MAKERS. "Kimberlé Crenshaw. The 2020 MAKERS Conference," 11:10.

32. Kimberlé Crenshaw, "Demarginalizing the Intersection of Race and Sex: A Black Feminist Critique of Antidiscrimination Doctrine, Feminist Theory, and Antiracist Politics," *University of Chicago Legal Forum* 1, no. 8 (1989): 139–167.

33. Jennifer C. Nash, "Re-Thinking Intersectionality," *Feminist Review*, no. 89 (2008): 3.

34. Kimberlé Crenshaw et al., "What Does Intersectionality Mean?" 2:04.

35. Kimberlé Crenshaw, "Mapping the Margins: Intersectionality, Identity Politics, and Violence against Women of Color," *Stanford Law Review* 43, no. 6 (July 1991): 1241–1299; Crenshaw, "Demarginalizing the Intersection of Race and Sex."

36. Crenshaw, "Mapping the Margins"; Crenshaw, "Demarginalizing the Intersection of Race and Sex"; Women of the World Festival 2016. "Kimberlé Crenshaw—On Intersectionality—Keynote—WOW 2016," 1:40; MAKERS. "Kimberlé Crenshaw. The 2020 MAKERS Conference."

37. Crenshaw, "Demarginalizing the Intersection of Race and Sex," 139.

38. Guided by the work of Lindsay Pérez Huber, I do not capitalize "white" to counter hegemonic grammatical norms and to "reject the grammatical representation of power capitalization brings to the term 'white'"; Lindsay Pérez Huber, "Using Latina/o Critical Race Theory (LatCrit) and Racist Nativism to Explore Intersectionality in the Educational Experiences of Undocumented Chicana College Students," *Educational Foundations* 24, no. 1–2 (2010): 93. I capitalize Asian American, Black, Latinx, and other minoritized racial groups, including Women of Color, as a form of linguistic empowerment.

39. Crenshaw, "Mapping the Margins," 1244.

40. Crenshaw, "Mapping the Margins."

41. Crenshaw, "Mapping the Margins."

42. Crenshaw, "Mapping the Margins," 1251.

43. Crenshaw, "Mapping the Margins."

44. Crenshaw, "Mapping the Margins"; Crenshaw, "Demarginalizing the Intersection of Race and Sex."

45. Andrea Smith, *Conquest: Sexual Violence and American Indian Genocide* (Cambridge, MA: South End Press, 2005); See also Hijin Park, "Interracial Violence, Western Racialized Masculinities, and the Geopolitics of Violence against Women," *Social & Legal Studies* 21, no. 4 (2012): 41–509; Victoria C. Olive, "Sexual Assault against Women of Color," *Journal of Student Research* 1 (2012): 1–9.

46. Armstrong et al., "Silence, Power, and Inequality"; Crenshaw, "Mapping the Margins."

47. Lorien S. Jordan, "Belonging and Otherness: The Violability and Complicity of Settler Colonial Sexual Violence," *Women & Therapy* 44 no. 3 (2021): 271–291; Andrea Smith, *Conquest: Sexual Violence and American Indian Genocide* (Cambridge, MA: South End Press, 2005).

48. Elizabeth A. Armstrong et al., "Silence, Power, and Inequality: An Intersectional Approach to Sexual Violence," *Annual Review of Sociology* 44

(2018): 99–122; Estelle B. Freedman, *Redefining Rape: Sexual Violence in the Era of Suffrage and Segregation* (Cambridge, MA: Harvard University Press, 2013); Jennifer Wriggins, "Rape, Racism, and the Law," *Harvard Women's Law Journal* 103, no. 6 (1983): 103–141.

49. Crenshaw, "Mapping the Margins."

50. Crenshaw, "Mapping the Margins," 1285.

51. Crenshaw, "Mapping the Margins," 1290.

52. Nash, "Re-Thinking Intersectionality," 3.

53. Linder et al., "What Do We Know about Campus Sexual Violence?"

54. Leah E. Adams-Curtis and Gordon B. Forbes, "College Women's Experiences of Sexual Coercion: A Review of Cultural, Perpetrator, Victim, and Situational Violence," *Trauma, Violence, & Abuse* 5, no. 2 (2004): 91–122; Christine A. Gidycz et al., "Sexual Victimization and Health-Risk Behaviors: A Prospective Analysis of College Women," *Journal of Interpersonal Violence* 23, no. 6 (2008): 744–763; Christina M. Hassija and Jessica A. Turchik, "An Examination of Disclosure, Mental Health Treatment Use, and Posttraumatic Growth among College Women Who Experienced Victimization," *Journal of Loss and Trauma* 21, no. 2 (2016): 124–136.

55. Gidycz et al., "Sexual Victimization and Health-Risk Behaviors: A Prospective Analysis of College Women," 751.

56. Annamma et al., "Conceptualizing Color-Evasiveness."

57. Brenda Lee Anderson Wadley and Sarah S. Hurtado, "Using Intersectionality to Reimagine Title IX Adjudication Policy," *Journal of Women and Gender in Higher Education* 16, no. 1 (2023): 52–66. Susan VanDeventer Iverson, "Mapping Identities: An Intersectional Analysis of Policies on Sexual Violence," in *Intersections of Identity and Sexual Violence on Campus: Centering Minoritized Students' Experiences*, ed. Jessica C. Harris and Chris Linder (Sterling, VA: Stylus, 2017), 214–232; Sara Carrigan Wooten, "Revealing a Hidden Curriculum of Black Women's Erasure in Sexual Violence Prevention Policy," *Gender and Education* 29, no. 3 (2017): 405–417.

58. Wadley and Hurtado, "Using Intersectionality to Reimagine Title IX Adjudication Policy."

59. Patricia Hill Collins, *Black Feminist Thought* (New York: Routledge, 2000); Roxanne Donovan and Michelle Williams, "Living at the Intersection," *Women & Therapy* 25, nos. 3–4 (2002): 95–105; Linda Kalof, "Ethnic Differences in Female Sexual Victimization," *Sexuality & Culture: An Interdisciplinary Quarterly* 4, no. 4 (2000): 75–97; Kelly H. Koo et al., "The Cultural Context of Nondisclosure of Alcohol-Involved Acquaintance Rape among Asian American College Women: A Qualitative Study," *Journal of Sex*

Research 52 (2015): 55–68; Victoria C. Olive, "Sexual Assault against Women of Color," *Journal of Student Research* 1 (2012): 1–9; Andrea Smith, *Conquest: Sexual Violence and American Indian Genocide* (Cambridge, MA: South End Press, 2005).

60. Koo et al., "The Cultural Context of Nondisclosure of Alcohol-Involved Acquaintance Rape among Asian American College Women," 63.

61. Kalof, "Ethnic Differences in Female Sexual Victimization"; Koo et al., "The Cultural Context of Nondisclosure of Alcohol-Involved Acquaintance Rape among Asian American College Women."

62. Kalof, "Ethnic Differences in Female Sexual Victimization," 92.

63. Wadley and Hurtado, "Using Intersectionality to Reimagine Title IX Adjudication Policy"; Iverson, "Mapping Identities"; Wooten, "Revealing a Hidden Curriculum of Black Women's Erasure in Sexual Violence Prevention Policy."

64. Luoluo Hong and Susan B. Marine, "Sexual Violence Through a Social Justice Paradigm: Framing and Applications," in *Addressing Sexual Violence in Higher Education and Student Affairs*, ed. Jody Jessup-Anger and Keith E. Edwards (San Francisco, CA: Jossey-Bass, 2018), 21–33; Culture of Respect, "Prevention Programming Matrix," https://cultureofrespect.org/programs-and-tools/matrix/. Most bystander intervention programs have not been found to impact rates of sexual assault perpetration; Kettrey et al., "Effects of Bystander Programs on the Prevention of Sexual Assault among Adolescents and College Students: A Systematic Review," *Campbell Systematic Reviews* 15, no. 1–2 (2019): 1–40; The few bystander intervention program evaluations that have demonstrated a change in rates of campus sexual violence involve student populations that are over 77% white; Ann L. Coker et al., "Evaluation of the Green Dot Bystander Intervention to Reduce Interpersonal Violence among College Students Across Three Campuses," *Violence Against Women* 21, no. 12 (2015): 1507–1527.

65. M. Candace Christensen and Richard J. Harris, "Correlates of Bystander Readiness to Help among a Diverse College Student Population: An Intersectional Perspective," *Research in Higher Education* 60, no. 8 (2019): 1195–1226; Jill C. Hoxmeier et al., "Students as Prosocial Bystanders to Sexual Assault: Demographic Correlates of Intervention Norms, Intentions, and Missed Opportunities," *Journal of Interpersonal Violence* 35, no. 3–4 (2020): 731–754; Jennifer Katz et al., "White Female Bystanders' Response to a Black Woman at Risk for Incapacitated Sexual Assault," *Psychology of Women Quarterly* 41, no. 2 (2017): 273–285; Sarah McMahon et al., "Bystander Intervention as a Prevention Strategy for Campus Sexual Violence: Perceptions

of Historically Minoritized College Students," *Prevention Science* 21 (2020): 795–806.

66. Katz et al., "White Female Bystanders' Response to a Black Woman at Risk for Incapacitated Sexual Assault."

67. Katz et al., "White Female Bystanders' Response to a Black Woman at Risk for Incapacitated Sexual Assault," 273.

68. McMahon et al., "Bystander Intervention as a Prevention Strategy for Campus Sexual Violence."

69. Harris et al., "Reimagining the Study of Campus Sexual Assault"; Iverson, "Mapping identities"; Linder et al., "What Do We Know about Campus Sexual Violence?"; Lundy-Wagner and Winkle-Wagner, "A Harassing Climate?"; Wadley and Hurtado, "Using Intersectionality to Reimagine Title IX Adjudication Policy"; Wooten, "Revealing a Hidden Curriculum of Black Women's Erasure in Sexual Violence Prevention Policy."

70. See Appendix for more information on each institutional site.

71. See Appendix for more on participant recruitment and survivor demographics; During the first few months of 2019, the doctoral student I was working with at the time, Dr. Nadeeka Karunaratne, interviewed the three final survivors from CU. I conducted all other interviews with survivors.

72. Two survivors were unable to complete the second interview due to scheduling issues. All Women of Color survivors were compensated for their time.

73. Some participants' quotes are not verbatim. Filler words, such as "um" and "like" and repeated words were edited out of some participants' quotes. This editing did not change the meaning of participants' stories.

74. MAKERS. "Kimberlé Crenshaw. The 2020 MAKERS Conference" 2:15.

75. Women of the World Festival 2016. "Kimberlé Crenshaw—On Intersectionality—Keynote—WOW 2016" 7:00.

76. See Appendix for more information on institutional context and the roles for each staff participant; Dr. Nadeeka Karunaratne interviewed two SVRC staff members at CU, two SVRC staff members at MU, and one SVRC staff member, the Title IX Coordinator, Women's Center Coordinator, and Cultural Center Director at RU.

77. Carly Parnitzke Smith and Jennifer J. Freyd, "Institutional Betrayal," *American Psychologist* 69, no. 6 (2014): 578.

78. U.S. Department of Education, "Dear Colleague Letter: Office of the Assistant Secretary."

79. Smith and Freyd, "Institutional Betrayal."

80. Alec M. Smidt and Jennifer J. Freyd, "Government-Mandated Institutional Betrayal," *Journal of Trauma & Dissociation* 19, no. 5 (2018): 491–499.

81. Jennifer J. Freyd, "When Sexual Assault Victims Speak Out, Their Institutions Often Betray Them," *The Conversation*, January 11, 2018, https://theconversation.com/when-sexual-assault-victims-speak-out-their -institutions-often-betray-them-87050; Alec M. Smidt and Jennifer J. Freyd, "Government-Mandated Institutional Betrayal."

82. Freyd, "When Sexual Assault Victims Speak Out."

83. Smidt and Freyd, "Government-Mandated Institutional Betrayal."

84. MAKERS. "Kimberlé Crenshaw. The 2020 MAKERS Conference," 11:10.

Chapter 1

1. Jessica C. Harris et al., "Reimagining the Study of Campus Sexual Assault," *Higher Education: Handbook of Theory and Research* 35 (2020): 1–47; Jessica C. Harris and Chris Linder, "Introduction," in *Sexual Violence and its Intersections on Campus: Centering Minoritized Students' Voices*, ed. Jessica C. Harris and Chris Linder (Sterling, VA: Stylus, 2017), 1–22; Chris Linder et al., "What Do We Know about Campus Sexual Violence? A Content Analysis of 10 Years of Research," *Review of Higher Education* 43, no. 4 (2020): 1017–1040.

2. Abigail H. Conley et al., "Prevalence and Predictors of Sexual Assault among a College Sample," *Journal of American College Health* 65, no. 1 (2017): 41–49; Elizabeth Culatta et al., "Sexual Revictimization: A Routine Activity Theory Explanation," *Journal of Interpersonal Violence* 35, nos. 15–16 (2017): 2800–2824; Leah E. Daigle et al., "The Violent and Sexual Victimization of College Women: Is Repeat Victimization a Problem?," *Journal of Interpersonal Violence* 23, no. 9 (2008): 1296–1313; Jennifer Katz et al., "Sexual Revictimization During Women's First Year of College: Self-Blame and Sexual Refusal Assertiveness as Possible Mechanisms," *Journal of Interpersonal Violence* 25, no. 11 (2010): 2113–2126; Jenna McCauley et al., "Binge Drinking and Rape: A Prospective Examination of College Women with a History of Previous Sexual Victimization," *Journal of Interpersonal Violence* 25, no. 9 (2010): 1655–1668; Terri L. Messman-Moore et al., "Substance Use and PTSD Symptoms Impact the Likelihood of Rape and Revictimization in College Women," *Journal of Interpersonal Violence* 24, no. 3 (2009): 499–521; Marla Reese-Weber and Dana M. Smith, "Outcomes of Child Sexual Abuse as Predictors of Later Sexual Victimization," *Journal of Interpersonal Violence* 26, no. 9 (2011): 1884–1905; Jonathan C. Waldron et al., "Sexual Victimization

History, Depression, and Task Physiology as Predictors of Sexual Revictimization: Results from a 6-Month Prospective Pilot Study," *Journal of Interpersonal Violence* 30, no. 4 (2015): 622–639.

3. Stephen Cranney, "The Relationships between Sexual Victimization and Year in School in U.S. Colleges: Investigating the Parameters of the 'Red Zone,'" *Journal of Interpersonal Violence* 30, no. 17 (2015): 3133–3145; William F. Flack, Jr. et al. "'The Red Zone': Temporal Risk for Unwanted Sex among College Students," *Journal of Interpersonal Violence* 23, no. 9 (2008): 1177–1196; Matthew Kimble et al., "Risk of Unwanted Sex for College Women: Evidence for a Red Zone," *Journal of American College Health* 57, no. 3 (2008): 331–338; Brian N. Sweeney, "The Allure of the Freshman Girl: Peers, Partying, and the Sexual Assault of First-Year College Women," *Journal of College and Character* 12, no. 4 (2011): 1–15.

4. Harris et al., "Reimagining the Study of Campus Sexual Assault"; Linder et al., "What Do We Know about Campus Sexual Violence?"

5. Antonia Abbey, "Alcohol-Related Sexual Assault: A Common Problem among College Students," *Journal of Studies on Alcohol and Drugs* 14 (2002): 118–128; Antonia Abbey et al., "Alcohol and Dating Risk Factors for Sexual Assault among College Women," *Psychology of Women Quarterly* 20, no. 1 (1996): 147–169.

6. Leah E. Daigle et al., "The Effectiveness of Sexual Victimization Prevention among College Students: A Summary of 'What Works,'" *Victims and Offenders* 4 (2009): 398–404; Jenny Dills et al., *Sexual Violence on Campus: Strategies for Prevention* (Atlanta, GA: National Center for Injury Prevention and Control, Centers for Disease Control and Prevention, 2016).

7. Kimberlé Crenshaw, "Mapping the Margins: Intersectionality, Identity Politics, and Violence against Women of Color," *Stanford Law Review* 43 no. 6 (1991): 1251.

8. Abbey et al., "Alcohol and Dating Risk Factors for Sexual Assault among College Women"; Christopher P. Krebs et al., "The Sexual Assault of Undergraduate Women at Historically Black Colleges and Universities (HBCU)," *Journal of Interpersonal Violence* 26, no. 18 (2011): 3640–3666.

9. Jeanette Wade and Robert L. Peralta, "Perceived Racial Discrimination, Heavy Episodic Drinking and Alcohol Abstinence among African American and White College Students," *Journal of Ethnicity in Substance Abuse* 16, no. 2 (2017): 165–180.

10. Cortney A. Franklin, "Sorority Affiliation and Sexual Assault Victimization: Assessing Vulnerability Using Path Analysis," *Violence Against Women* 22, no. 8 (2015): 895–922.

11. J.B. Kingree and Martie Thompson, "Sorority Membership and Sexual Victimization: An Examination of Potential Mediators of the Association," *Journal of Interpersonal Violence* 35, nos. 23–24 (2020): 5834–5852.

12. Jacqueline Chevalier Minow and Christopher J. Einolf, "Sorority Participation and Sexual Assault Risk," *Violence Against Women* 15, no. 7 (2009): 835–851.

13. Franklin, "Sorority Affiliation and Sexual Assault Victimization"; Kingree and Thompson, "Sorority Membership"; Minow and Einolf, "Sorority Participation."

14. Jessica C. Harris et al., "The Property Functions of Whiteness within Fraternity/Sorority Culture on Campus," in *Critical Considerations of Race, Ethnicity, and Culture in Fraternity/Sorority Life*, ed. Kathleen E. Gillon et al. (San Francisco, CA: Jossey Bass, 2019), 17–27; Annemarie Vacarro and Melissa J. Camba-Kelsay, *Centering Women of Color in Academic Counterspaces: A Critical Race Analysis of Teaching, Learning, and Classroom Dynamics* (Lanham, MD: Lexington Books, 2016).

15. In addition to their stories of sexual health education, many women also conveyed that the culture of their institution placed them at risk for sexual violence. These campus cultures and their influence on sexual violence are explored in more depth in Chapters 2 through 4. According to the World Health Organization, sexual health is "a state of physical, emotional, mental and social well-being in relation to sexuality; it is not merely the absence of disease, dysfunction or infirmity. Sexual health requires a positive and respectful approach to sexuality and sexual relationships, as well as the possibility of having pleasurable and safe sexual experiences, free of coercion, discrimination and violence. For sexual health to be attained and maintained, the sexual rights of all persons must be respected, protected and fulfilled." World Health Organization, *Sexual and Reproductive Health and Research*, 2023, https://www.who.int/teams/ sexual-and-reproductive-health-and-research-(srh)/areas-of-work/ sexual-health, para. 1. Sexual health education, then, includes education on sexuality, sexual relationships, sexual violence, sexual rights, and sexually transmitted infections.

16. Throughout the research, I observed that Women of Color survivors did not often use the word "sex" when referring to sex. Survivors often referred to sex as "it" or "that." This semantic substitution made me wonder, is sex so unknown, or perhaps taboo, that some participants hesitate to say the word?

17. Kristen Luker, *When Sex Goes to School: Warring Views on Sex—and Sex Education—since the Sixties* (New York: W.W. Norton & Company, 2006), 22.

18. Charlene L. Muehlenhard et al., "The Complexities of Sexual Consent among College Students: A Conceptual and Empirical Review," *The Journal of Sex Research* 53, nos. 4–5 (2016): 457–487; Mary A. Ott and John S. Santelli, "Abstinence and Abstinence-Only Education," *Current Opinion in Obstetrics and Gynecology* 19, no. 5 (2007): 446–452; John Santelli et al., "Abstinence and Abstinence-Only Education: A Review of U.S. Policies and Programs," *Journal of Adolescent Health* 38 (2006): 72–81.

19. Sharon E. Hoefer and Richard Hoefer, "Worth the Wait? The Consequences of Abstinence-Only Sex Education for Marginalized Students," *American Journal of Sexuality Education* 12, no. 3 (2017): 257–276.

20. Hoefer and Hoefer, "Worth the Wait?"; Samantha Y. Sneen, "The Current State of Sex Education and its Perpetuation of Rape Culture," *California Western International Law Journal* 49 (2019): 463–490.

21. William Ryan, *Blaming the Victim* (New York: Pantheon Books, 1971).

22. Sneen, "The Current State of Sex Education," 472.

23. Sneen, "The Current State of Sex Education."

24. Madeline Schneider and Jennifer S. Hirsch, "Comprehensive Sexuality Education as a Primary Prevention Strategy for Sexual Violence Perpetration," *Trauma, Violence, & Abuse* 21, no. 3 (2020): 439–455.

25. Jennifer S. Hirsch and Claude A. Mellins, "Sexual Health Initiative to Foster Transformation (SHIFT)," Columbia University, March 2019, www.publichealth.columbia.edu/sites/default/files/shift_final_report_4 -11-19.pdf; John S. Santelli et al., "Does Sex Education before College Protect Students from Sexual Assault in College?" *PloS One* 13, no. 11 (2018): e0205951–e0205951.

26. Hirsch and Mellins, "Sexual Health Initiative."

27. Hirsch and Mellins, "Sexual Health Initiative," 11.

28. Hirsch and Mellins, "Sexual Health Initiative"; Sneen, "The Current State of Sex Education."

29. Hirsch and Mellins, "Sexual Health Initiative."

30. "Sex Ed State Law and Policy Chart: SIECUS State Profiles, July 2022," SIECUS: Sex Ed for Social Change, 2022, https://siecus.org/wp -content/uploads/2021/09/2022-Sex-Ed-State-Law-and-Policy-Chart.pdf.

31. "Sex Ed State Law."

32. Definitions of consent vary across state legislation.

33. "Sex Ed State Law."

34. Mariotta Gary-Smith et al., "Sex, Race, and Politics in the U.S.: A Call to Action to Address Racial Justice in Sexuality Education," SIECUS: Sex Ed for Social Change, 2022, https://siecus.org/wp-content/uploads/2022/06/2022-Racial-Justice-Resource.pdf, 41.

35. Hoefer and Hoefer, "Worth the Wait?"

36. Hoefer and Hoefer, "Worth the Wait?"

37. Luker, *When Sex Goes to School*.

38. Laura Duberstein Lindberg et al., "Changes in Adolescents' Receipt of Sex Education, 2006–2013," *Journal of Adolescent Health* 58, no. 6 (2016): 621–627; Scott Edward Rutledge et al., "Information about Human Sexuality: Sources, Satisfaction, and Perceived Knowledge among College Students," *Sex Education* 11, no. 4 (2011): 471–487.

39. Lindberg et al., "Changes in Adolescents' Receipt of Sex Education."

40. Linda G. Castillo et al., "Construction and Initial Validation of the Marianismo Beliefs Scale," *Counselling Psychology Quarterly* 23, no. 2 (2010): 165.

41. Michael Lipka, "A Snapshot of Catholics in Mexico, Pope Francis' Next Stop," Pew Research Center, 2016, www.pewresearch.org/fact-tank/2016/02/10/a-snapshot-of-catholics-in-mexico-pope-francis-next-stop.

42. Lipka, "A Snapshot of Catholics," para 1.

43. Maria Cristina Alcalde and Ana Maria Quelopana, "Latin American Immigrant Women and Intergenerational Sex Education," *Sex Education* 13, no. 3 (2013): 291–304; Mariel Rouvier et al., "Factors that Influence Communication about Sexuality between Parents and Adolescents in the Cultural Context of Mexican Families," *Sex Education* 11, no. 2 (2011): 175–191.

44. Rouvier at al., "Factors that Influence Communication about Sexuality."

45. Vijay Mishra, "The Diasporic Imaginary: Theorizing the Indian Diaspora," *Textual Practice* 10, no. 3 (1996): 421–447.

46. Amy E. Heberle et al., "An Intersectional Perspective on the Intergenerational Transmission of Trauma and State-Perpetrated Violence," *Journal of Social Issues* 76, no. 4 (2020): 814–834; Simone Jacobs and Chandra Davis, "Challenging the Myths of Black Women—A Short-Term, Structured, Art Experience Group: Exploring the Intersections of Race, Gender, and Intergenerational Trauma," *Smith College Studies in Social Work* 87, nos. 2–3 (2017): 200–219.

47. Mallory E. Bowers and Rachel Yehuda, "Intergenerational Transmission of Stress in Humans," *Neuropsychopharmacology* 41 (2016): 232–244; Rachel Yehuda et al., "Maternal, Not Paternal, PTSD is Related to Increased

Risk for PTSD in Offspring of Holocaust Survivors," *Journal of Psychiatric Research* 42, no. 13 (2008): 1104–1111.

48. Miriam K. Ehrensaft et al., "Intergenerational Transmission of Partner Violence: A 20-Year Prospective Study," *Journal of Consulting and Clinical Psychology* 71, no. 4 (2003): 741–753; Rachel Lev-Wiesel, "Intergenerational Transmission of Sexual Abuse? Motherhood in the Shadow of Incest," *Journal of Child Sexual Abuse* 15, no. 2 (2006): 75–101; Laura Ann McCloskey, "The Intergenerational Transfer of Mother–Daughter Risk for Gender-Based Abuse," *Psychodynamic Psychiatry* 41, no. 2 (2013): 303–328; Laura Ann McCloskey and Jennifer A. Bailey, "The Intergenerational Transmission of Risk for Child Sexual Abuse," *Journal of Interpersonal Violence* 15, no. 10 (2000): 1019–1035; Maria Testa et al., "Intergenerational Transmission of Sexual Victimization Vulnerability as Mediated Via Parenting," *Child Abuse & Neglect* 35, no. 5 (2011): 363–371.

49. Ehrensaft et al., "Intergenerational Transmission of Partner Violence."

50. Testa et al., "Intergenerational Transmission of Sexual Victimization Vulnerability as Mediated Via Parenting."

51. Douglas A. Brownridge, "Intergenerational Transmission and Dating Violence Victimization: Evidence from a Sample of Female University Students in Manitoba," *Canadian Journal of Community Mental Health* 25, no. 1 (2006): 75–93.

52. Brownridge, "Intergenerational Transmission and Dating Violence Victimization."

53. Maria Yellow Horse Brave Heart, "The Historical Trauma Response among Natives and its Relationship with Substance Abuse: A Lakota Illustration," *Journal of Psychoactive Drugs* 35, no. 1 (2003): 7.

54. Huma Ahmed-Ghosh, "Chattels of Society: Domestic Violence in India," *Violence Against Women* 10, no. 1 (2004): 94–118.

55. Lorien S. Jordan, "Belonging and Otherness: The Violability and Complicity of Settler Colonial Sexual Violence," *Women & Therapy* 44 no. 3 (2021): 271–291; Andrea Smith, *Conquest: Sexual Violence and American Indian Genocide* (Cambridge, MA: South End Press, 2005); Andrea Smith, "Not an Indian Tradition: The Sexual Colonization of Native Peoples," *Hypatia* 18, no. 2 (2003): 70–85.

56. Jordan, "Belonging and Otherness," 274.

57. Jordan, "Belonging and Otherness"; Smith, *Conquest*; Smith, "Not an Indian Tradition."

58. Evelyn Nakano Glenn, "Settler Colonialism as Structure: A Framework for Comparative Studies of U.S. Race and Gender Formation," *Sociology of Race and Ethnicity* 1, no. 1 (2015): 52–72; Jordan, "Belonging and Otherness"; Smith, "Not an Indian Tradition."

59. Brave Heart, "The Historical Trauma Response," 7.

60. Michelle Sotero, "A Conceptual Model of Historical Trauma: Implications for Public Health Practice and Research," *Journal of Health Disparities Research and Practice* 1, no. 1 (2006): 93–108; Brave Heart, "The Historical Trauma Response."

61. Sotero, "A Conceptual Model of Historical Trauma," 96.

62. Ahmed-Ghosh, "Chattels of Society," 109.

63. Conley et al., "Prevalence and Predictors of Sexual Assault"; Culatta et al., "Sexual Revictimization"; Daigle et al., "The Violent and Sexual Victimization of College Women: Is Repeat Victimization a Problem?"; Katz et al., "Sexual Revictimization"; McCauley et al., "Binge Drinking"; Messman-Moore et al., "Substance Use"; Reese-Weber and Smith, "Outcomes of Child Sexual Abuse"; Waldron et al., "Sexual Victimization History."

64. Randolph D. Hubach et al., "'What Should Sex Look Like?' Students' Desires for Expanding University Sexual Assault Prevention Programs to Include Comprehensive Sex Education," *Qualitative Health Research* 29, no. 13 (2019): 1967–1977.

65. World Health Organization, *Sexual and Reproductive Health and Research*, 2023, https://www.who.int/teams/sexual-and-reproductive-health-and-research-(srh)/areas-of-work/sexual-health.

66. Hubach et al., "'What Should Sex Look Like?'"; Muehlenhard et al., "The Complexities of Sexual Consent"; Santelli et al., "Abstinence and Abstinence-Only Education."

67. Carly Parnitzke Smith and Jennifer J. Freyd, "Institutional Betrayal," *American Psychologist* 69, no. 6 (2014): 575–587.

68. Kelly H. Koo et al., "The Cultural Context of Nondisclosure of Alcohol-Involved Acquaintance Rape among Asian American College Women: A Qualitative Study," *Journal of Sex Research* 52 (2015): 55–68; Sarah McMahon and Rita C. Seabrook, "Reasons for Nondisclosure of Campus Sexual Violence by Sexual and Racial/Ethnic Minority Women," *Journal of Student Affairs Research and Practice* 57, no. 4 (2020): 417–431; Jane E. Palmer and Noelle M. St. Vil, "Sexual Assault Disclosure by College Women at Historically Black Colleges and Universities and Predominantly White Institutions," *NASPA Journal About Women in Higher Education* 11, no. 1 (2018): 33–55.

69. Crenshaw, "Mapping the Margins"; Koo et al., "The Cultural Context of Nondisclosure of Alcohol-Involved Acquaintance Rape among Asian American College Women"; Sexual Assault Disclosure by College Women at Historically Black Colleges and Universities and Predominantly White Institutions."

70. Crenshaw, "Mapping the Margins"; see also McMahon and Seabrook, "Reasons for Nondisclosure of Campus Sexual Violence by Sexual and Racial/Ethnic Minority Women."

71. U.S. Department of Education, "Dear Colleague Letter: Office of the Assistant Secretary," 2011, https://www2.ed.gov/about/offices/list/ocr/letters/colleague-201104.html, 14.

72. U.S. Department of Education, "Dear Colleague Letter," 14–15.

73. Veronica Shepp et al., "The Carceral Logic of Title IX," *Journal of Women and Gender in Higher Education* 16, no. 1 (2023): 4.

74. Smith and Freyd, "Institutional Betrayal," 582.

75. Education, H.B. 1069, 2023 Session of the Florida Legislature. (2023), https://legiscan.com/FL/text/H1069/2023, 4.

76. Christine Soyong Harley, "Sex Ed is a Vehicle for Social Change. Full Stop." SIECUS: Sex Ed for Social Change, January 2019, https://siecus.org/sex-ed-is-a-vehicle-for-social-change; Hirsch and Mellins, "Sexual Health Initiative"; Santelli et al., "Does Sex Education before College Protect Students from Sexual Assault in College?"

77. Harley, "Sex Ed is a Vehicle," para 9.

78. Harley, "Sex Ed is a Vehicle"; Hirsch and Mellins, "Sexual Health Initiative"; "Sex Ed State Law."

79. Bruce M. King et al., "Promoting Sexual Health: Sexuality and Gender/Women's Studies Courses in U.S. Higher Education," *Health Behavior Policy Review* 4, no. 3 (2017): 213–223; Bruce M. King et al., "Reasons Students at a U.S. University Do or Do Not Enrol in a Human Sexuality Course," *Sex Education* 20, no. 1 (2020): 101–109.

80. King et al., "Reasons Students at a U.S. University Do or Do Not Enrol in a Human Sexuality Course," 2020.

81. King et al., "Reasons Students at a U.S. University Do or Do Not Enrol in a Human Sexuality Course," 2020.

82. King et al., "Reasons Students at a U.S. University Do or Do Not Enrol in a Human Sexuality Course," 2020.

Chapter 2

1. See Appendix for more about the RU campus environment.

2. Kathryn J. Holland et al., "'Serious Enough?' A Mixed Method Examination of the Minimization of Sexual Assault as a Service Barrier for College Sexual Assault Survivors," *Psychology of Violence* 11, no. 3 (2021): 277; Kathryn J. Holland and Lilia M. Cortina, "'It Happens to Girls All the Time': Examining Sexual Assault Survivors' Reasons for Not Using Campus Supports," *American Journal of Community Psychology* 59, nos. 1–2 (2017): 50–64.

3. Some women survivors, such as Felecia, mentioned an incident where several RU men students drugged and raped a Black woman student. I was able to locate one institutional message stating that RU leaders were aware about the incident but they could not share more information with the community due to an ongoing police investigation. I did not locate any other institutional messages about the alleged assault. In her interview, the RU Title IX Coordinator acknowledged the incident, but policies concerning confidentiality precluded the coordinator from sharing more information with me or with the campus community. Women survivors, however, pointed me to the RU Confessions Facebook page and a Reddit thread. These online forums provided vague details about the alleged drugging and rape. In both forums, commenters were frustrated by the lack of institutional action and believed the institution "swept [victim's name] under the rug to protect River University."

4. Carly Parnitzke Smith and Jennifer J. Freyd, "Institutional Betrayal," *American Psychologist* 69, no. 6 (2014): 575–587; Carly Parnitzke Smith and Jennifer J. Freyd, "Dangerous Safe Havens: Institutional Betrayal Exacerbates Sexual Trauma," *Journal of Traumatic Stress* 26, no. 1 (2013): 119–124.

5. Kaitlin Walsh Carson et al., "Why Women Are Not Talking about It: Reasons for Nondisclosure of Sexual Victimization and Associated Symptoms of Posttraumatic Stress Disorder and Depression," *Violence Against Women* 26, nos. 3–4 (2020): 271–295; Katie M. Edwards et al., "In Their Own Words: A Content-Analytic Study of College Women's Resistance to Sexual Assault," *Journal of Interpersonal Violence* 29, no. 14 (2014): 2527–2547; Kathryn J. Holland and Allison E. Cipriano, "Does a Report = Support? A Qualitative Analysis of College Sexual Assault Survivors' Title IX Office Knowledge, Perceptions, and Experiences," *Analysis of Social Issues and Public Policy* 21 (2021): 1054–1081; Holland and Cortina, "'It Happens to Girls All the Time'"; Holland et al., "'Serious Enough?'"

6. Although no RU survivors I spoke with reported their experiences with violence to the institution, one survivor did visit the RU SVRC. This survivor met with an advocate for one session and was looking for "resources" and "a check-in." The survivor did not disclose her assault to the SVRC Advocate.

7. Smith and Freyd, "Institutional Betrayal"; Smith and Freyd, "Dangerous Safe Havens."

8. Chris Linder and Jess S. Myers, "Institutional Betrayal as a Motivator for Campus Sexual Assault Activism," *NASPA Journal About Women in Higher Education* 11, no. 1 (2018): 1–16.

9. Linder and Myers, "Institutional Betrayal."

10. Corey Rayburn Yung, "Concealing Campus Sexual Assault: An Empirical Examination," *Psychology, Public Policy, and Law* 21, no. 1 (2015): 5.

11. Yung, "Concealing Campus Sexual Assault."

12. Nancy Chi Cantalupo, "Burying Our Heads in the Sand: Lack of Knowledge, Knowledge Avoidance, and the Persistent Problem of Campus Peer Sexual Violence," *Loyola University Chicago Law Journal* 43 (2011): 244.

13. Linder and Myers, "Institutional Betrayal," 10.

14. Sandra H. Sulzer et al., "A Missed Research Opportunity for Effective Prevention: Clery Act Timely Warning Notices," *Journal of American College Health* 70, no. 5 (2020): 1359–1362.

15. U.S. Department of Education, "Dear Colleague Letter: Office of the Assistant Secretary," 2011, https://www2.ed.gov/about/offices/list/ocr/letters/colleague-201104.html.

16. The Clery Center "The Jeanne Cleary Act: Summary, Reporting Requirements, and Clery Center Resources," 2022, https://clerycenter.org/policy/the-clery-act.

17. "Yesterday: Jeanne Clery," Clery Center, 2022, http://clery.clerycenter.org/home-2.

18. Beverly Beyette, "Campus Crime Crusade: Howard and Connie Clery Lost Their Daughter to a Crazed Thief; Now They're Angry and Fighting Back," *Los Angeles Times*, August 10, 1989, https://www.latimes.com/archives/la-xpm-1989-08-10-vw-301-story.html, para. 8.

19. Beyette, "Campus Crime Crusade," para. 47.

20. Clery Act crimes include criminal homicide, sex offenses, robbery, aggravated assault, burglary, motor vehicle theft, and arson (U.S. Department of Education, "Dear Colleague"); Beyette, "Campus Crime Crusade," para. 47.

21. "Timely Warning Guide," Clery Center, 2018, https://www.clerycenter.org/assets/docs/NCSAM18_Timely-Warning-Guide.pdf, 2; Sulzer et al., "A Missed Research Opportunity."

22. Clery Center, "Timely Warning Guide," 1.

23. Alison Kiss and Kiersten N. Feeney White, "Looking beyond the Numbers: Understanding the Jeanne Clery Act and Sexual Violence," in *The*

Crisis of Campus Sexual Violence: Critical Perspectives on Prevention And Response, ed. Sara Carrigan Wooten and Roland W. Mitchell (New York: Routledge, 2016), 95–112; Laura R. McNeal, "Clery Act: Road to Compliance," *Journal of Personnel Evaluation in Education* 19 (2007): 105–113; Sulzer et al., "A Missed Research Opportunity."

24. "Clery Act Reports By Year," U.S. Department of Education, 2022, https://studentaid.gov/data-center/school/clery-act-reports/clery-by-year.

25. Original documents pertaining to each institutional review and settlement agreements can be found at https://studentaid.gov/data-center/school/clery-act-reports/clery-by-year.

26. Cantalupo, "Burying Our Heads in the Sand"; Vanessa Woodward Griffin et al., "Campus Sexual Violence Elimination Act: Saving Lives or Saving Face?" *American Journal of Criminal Justice* 42 (2017): 401–425; Yung, "Concealing Campus Sexual Assault."

27. Smith and Freyd, "Institutional Betrayal."

28. Linder and Myers, "Institutional Betrayal."

29. Holland and Cortina, "'It Happens to Girls All the Time,'" 61.

30. Bonnie S. Fisher et al., "The Discovery of Acquaintance Rape: The Salience of Methodological Innovation and Rigor," *Journal of Interpersonal Violence* 20, no. 4 (2005): 494.

31. Elizabeth A. Armstrong et al., "Silence, Power, and Inequality: An Intersectional Approach to Sexual Violence," *Annual Review of Sociology* 44 (2018): 99–122; Kimberlé Crenshaw, "Mapping the Margins: Intersectionality, Identity Politics, and Violence against Women of Color," *Stanford Law Review* 43, no. 6 (July 1991): 1241–1299; Estelle B. Freedman, *Redefining Rape: Sexual Violence in the Era of Suffrage and Segregation* (Cambridge, MA: Harvard University Press, 2013); Jennifer Wriggins, "Rape, Racism, and the Law," *Harvard Women's Law Journal* 103, no. 6 (1983): 103–141.

32. Freedman, *Redefining Rape*; Crenshaw, "Mapping the Margins."

33. Freedman, *Redefining Rape*, p. 15.

34. Freedman, *Redefining Rape*; Crenshaw, "Mapping the Margins."

35. Armstrong et al., "Silence, Power, and Inequality," p. 104; see also Freedman, *Redefining Rape*; Wriggins, "Rape, Racism, and the Law."

36. Fisher et al., "The Discovery of Acquaintance Rape"; Heidi L.M. DeLoveh and Lauren Bennett Cattaneo, "Deciding Where to Turn: A Qualitative Investigation of College Students' Helpseeking Decision after Sexual Assault," *American Journal of Community Psychology* 59 (2017): 65–79; Bonnie S. Fisher et al., "Reporting Sexual Victimization to the Police and Others:

Results from a National-Level Study of College Women," *Criminal Justice and Behavior* 30 (2003): 6–38.

37. Smith and Freyd, "Institutional Betrayal."

38. For Uniform Crime Reports, the FBI defines rape as "penetration, no matter how slight, of the vagina or anus with any body part or object, or oral penetration by a sex organ of another person, without the consent of the victim" (Criminal Justice Information Services, 2012, para. 1; see also RAINN, 2022).

39. Smith and Freyd, "Institutional Betrayal."

40. Bonnie S. Fisher et al., *The Sexual Victimization of College Women: Research Report* (Washington, DC: U.S. Department of Justice, 2000); Fisher et al., "The Discovery of Acquaintance Rape."

41. Smith and Freyd, "Institutional Betrayal," 583.

42. On some level, Jane knew her experience qualified as sexual violence. She responded to my call for participation in the research. I recruited for women who "experienced sexual assault, which includes any physical, sexual activity that occurs without your consent." Jane also described how she did not label her experience as "assault," but that she understands that some might label it as "rape" or "sexual assault."

43. "Don't walk alone" was one of the safety tips that the RU Police Department offered to the RU community after the stabbing that multiple survivors mentioned.

44. Smith and Freyd, "Institutional Betrayal," 583.

45. Linder and Myers, "Institutional Betrayal."

46. Fisher et al., *The Sexual Victimization of College Women*; Fisher et al., "The Discovery of Acquaintance Rape."

47. Antonia Abbey, "Alcohol-Related Sexual Assault: A Common Problem among College Students," *Journal of Studies on Alcohol and Drugs* 14 (2002): 118–128; Antonia Abbey et al., "Alcohol and Dating Risk Factors for Sexual Assault among College Women," *Psychology of Women Quarterly* 20, no. 1 (1996): 147–169.

Chapter 3

1. Kyle C. Ashlee and Rachel Wagner, "Toward an Intersectional Model of College Men and Masculinities Programming," In *Men and Masculinities: Theoretical Foundations and Promising Practices for Supporting College Men's Development*, ed. Daniel Tillapaugh and Brian L. McGowan (Sterling, VA: Stylus, 2019), 74; see also Sam de Boise, "Editorial: Is Masculinity Toxic?"

NORMA 14, no. 3 (2019): 147–151; Michael Kimmel and Lisa Wade, "Ask a Feminist: Michael Kimmel and Lisa Wade Discuss Toxic Masculinity," *Signs: Journal of Women in Culture and Society* 44, no. 1 (2018): 233–254.

2. de Boise, "Editorial"; Kimmel and Wade, "Ask A Feminist."

3. Kimmel and Wade, "Ask A Feminist"; Andrea Waling, "Problematis-ing 'Toxic' and 'Healthy' Masculinity for Addressing Gender Inequalities," *Australian Feminist Studies* 34, no. 101 (2019): 362–375.

4. Waling, "Problematising 'Toxic' and 'Healthy' Masculinity."

5. Sarah McMahon and Victoria L. Banyard, "When Can I Help? A Con-ceptual Framework for the Prevention of Sexual Violence through Bystander Intervention," *Trauma, Violence, & Abuse* 13, no. 1 (2012): 3–14.

6. McMahon and Victoria L. Banyard, "When Can I Help?"

7. Vanessa Woodward Griffin et al., "Explaining the Why in #Whyidid-ntreport: An Examination of Common Barriers to Formal Disclosure of Sexual Assault in College Students," *Journal of Interpersonal Violence* 37, nos. 15–16 (2022): NP14716–NP14745; Lindsay M. Orchowski et al., "Social Reactions to Disclosure of Sexual Victimization and Adjustment among Survivors of Sexual Assault," *Journal of Interpersonal Violence* 28, no. 10 (2013): 2006–2023; Roseann Pluretti and Joseph L. Chesebro, "Managing Privacy and the Decision to Disclose: Disclosures of Sexual Victimization," *Communication Quarterly* 63, no. 5 (2015): 550–567.

8. SVRC is not a reporting unit. It is a campus unit that offers support and resources to survivors, including help with navigating formal on and off campus reporting processes.

9. Alec M. Smidt and Jennifer J. Freyd, "Government-Mandated Institu-tional Betrayal," *Journal of Trauma & Dissociation* 19, no. 5 (2018): 491–499.

10. Smidt and Freyd, "Government-Mandated Institutional Betrayal."

11. Freyd, "When Sexual Assault Victims Speak Out"; Smidt and Freyd, "Government-Mandated Institutional Betrayal."

12. Ari Shapiro, "The Fine Line between a Bad Date and Sexual Assault: 2 Views on Aziz Ansari," *National Public Radio*, January 16, 2018, https://www .npr.org/2018/01/16/578422491/the-fine-line-between-a-bad-date-and -sexual-assault-two-views-on-aziz-ansari.

13. Katie Way, "I Went on a Date with Aziz Ansari. It Turned into the Worst Night of My Life," *Babe*, January 13, 2018, https://babe.net/2018/01/13/ aziz-ansari-28355, para. 7.

14. Way, "I Went on a Date," para. 7.

15. Sonora Jha, "To Raise a Feminist Son, Talk to Him about Aziz Ansari," *Medium*, 2018, https://medium.com/the-establishment/to-raise-a

-feminist-son-talk-to-him-about-aziz-ansari-1ae7fd41b074; Shapiro, "The Fine Line."

16. Jha, "To Raise a Feminist Son," para. 21.

17. de Boise, "Editorial"; Kimmel and Wade, "Ask A Feminist"; Michael Salter, "The Problem with a Fight against Toxic Masculinity," *The Atlantic*, 2019, https://www.theatlantic.com/health/archive/2019/02/toxic-masculinity-history/583411.

18. Salter, "The Problem," para 6.

19. Salter, "The Problem," para 6.

20. See Appendix for more about the MU campus environment and MU as a community-oriented campus.

21. McMahon and Banyard, "When Can I Help?"

22. Victoria L. Banyard, "Who Will Help Prevent Sexual Violence: Creating an Ecological Model of Bystander Intervention," *Psychology of Violence* 1, no. 3 (2011): 216–229. Sarah McMahon, "Call for Research on Bystander Intervention to Prevent Sexual Violence: The Role of Campus Environments," *American Journal of Community Psychology* 55 (2015): 472–489.

23. McMahon and Banyard, "When Can I Help?"

24. McMahon and Banyard, "When Can I Help?"

25. Langan Denhard et al., "A Review of Alcohol Use Interventions on College Campuses and Sexual Assault Outcomes," *Current Epidemiology Reports* 7 (2020): 363–375; Jessica C. Harris and Chris Linder, "Introduction," in *Sexual Violence and its Intersections on Campus: Centering Minoritized Students' Voices*, ed. Jessica C. Harris and Chris Linder (Sterling, VA: Stylus, 2017), 1–22.

26. Sidney Bennett et al., "To Act or Not to Act, That is the Question? Barriers and Facilitators of Bystander Intervention," *Journal of Interpersonal Violence* 29, no. 3 (2014): 476–496.

27. Ruschelle M. Leone and Dominic J. Parrott, "Misogynistic Peers, Masculinity, and Bystander Intervention for Sexual Aggression: Is It Really Just 'Locker-Room Talk?'" *Aggressive Behavior* 45 (2019): 42–51; Ruschelle M. Leone et al., "When is it 'Manly' to Intervene?" Examining the Effects of a Misogynistic Peer Norm on Bystander Intervention for Sexual Aggression," *Psychology of Violence* 7, no. 2 (2017): 286–295.

28. Elise Kramer, "The Playful is Political: The Metapragmatics of Internet Rape-Joke Arguments," *Language in Society* 40 (2011): 137–168; Raúl Pérez and Viveca S. Greene, "Debating Rape Jokes vs. Rape Culture: Framing and Counter-Framing Misogynistic Comedy," *Social Semiotics* 26, no. 3 (2016): 265–282.

29. Pérez and Greene, "Debating Rape Jokes," 266.

30. Kramer, "The Playful is Political."

31. Kramer, "The Playful is Political."

32. Meredith D. Clark, "DRAG THEM: A Brief Etymology of So-Called 'Cancel Culture,'" *Communication and the Public* 5, nos. 3–4 (2020): 89.

33. Clark, "DRAG THEM."

34. Clark, "DRAG THEM."

35. Clark, "DRAG THEM," 89.

36. Leone and Parrott, "Misogynistic Peers"; Leone et al., "When is it 'Manly' to Intervene?")

37. Earlier in the chapter, however, Ananya suggested that she did not engage secondary interventions. Intervening in sexual violence is complex and should not be reduced to *only* one's gender identity; Victoria L. Banyard, "Measurement and Correlates of Pro-social Bystander Behavior: The Case of Interpersonal Violence," *Violence and Victims* 23 (2008): 85–99; Amy L. Brown et al., "College Students as Helpful Bystanders against Sexual Violence: Gender, Race, and Year in College Moderate the Impact of Perceived Peer Norms," *Psychology of Women Quarterly* 38, no. 3 (2014): 350–362; Jill C. Hoxmeier et al., "Students as Prosocial Bystanders to Sexual Assault: Demographic Correlates of Intervention Norms, Intentions, and Missed Opportunities," *Journal of Interpersonal Violence* 35, nos. 3–4 (2020): 731–754; Sarah McMahon, "Rape Myth Beliefs and Bystander Attitudes among Incoming College Students," *Journal of American College Health* 59, no. 1 (2010): 3–11; McMahon, "Call for Research."

38. Michael Kimmel, *Guyland: The Perilous World Where Boys Become Men* (New York: HarperCollins Publishers, 2008).

39. Banyard, "Measurement and Correlates."

40. McMahon and Banyard, "When Can I Help?"

41. Aylin Kaya et al., "Men Who Intervene to Prevent Sexual Assault: A Grounded Theory Study on the Role of Masculinity in Bystander Intervention," *Psychology of Men and Masculinities* 21, no. 3 (2020): 463–478; McMahon, "Rape Myth Beliefs."

42. Banyard, "Measurement and Correlates"; McMahon, "Rape Myth Beliefs."

43. Bennett et al., "To Act or Not to Act."

44. Lindsay Orchowski and Christine A. Gidycz, "Psychological Consequences Associated with Positive and Negative Responses to Disclosure of Sexual Assault among College Women: A Prospective Study," *Violence Against Women* 21, no. 7 (2015): 803–823; Orchowski et al., "Social Reactions";

Pluretti and Chesebro, "Managing Privacy"; Sarah E. Ullman and Liana Peter-Hagene, "Social Reactions to Sexual Assault Disclosure, Coping, Perceived Control, and PTSD Symptoms in Sexual Assault Victims," *Journal of Community Psychology* 42, no. 4 (2014): 495–508.

45. Cortney A. Franklin and Alondra D. Garza, "Sexual Assault Disclosure: The Effect of Victim Race and Perpetrator Type on Empathy, Culpability, and Service Referral for Survivors in a Hypothetical Scenario," *Journal of Interpersonal Violence* 36, nos. 5–6 (2021): 2327–2352.

46. Smidt and Freyd, "Government-Mandated Institutional Betrayal."

47. Amy C. Graham et al., "Sexual Assault Survivors' Perceived Helpfulness of University-Affiliated Resources," *Violence Against Women* 27, no. 10 (2021): 1758–1773; Chiara Sabina and Lavina Y. Ho, "Campus and College Victim Responses to Sexual Assault and Dating Violence: Disclosure, Service Utilization, and Service Provision," *Trauma, Violence, & Abuse* 15, no. 3 (2014): 201–226; Julie E. Stoner and Robert J. Cramer, "Sexual Violence Victimization among College Females: A Systematic Review of Rates, Barriers, and Facilitators of Health Service Utilization on Campus," *Trauma, Violence, & Abuse* 20, no. 4 (2019): 520–533.

48. Wendy A. Walsh et al., "Disclosure and Service Use on a College Campus after an Unwanted Sexual Experience," *Journal of Trauma & Dissociation* 11, no. 2 (2010): 134–151.

49. Sabina and Ho, "Campus and College Victim Responses"; Stoner and Cramer, "Sexual Violence Victimization."

50. Bonnie S. Fisher et al., "Reporting Sexual Victimization to the Police and Others: Results from a National-Level Study of College Women," *Criminal Justice and Behavior* 30, no. 1 (2003): 6–38.

51. These rates for service utilization and reporting may be influenced by sampling selection bias. I recruited participants through the MU SVRC LISTSERV, as well as many other spaces and places on the MU campus. It may be possible that Women of Color survivors who used SVRC were more likely to respond to my call for participation. I did, however, also recruit participants in the same manner via the SVRC LISTSERV at RU and CU. See Appendix for more information on participant recruitment methods.

52. Smidt and Freyd, "Government-Mandated Institutional Betrayal," 495.

53. Jennifer J. Freyd, "When Sexual Assault Victims Speak Out, Their Institutions Often Betray Them," *The Conversation*, January 11, 2018, https://theconversation.com/when-sexual-assault-victims-speak-out-their -institutions-often-betray-them-87050.

54. Sara Ahmed, *Complaint!* (Durham, NC: Duke University Press, 2021), 37.

55. Ahmed, *Complaint!*, 92.

56. Graham et al., "Sexual Assault Survivors' Perceived Helpfulness."

57. Leila Wood et al., "Exploring Advocacy Practices for Interpersonal Violence Survivors on College Campuses: Approaches and Key Factors," *Psychology of* Violence 11, no. 1 (2021): 29–30.

58. Atreyi Mitra et al., "Structural Barriers to Accessing the Campus Assault Resources and Education (CARE) Offices at the University of California (UC) Campuses," *Journal of Interpersonal Violence* 37, no. 21–22 (2022): NP19468–NP19490; Michelle L. Munro-Kramer et al., "What Survivors Want: Understanding the Needs of Sexual Assault Survivors," *Journal of American College Health* 65, no. 5 (2017): 297–305; Wood et al., "Exploring Advocacy Practices for Interpersonal Violence Survivors on College Campuses."

59. Rebecca Campbell, "Rape Survivors' Experiences with the Legal and Medical Systems: Do Rape Victim Advocates Make a Difference?" *Violence Against Women* 12, no. 1 (2006): 30–45; Debra Patterson and Brenda Tringali, "Understanding How Advocates Can Affect Sexual Assault Victim Engagement in the Criminal Justice Process," *Journal of Interpersonal Violence* 30, no. 12 (2015): 1987–1997.

60. Campbell, "Rape Survivors' Experiences."

61. Freyd, "When Sexual Assault Victims Speak Out."

62. Smidt and Freyd, "Government-Mandated Institutional Betrayal," 494.

63. Brenda Lee Anderson Wadley and Sarah S. Hurtado, "Using Intersectionality to Reimagine Title IX Adjudication Policy," *Journal of Women and Gender in Higher Education* 16, no. 1 (2023): 52–66.

64. Atreyi Mitra et al., "Structural Barriers to Accessing the Campus Assault Resources and Education (CARE) Offices at the University of California (UC) Campuses"; Munro-Kramer et al., "What Survivors Want"; Wood et al., "Exploring Advocacy Practices for Interpersonal Violence Survivors on College Campuses."

65. McMahon and Banyard, "When Can I Help?"

66. Heather Hensman Kettrey et al., "Effects of Bystander Programs on the Prevention of Sexual Assault among Adolescents and College Students: A Systematic Review," *Campbell Systematic Reviews* 15, no. 1–2 (2019): 1–40.

67. Banyard, "Measurement and Correlates."

68. Wadley and Hurtado, "Using Intersectionality to Reimagine Title IX Adjudication Policy."

69. Suggestions for enhancing, or, rather, dismantling the reporting process are explored in more depth in Chapter 5.

Chapter 4

1. Charles T. Clotfelter, *Big-Time Sports in American Universities*, 2nd ed. (New York: Cambridge University Press, 2019); Caitlin Flanagan, "The Dark Power of Fraternities," *The Atlantic*, March 2014, https://www.theatlantic.com/magazine/archive/2014/03/the-dark-power-of-fraternities/357580; Willian B. Harrison et al., "Alumni Donations and Colleges' Development Expenditures: Does Spending Matter?" *The American Journal of Economics and Sociology* 54, no. 4 (1995): 397–412; Daniel Diaz Vidal and Thomas G. Pittz, "Educating beyond the Classroom: Alumni Giving and the Value of Campus Culture," *Studies in Higher Education* 44, no. 12 (2019): 2208–2222.

2. Lee Ellis and Charles Beattie, "The Feminist Explanation for Rape: An Empirical Test," *The Journal of Sex Research* 19, no. 1 (1983): 74–93; Diana E.H. Russell, *The Politics of Rape: The Victim's Perspective* (Lincoln, NB: iUniverse, 1984); see also Susan Brownmiller, *Against Our Will: Men, Women, and Rape* (New York: Random House, 1975).

3. Ellis and Beattie, "The Feminist Explanation," 75.

4. Elizabeth A. Armstrong et al., "Sexual Assault on Campus: A Multilevel, Integrative Approach to Party Rape," *Social Problems* 53, no. 4 (2006): 483–499; Kristen N. Jozkowski and Jacquelyn D. Wiersma-Mosley, "The Greek System: How Gender Inequality and Class Privilege Perpetuate Rape Culture," *Interdisciplinary Journal of Applied Family Studies* 66, no. 1 (2017): 89–103; Mindy Stombler and Patricia Yancey Martin, "Bringing Women in, Keeping Women down: Fraternity 'Little Sister' Organizations," *Journal of Contemporary Ethnography* 23, no. 2 (1994): 150–184.

5. Patricia Hill Collins, *Black Feminist Thought* (New York: Routledge, 2000); Roxanne Donovan and Michelle Williams, "Living at the Intersection," *Women & Therapy* 25, nos. 3–4 (2002): 95–105; Victoria C. Olive, "Sexual Assault against Women of Color," *Journal of Student Research* 1 (2012): 1–9; Andrea Smith, *Conquest: Sexual Violence and American Indian Genocide* (Cambridge, MA: South End Press, 2005).

6. Carly Parnitzke Smith and Jennifer J. Freyd, "Institutional Betrayal," *American Psychologist* 69, no. 6 (2014): 580.

7. Elizabeth A. Armstrong and Laura Hamilton, *Paying for the Party: How College Maintains Inequality* (Cambridge, MA: Harvard University Press, 2013); Danielle Paquette, "Why Frat Bros Can Throw Parties but Sorority Sisters Aren't Allowed To," *Washington Post*, January 22, 2016, https://www

.washingtonpost.com/news/wonk/wp/2016/01/22/why-frats-can-throw
-parties-but-sororities-cant.

8. Paquette, "Why Frat Bros Can Throw Parties."

9. Jessica Bennet, "The Problem with Frats isn't Just Rape. It's Power," *TIME*, December 3, 2014, https://time.com/3616158/fraternity-rape-uva -rolling-stone-sexual-assault; Jozkowski and Wiersma-Mosley, "The Greek System."

10. Jozkowski and Wiersma-Mosley, "The Greek System."

11. See Appendix for more about the CU campus environment and CU campus geography.

12. Nolan L. Cabrera et al., "Whiteness in Higher Education: The Invisible Missing Link in Diversity and Racial Analyses," *ASHE Higher Education Report Series* 42, no. 6 (San Francisco, CA: Jossey-Bass, 2016); Lori D. Patton, "Disrupting Postsecondary Prose: Toward a Critical Race Theory of Higher Education," *Urban Education* 51 (2016): 315–342.

13. Jessica C. Harris et al., "The Property Functions of Whiteness within Fraternity/Sorority Culture on Campus," in *Critical Considerations of Race, Ethnicity, and Culture in Fraternity/Sorority Life*, ed. Kathleen E. Gillon et al. (San Francisco, CA: Jossey Bass, 2019), 17–27; Nicholas L. Syrett, *The Company He Keeps: A History of White College Fraternities* (Chapel Hill, NC: University of North Carolina Press, 2009).

14. Ryan P. Barone, "White Clauses in Two Historically White Fraternities: Documenting the Past and Exploring Future Implications," *Oracle: The Research Journal of the Association of Fraternity/Sorority Advisors* 8, no. 1 (2014): 54–73; Harris et al., "The Property Functions of Whiteness"; Syrett, *The Company He Keeps*.

15. Women of the World Festival 2016. "Kimberlé Crenshaw—On Intersectionality—Keynote—WOW 2016," YouTube Video, 30:46, March 14, 2016, https://www.youtube.com/watch?v=-DW4HLgYPlA&t=245s.

16. Women of the World Festival 2016. "Kimberlé Crenshaw—On Intersectionality—Keynote—WOW 2016," 7:00.

17. Armstrong and Hamilton, *Paying for the Party*; Jozkowski and Wiersma-Mosley, "The Greek System."

18. North American Interfraternity Conference, "Greek Members of Congress (117th Congress- updated 01/2021)," 2021, https://nicfraternity .org/ufaqs/greek-members-of-congrestt.

19. Forbes, "Best Fraternities for Future CEOs," *Forbes*, January 31, 2003, https://www.forbes.com/2003/01/31/cx_dd_0131frat.html.

20. Jozkowski and Wiersma-Mosley, "The Greek System," 90.

21. Bennet, "The Problem with Frats," para. 11.

22. Bennet, "The Problem with Frats," para. 20.

23. In 2022, for instance, several IFC organizations at the University of Southern California (USC) disaffiliated from the institution and formed the University Park Interfraternity Council (UPIFC). UPIFC is not affiliated in any way with USC. There were multiple reasons why the fraternities disaffiliated, one being the strict "event management rules" handed down by the institution after multiple allegations of sexual assault at USC fraternities surfaced; USC Office of the Provost, 2022, "USC IFC Affiliation/Disaffiliation FAQ," https://greeklife.usc.edu/unaffiliated-organizations/disafffiliation-frequently-asked-questions/, np. The presence of many disaffiliated fraternities remains at USC, for example, chapter houses and some forms of recruitment still exist, but the institution has no oversight over the organizations. In their official communication about the mass disaffiliation, USC administrators explained, "We no longer have access to these houses, we don't know who lives there, nor do we know how the leaders are handling issues of training and whether they are meeting the requirements set forth by their national governing bodies"; USC Office of the Provost, "USC IFC Affiliation/Disaffiliation FAQ," np.

24. Jaclyn Diaz, "Cornell Suspends Frat Parties after Reports of Drugged Drinks and Sexual Assault," *NPR*, November 9, 2022, https://www.npr.org/2022/11/09/1135237114/cornell-university-suspends-fraternity-parties-sexual-assault; Martha Pollack and Ryan Lombardi, "Response to Recent Crime Alerts," November 7, 2022, https://statements.cornell.edu/2022/20221107-crime-alerts.cfm.

25. Gabriella Pacitto, "IFC Lifts Ban on Fraternity Parties and Social Events, Implements New Safety Measures," *The Cornell Daily Sun*, February 2, 2023, https://cornellsun.com/2023/02/02/ifc-lifts-ban-on-fraternity-parties-and-social-events-implements-new-safety-measures.

26. Jake New, "Alcohol Bans and Sexual Assault," *Inside Higher Ed*, August 23, 2016, https://www.insidehighered.com/news/2016/08/24/stanfords-ban-large-containers-hard-alcohol-sparks-debate-about-sexual-assault.

27. New, "Alcohol Bans," para. 12.

28. Harrison et al., "Alumni Donations"; Vidal and Pittz, "Educating Beyond the Classroom."

29. Flanagan, "The Dark Power of Fraternities," para. 17.

30. Flanagan, "The Dark Power of Fraternities," para. 17.

31. Flanagan, "The Dark Power of Fraternities."

32. Smith and Freyd, "Institutional Betrayal," 580.

33. Jeff Borzello, "Alabama's Brandon Miller OK'd to Play, Scores Career-High 41," *ESPN*, February 22, 2023, https://www.espn.com/mens -college-basketball/story/_/id/35713382/alabama-says-brandon-miller-play -south-carolina; Lindsay Schnell, "Brandon Miller, Alabama Basketball, Murder and Controversy. Here Is What We Know," *USA TODAY*, February 24, 2023, https://www.usatoday.com/story/sports/ncaab/2023/02/24/ alabama-basketball-brandon-miller-murder-what-we-know/11334563002.

34. Borzello, "Alabama's Brandon Miller"; Austin Hannon, "Brandon Miller's Attorney, UA Athletics Release Statements Surrounding Darius Miles Case," *FanNation*, February 22, 2023, https://www.si.com/college/alabama/ bamacentral/brandon-millers-attorney-ua-athletics-release-statements -surrounding-darius-miles-case-hannon; Schnell, "Brandon Miller."

35. Borzello, "Alabama's Brandon Miller."

36. Chris Low, "Wrongful Death Lawsuit Filed Against Ex-Alabama Star Brandon Miller," *ESPN*, October 20, 2023, https://www.espn.com/mens -college-basketball/story/_/id/38704027/wrongful-death-lawsuit-filed-ex -alabama-star-brandon-miller.

37. Jessica Luther and Dan Solomon, "Silence at Baylor," *Texas Monthly*, August 20, 2015, https://www.texasmonthly.com/arts-entertainment/ silence-at-baylor.

38. Luther and Solomon, "Silence at Baylor."

39. Luther and Solomon, "Silence at Baylor"; Katherine Mangan, "A Wave of Sexual-Assault Cases Kindles Anger on Baylor's Campus," *The Chronicle of Higher Education*, March 27, 2016, https://www.chronicle.com/article/a -wave-of-sexual-assault-cases-kindles-anger-on-baylors-campus.

40. Luther and Solomon, "Silence at Baylor"; Mangan, "A Wave of Sexual-Assault Cases."

41. Clotfelter, *Big-Time Sports*.

42. Carly Parnitzke Smith and Jennifer J. Freyd, "Dangerous Safe Havens: Institutional Betrayal Exacerbates Sexual Trauma," *Journal of Traumatic Stress* 26, no. 1 (2013): 119–124; Smith and Freyd, "Institutional Betrayal."

43. Carly P. Smith et al., "Sexual Violence, Institutional Betrayal, and Psychological Outcomes for LGB College Students," *Translational Issues in Psychological Science* 2 (2016): 353.

44. *USA TODAY* analyzed aggregate statistics from sexual misconduct reports received over a seven-year period (2014–2020) at 56 public U.S. institutions of higher education. The reports included statistics on the number of formal investigations, number of students found responsible, and resulting

sanctions. From their investigation, *USA TODAY* found that across the 56 schools, for a seven-year period, 1,094 students were suspended and 594 were expelled. This averages about 2.8 students suspended and 1.5 students expelled each year at any given institution, with an average enrollment of 36,000 students.

45. Kenny Jacoby, "Despite Men's Rights Claims, Colleges Expel Few Sexual Misconduct Offenders While Survivors Suffer," *USA TODAY*, November 16, 2022, https://www.usatoday.com/in-depth/news/investigations/2022/11/16/title-ix-campus-rape-colleges-sexual-misconduct-expel-suspend/7938853001.

46. Jacoby, "Despite Men's Rights Claims."

47. Collins, *Black Feminist Thought*; Donovan and Williams, "Living at the Intersection"; Olive, "Sexual Assault"; Smith, *Conquest*.

48. Jennifer Lynn Gossett and Sarah Byrne, "'Click Here': A Content Analysis of Internet Rape Sites," *Gender & Society* 16, no. 5 (2002): 703.

49. Hijin Park, "Interracial Violence, Western Racialized Masculinities, and the Geopolitics of Violence against Women," *Social & Legal Studies* 21, no. 4 (2012): 495.

50. Donovan and Williams, "Living at the Intersection," 97; see also Collins, *Black Feminist Thought*; Olive, "Sexual Assault."

51. Smith, *Conquest*, 10.

52. Park, "Interracial Violence"; Smith, *Conquest*.

53. Sarah Jane Brubaker et al., "Measuring and Reporting Campus Sexual Assault: Privilege and Exclusion in What We Know and What We Do," *Sociology Compass* 11, no. 12 (2017): 1–19; Roxanne A. Donovan, "To Blame or Not to Blame: Influences of Target Race and Observer Sex on Rape Blame Attribution," *Journal of Interpersonal Violence* 22, no. 6 (2007): 722–736; Kelly H. Koo et al., "The Cultural Context of Nondisclosure of Alcohol-Involved Acquaintance Rape among Asian American College Women: A Qualitative Study," *Journal of Sex Research* 52 (2015): 55–68; Sarah McMahon and Rita C. Seabrook, "Reasons of Nondisclosure of Campus Sexual Violence by Sexual and Racial/Ethnic Minority Women," *Journal of Student Affairs Research and Practice* 57, no. 4 (2020): 417–431.

54. Donovan, "To Blame or Not to Blame," 733.

55. Linda A. Foley et al., "Date Rape: Effects of Race of Assailant and Victim and Gender of Subjects on Perceptions," *Journal of Black Psychology* 21, no. 1 (1995): 6–18.

56. Koo et al., "The Cultural Context of Nondisclosure"; McMahon and Seabrook, "Reasons of Nondisclosure."

57. Koo et al., "The Cultural Context of Nondisclosure," 63.

58. Kimberlé Crenshaw, "Mapping the Margins: Intersectionality, Identity Politics and Violence against Women of Color," *Stanford Law Review* 43, no. 6 (1991): 1266.

59. Margaret Hunter, "The Consequences of Colorism," In *The Melanin Millennium: Skin Color as 21st Century International Discourse*, ed. Ronald E. Hall (New York: Springer, 2013), 247.

60. Margaret Hunter, "'If You're Light You're Alright': Light Skin Color as Social Capital for Women of Color," *Gender & Society* 16 (2002): 175–193; Margaret Hunter, *Race, Gender, and the Politics of Skin Tone* (New York: Routledge, 2005); Hunter, "The Consequences of Colorism."

61. Hunter, "'If You're Light'"; Hunter, *Race*; Hunter, "The Consequences of Colorism"; see also Eduardo Bonilla-Silva, "From Bi-Racial to Tri-Racial: Towards a New System of Racial Stratification in the USA," *Ethnic and Racial Studies* 27, no. 6 (2004): 931–950.

62. Hunter, "'If You're Light,'" 188.

63. Crenshaw, "Mapping the Margins"; Donovan, "To Blame or Not to Blame"; Chelsea Hale and Meghan Matt, "The Intersection of Race and Rape Viewed through the Prism of a Modern-Day Emmett Till," *The American Bar Association*, July 16, 2019, https://www.americanbar.org/groups/litigation/committees/diversity-inclusion/articles/2019/summer2019-intersection-of-race-and-rape; Jennifer Wriggins, "Rape, Racism, and the Law," *Harvard Women's Law Journal* 6 (1983): 103–141.

64. Valerie Smith, "Split Affinities: The Case of Interracial Rape," in *Conflicts in Feminism*, ed. Marianne Hirsch and Evelyn Fox Keller (New York: Routledge, 1990), 271–287.

65. Collins, *Black Feminist Thought*; Donovan and Williams, "Living at the Intersection"; Smith, *Conquest*.

66. Nicole T. Buchanan et al., "Comparing Sexual Harassment Subtypes among Black and White Women in Military Rank: Double Jeopardy, the Jezebel, and the Cult of True Womanhood," *Psychology of Women Quarterly* 32 (2008): 347–361; Collins, *Black Feminist Thought*; Ruth Frankenberg, *White Women, Race Matters: The Social Construction of Whiteness* (Minneapolis, MN: University of Minnesota Press, 1993).

67. Smith, "Split Affinities," 276.

68. Veronica Shepp et al., "The Carceral Logic of Title IX," *Journal of Women and Gender in Higher Education* 16, no. 1 (2023): 4–24; Deborah Tuerkheimer, "Incredible Women: Sexual Violence and the Credibility Discount," *University of Pennsylvania Law Review* 166, no. 1 (2017): 1–58.

69. Smith et al., "Sexual Violence."

70. From the documents I could locate, Patrick did not attract money, prestige, or students to the institution. Patrick is also a Man of Color. As a Man of Color, he held little value to the institution; there may have been little-to-no reason for the institution to protect Patrick. See Crenshaw, "Mapping the Margins"; Hale and Matt, "The Intersection"; Smith, "Split Affinities"; Wriggins, "Rape, Racism, and the Law."

71. Harris et al., "The Property Functions of Whiteness."

72. Women of the World Festival .2016. "Kimberlé Crenshaw—On Intersectionality—Keynote—WOW 2016."

Chapter 5

1. Kimberlé Crenshaw, "Mapping the Margins: Intersectionality, Identity Politics, and Violence against Women of Color," *Stanford Law Review* 43, no. 6 (July 1991): 1241–1299; Kimberlé Crenshaw, "Demarginalizing the Intersection of Race and Sex: A Black Feminist Critique of Antidiscrimination Doctrine, Feminist Theory, and Antiracist Politics," *University of Chicago Legal Forum* 1, no. 8 (1989): 139–167.

2. Kelly H. Koo et al., "The Cultural Context of Nondisclosure of Alcohol-Involved Acquaintance Rape among Asian American College Women: A Qualitative Study," *Journal of Sex Research* 52, no. 1 (2015): 55–68; Jane E. Palmer and Noelle M. St. Vil, "Sexual Assault Disclosure by College Women at Historically Black Colleges and Universities and Predominantly White Institutions," *NASPA Journal About Women in Higher Education* 11, no. 1 (2018): 33–55; Martie Thompson et al., "Reasons for Not Reporting Victimizations to the Police: Do They Vary for Sexual Incidents?" *Journal of American College Health* 55 (March-April 2007): 277–282.

3. Crenshaw, "Mapping the Margins"; see also Sarah McMahon and Rita C. Seabrook, "Reasons for Nondisclosure of Campus Sexual Violence by Sexual and Racial/Ethnic Minority Women," *Journal of Student Affairs Research and Practice* 57, no. 4 (2020): 417–431.

4. Jessica C. Harris et al., "Re-imagining the Study of Campus Sexual Assault," in *Higher Education: Handbook of Theory and Research*, ed. Laura W. Perna (New York: Springer Publishing, 2020); Chris Linder et al., "What Do We Know About Campus Sexual Violence? A Content Analysis of 10 Years of Research," *The Review of Higher Education* 43, no. 4 (Summer 2020): 1017–1040.

5. Lindsay M. Orchowski and Christine A. Gidycz, "To Whom Do College Women Confide Following Sexual Assault? A Prospective Study of

Predictors of Sexual Assault Disclosure and Social Reactions," *Violence Against Women* 18, no. 3 (March 2012): 265.

6. *People v. Brock Allen Turner*, case no. B1577162 (Santa Clara County Super. Ct., 2016).

7. *People v. Brock Allen Turner*, case no. B1577162.

8. *People v. Brock Allen Turner*, case no. B1577162.

9. *People v. Brock Allen Turner*, case no. B1577162.

10. *People v. Brock Allen Turner*, case no. B1577162.

11. Bethy Squires, "Brock Turner Court Documents Reveal He Lied about History of Drinking, Drugs," *Vice*, June 14, 2016, https://www.vice.com/en/article/nz88bz/brock-turner-court-documents-reveal-he-lied-about-history-of-drinking-drugs.

12. Chanel Miller, *Know My Name: A Memoir* (New York: Viking Press, 2019).

13. Miller, *Know My Name*, 241.

14. *People v. Brock Allen Turner*, case no. B1577162.

15. Richard Gonzalez and Camila Domonoske, "Voters Recall Aaron Persky, Judge Who Sentenced Brock Turner," National Public Radio, June 5, 2018, www.npr.org/sections/thetwo-way/2018/06/05/617071359/voters-are-deciding-whether-to-recall-aaron-persky-judge-who-sentenced-brock-tur, para. 8; Marina Koren, "Telling the Story of the Stanford Rape Case," *The Atlantic*, June 6, 2016, www.theatlantic.com/news/archive/2016/06/stanford-sexual-assault-letters/485837, para. 3.

16. Katie J.M. Baker, "Here's the Powerful Letter the Stanford Victim Wrote to Her Attacker," *BuzzFeed News*, June 3, 2016, www.buzzfeednews.com/article/katiejmbaker/heres-the-powerful-letter-the-stanford-victim-read-to-her-ra.

17. "Know My Name: A Memoir by Chanel Miller," Penguin Random House, accessed May 9, 2023, www.penguinrandomhouse.com/books/553663/know-my-name-by-chanel-miller/9780735223707.

18. Koren, "Telling the Story," para. 6; see also Gonzalez and Domonoske, "Voters Recall Aaron Persky."

19. Maggie Astor, "California Voters Remove Judge Aaron Persky, Who Gave a 6-Month Sentence for Sexual Assault," *New York Times*, June 6, 2018, www.nytimes.com/2018/06/06/us/politics/judge-persky-brock-turner-recall.html; Gonzalez and Domonoske, "Voters Recall Aaron Persky."

20. Chanel Miller, "I Thought Anonymity Was a Shield After My Sexual Assault. But Coming Forward Brought Me Back to Myself," *TIME*, July 27,

2020, https://time.com/5879561/chanel-miller-on-coming-forward-know-my-name/, para. 4.

21. Sara Ahmed, *Complaint!* (Durham, NC: Duke University Press, 2021), 74.

22. Sara Ahmed, *Complaint!*, 75.

23. Sara Ahmed, *Complaint!*

24. Crenshaw, "Mapping the Margins."

25. Crenshaw, "Mapping the Margins," 1266.

26. David Lisak et al., "False Allegations of Sexual Assault: An Analysis of Ten Years of Reported Cases," *Violence Against Women* 16, no. 12 (December 2010): 1318–1334.

27. Sara Ahmed, *Complaint!*

28. CNN, "Read the Letter Christine Blasey Ford Sent Accusing Brett Kavanaugh of Sexual Misconduct," *CNN*, September 17, 2018, https://www.cnn.com/2018/09/16/politics/blasey-ford-kavanaugh-letter-feinstein/index.html; Meg Anderson, "Who is Christine Blasey Ford, the Woman Accusing Brett Kavanaugh of Sexual Assault?" *NPR*, September 17, 2018, https://www.npr.org/2018/09/17/648803684/who-is-christine-blasey-ford-the-woman-accusing-brett-kavanaugh-of-sexual-assaul.

29. Li Zhou, "Christine Blasey Ford Shows the Lengths Women Have to go to be Believed," *Vox*, September 27, 2018, https://www.vox.com/policy-and-politics/2018/9/27/17880490/supreme-court-nominee-christine-blasey-ford-kavanaugh.

30. For example, Margot Cleveland, "Christine Blasey Ford's Changing Kavanaugh Assault Story Leaves Her Short on Credibility," *USA TODAY*, October 3, 2018, https://www.usatoday.com/story/opinion/2018/10/03/christine-blasey-ford-changing-memories-not-credible-kavanaugh-column/1497661002/; Kevin Roose, "Debunking 5 Viral Rumors About Christine Blasey Ford, Kavanaugh's Accuser," *New York Times*, September 19, 2018, https://www.nytimes.com/2018/09/19/us/politics/christine-blasey-ford-kavanaughs-fact-check.html; Emily Stewart, "Susan Collins Says She Doesn't Think Kavanaugh Was Ford's Assailant," *Vox*, October 7, 2018, https://www.vox.com/policy-and-politics/2018/10/7/17947734/brett-kavanaugh-confirmation-reaction-susan-collins-ford.

31. Anne Helen Petersen, "Would You Be Believed?" *BuzzFeed News*, September 27, 2018, https://www.buzzfeednews.com/article/annehelenpetersen/christine-blasey-ford-brett-kavanaugh-hearing-testimony, para. 13.

32. Crenshaw, "Mapping the Margins."

33. Crenshaw, "Mapping the Margins"; Roxanne A. Donovan, "To Blame or Not To Blame: Influences of Target Race and Observer Sex on Rape Blame Attribution," *Journal of Interpersonal Violence* 22, no. 6 (June 2007): 722–736; Chelsea Hale and Meghan Matt, "The Intersection of Race and Rape Viewed Through the Prism of a Modern-Day Emmett Till," The American Bar Association, July 16, 2019, www.americanbar.org/groups/litigation/committees/diversity-inclusion/articles/2019/summer2019-intersection-of-race-and-rape.

34. Rebecca Campbell et al., "The Detroit Sexual Assault Kit (SAK) Action Research Project, Final Report," February 2015, https://nij.ojp.gov/library/publications/detroit-sexual-assault-kit-sak-action-research-project-arp-final-report; Crenshaw, "Mapping the Margins"; Hale and Matt, "The Intersection"; Jennifer Wriggins, "Rape, Racism, and the Law," *Harvard Women's Law Journal* 6 (1983): 103–141.

35. Crenshaw, "Mapping the Margins"; Veronica Shepp et al., "The Carceral Logic of Title IX," *Journal of Women and Gender in Higher Education* 16, no. 1 (2023): 4–24; Deborah Tuerkheimer, "Incredible Women: Sexual Violence and the Credibility Discount," *University of Pennsylvania Law Review* 166, no. 1 (2017): 1–58; Wriggins, "Rape, Racism, and the Law."

36. Crenshaw, "Mapping the Margins," 1270.

37. Alyssa Milano (@Alyssa_Milano), Twitter, October 15, 2017, https://twitter.com/Alyssa_Milano/status/919659438700670976.

38. Stephanie Zacharek et al., "The Silence Breakers," *TIME*, December 18, 2017, https://time.com/time-person-of-the-year-2017-silence-breakers/.

39. Constance Grady, "The Black Gowns on the Golden Globes Red Carpet Weren't Just a Gimmick," *Vox*, January 8, 2018, https://www.vox.com/culture/2018/1/7/16861532/black-gowns-golden-globes-red-carpet; Linda Holmes and Nicole Werbeck, "At the Golden Globes, Not Just Another Red Carpet," National Public Radio, January 7, 2018, www.npr.org/2018/01/07/576036145/at-the-golden-globes-not-just-another-red-carpet.

40. *The Morning Show*, directed by Mimi Leder, aired 2019–2021, on Apple TV+.

41. Audrey Carlsen et al., "#MeToo Brought Down 201 Powerful Men. Nearly Half of Their Replacements Are Women," *New York Times*, October 29, 2018, www.nytimes.com/interactive/2018/10/23/us/metoo-replacements.html.

42. Zacharek et al., "The Silence Breakers," para. 9.

43. Tarana Burke, "Me Too is a Movement, Not a Moment," filmed November 2016 at TEDWomen, Palm Springs, CA, video, 16:06, www.ted

.com/talks/tarana_burke_me_too_is_a_movement_not_a_moment; Chaz Thorne, "Stop Calling #MeToo a Witch Hunt," *Medium*, March 27, 2020, https://medium.com/equality-includes-you/stop-calling-metoo-a-witch -hunt-e98f4ed2f5b.

44. Caitlin Flanagan, "The Humiliation of Aziz Ansari," *The Atlantic*, January 14, 2018, https://www.theatlantic.com/entertainment/archive/ 2018/01/the-humiliation-of-aziz-ansari/550541, para. 9.

45. "History and Inceptions," me too, accessed May 9, 2023, https:// metoomvmt.org/get-to-know-us/history-inception.

46. "Tarana Burke: Founder," me too, accessed May 9, 2023, https:// metoomvmt.org/get-to-know-us/tarana-burke-founder, para. 1.

47. Elizabeth Adetiba, "Tarana Burke Says #MeToo Should Center Marginalized Communities," *The Nation*, November 17, 2017, https://www .thenation.com/article/archive/tarana-burke-says-metoo-isnt-just-for -white-people/, para. 7.

48. Richard Gregory Johnson III and Hugo Renderos, "Invisible Population and the #MeToo Movement," *Public Administration Review* 80, no. 6 (2020): 1123–1126; Hannah McCann and Megan Sharp, "#MeToo, Cisheteropatriarchy and LGBTQ+ Sexual Violence on Campus," *Sexualities* 0, no. 0 (2023): 1–15; Tiina Rosenberg, "It Happened to #MeToo: Queer Feminist Critique of Cisgender White Feminism," in *The Palgrave Handbook of Queer and Trans Feminisms in Contemporary Performance*, ed. Tiina Rosenberg et al. (Cham: Palgrave Macmillan, 2021) 223–242.

49. Crenshaw, "Mapping the Margins," 1271.

50. Crenshaw, "Mapping the Margins."

51. Crenshaw, "Mapping the Margins."

52. Jennifer M. Gómez and Jennifer J. Freyd, "Psychological Outcomes of Within-Group Sexual Violence: Evidence of Cultural Betrayal," *Journal of Immigrant and Minority Health* 20 (2018): 1458–1467; Jennifer M. Gómez and Robyn L. Gobin, "Black Women and Girls & #MeToo: Rape, Cultural Betrayal, & Healing," *Sex Roles* 82 (2020): 1–12.

53. Gómez and Gobin, "Black Women and Girls & #MeToo," 3.

54. Jennifer M. Gómez, "Group Dynamics as a Predictor of Dissociation for Black Victims of Violence: An Exploratory Study of Cultural Betrayal Trauma Theory," *Transcultural Psychiatry* 56, no. 5 (2019): 878–894; Gómez and Freyd, "Psychological Outcomes of Within-Group Sexual Violence"; Gómez and Gobin, "Black Women and Girls & #MeToo."

55. Crenshaw, "Mapping the Margins."

56. Veronica Shepp et al., "The Carceral Logic of Title IX," *Journal of Women and Gender in Higher Education* 16, no. 1 (2023): 5.

57. Guillermo Miguel Arciniega et al., "Toward a Fuller Conception of Machismo: Development of a Traditional Machismo and Caballerismo Scale," *Journal of Counseling Psychology* 55, no. 1 (January 2008): 19.

58. Arciniega et al., "Toward a Fuller Conception of Machismo."

59. Arciniega et al., "Toward a Fuller Conception of Machismo."

60. Linda G. Castillo et al., "Construction and Initial Validation of the Marianismo Beliefs Scale," *Counselling Psychology Quarterly* 23, no. 2 (June 2010): 163–175.

61. Castillo et al., "Construction and Initial Validation," 165.

62. Crenshaw, "Mapping the Margins," 1257.

63. Crenshaw, "Mapping the Margins."

64. Crenshaw, "Mapping the Margins," 1257.

65. Xhercis Méndez, "Beyond Nassar: A Transformative Justice and Decolonial Feminist Approach to Campus Sexual Assault," *Frontiers: A Journal of Women Studies* 41, no. 2 (2020): 83.

66. Harris, "Heteropatriarchy Kills"; Mimi E. Kim, "Transformative Justice and Restorative Justice: Gender-Based Violence and Alternative Visions of Justice in the United States," *International Review of Victimology* 27, no. 2 (May 2021): 162–172; Méndez, "Beyond Nassar."

67. Kelly Hayes and Miriam Kaba, "The Sentencing of Larry Nassar Was Not 'Transformative Justice.' Here's Why." *The Appeal*, February 5, 2018, https://theappeal.org/the-sentencing-of-larry-nassar-was-not-transformative-justice-here-s-why-a2ea323a6645/.

68. Julia Wade, "We're Ready: Restorative Justice for College Sexual Misconduct," UCLA School of Education & Information Studies: Educational Leadership Program, March 2023, https://ucla.app.box.com/s/z4flle4dphe7s2wak91rmd38yhlcckoz.

69. Harris, "Heteropatriarchy Kills"; Mimi E. Kim, "From Carceral Feminism to Transformative Justice: Women of Color Feminism and Alternatives to Incarceration," *Journal of Ethnic & Cultural Diversity in Social Work* 27, no. 3 (2018): 219–233; Kim, "Transformative Justice."

70. Angela P. Harris, "Heteropatriarchy Kills: Challenging Gender Violence in a Prison Nation," *Washington University Journal of Law & Policy* 37, no. 1 (January 2011): 40.

71. Kim, "From Carceral Feminism"; Kim, "Transformative Justice"; Mia Mingus, "Transformative Justice: A Brief Description," *Leaving*

Evidence, January 9, 2019, https://leavingevidence.wordpress.com/2019/01/09/transformative-justice-a-brief-description/.

72. Kim, "From Carceral Feminism."

73. Harris, "Heteropatriarchy Kills," 58.

74. Sara Kershner et al., *Toward Transformative Justice: A Liberatory Approach to Child Sexual Abuse and Other Forms of Intimate and Community Violence*, generation FIVE (June 2007), https://azinelibrary.org/zines/Towards-Transformative-Justice-Generation-Five; Harris, "Heteropatriarchy Kills"; Mingus, "Transformative Justice."

75. Generation FIVE, *Toward Transformative Justice*; Méndez, "Beyond Nassar."

76. Generation FIVE, *Toward Transformative Justice*.

77. Generation FIVE, *Toward Transformative Justice*; Hayes and Kaba, "The Sentencing."

78. Harris, "Heteropatriarchy Kills"; Kim, "Transformative Justice"; Méndez, "Beyond Nassar."

79. Kim, "Transformative Justice," 168.

80. Méndez, "Beyond Nassar."

81. Generation FIVE, *Toward Transformative Justice*; Mingus, "Transformative Justice."

82. Generation FIVE, *Toward Transformative Justice*, 29; see also Mingus, "Transformative Justice."

83. Generation FIVE, *Toward Transformative Justice*; Méndez, "Beyond Nassar."

84. U.S. Department of Education, "Summary of Major Provisions of the Title IX Final Rule," accessed May 9, 2023, https://www2.ed.gov/about/offices/list/ocr/docs/titleix-summary.pdf.

85. Méndez, "Beyond Nassar."

Chapter 6

1. Julie A. Gameon et al., "College Students' Perspectives on Healing following an Unwanted Sexual Experience," *Current Psychology* 40, no. 6 (June 2021): 2570–2580; Chiara Sabina and Lavina Y. Ho, "Campus and College Victim Responses to Sexual Assault and Dating Violence: Disclosure, Service Utilization, and Service Provision," *Trauma, Violence, & Abuse* 15, no. 3 (February 2014): 201–226; Chiara Sabina et al., "Campus Responses to Dating Violence and Sexual Assault: Information from University Representatives," *Journal of Aggression, Maltreatment and Trauma* 26, no. 1 (February 2017): 88–102.

2. Shaun Ginwright, *Hope and Healing in Urban Education: How Urban Activists and Teachers are Reclaiming Matters of the Heart* (New York: Routledge/Taylor & Francis, 2016).

3. Ginwright, *Hope and Healing*.

4. Ginwright, *Hope and Healing*.

5. Ginwright, *Hope and Healing*.

6. Anika signed up for the yoga program but did not show up for the first class. She found healing through other avenues, such as activism, journaling, reading, and spending time in nature.

7. Peter A. Levine, *In an Unspoken Voice: How the Body Releases Trauma and Restores Goodness* (Berkeley, CA: North Atlantic Books, 2010).

8. Ananda Balayogi Bhavanani, "Understanding Yoga as Therapy," *Journal of Yoga & Physiotherapy* 1, no. 1 (September 2016): 1–2; Laura Douglass, "How Did We Get Here? A History of Yoga in America, 1800–1970," *International Journal of Yoga Therapy* 17, no. 1 (October 2007): 35–42; Pallav Sengupta, "Health Impacts of Yoga and Pranayama: A State-of-the-Art Review," *International Journal of Preventative Medicine* 3, no. 7 (July 2012): 444–458.

9. Stanley Williford, "Yoga: Something for Everyone," *EBONY* (September 1975): 96–102.

10. American Psychological Association, "Apology to People of Color for APA's Role in Promoting, Perpetuating, and Failing to Challenge Racism, Racial Discrimination, and Human Hierarchy in U.S.," 2021, https://www.apa.org/about/policy/racism-apology; Kimberly Gordon-Achebe et al., "Origins of Racism in American Medicine and Psychiatry," in *Racism and Psychiatry: Contemporary Issues and Interventions*, ed. Morgan M. Medlock et al. (Cham: Humana Press, 2019), 3–19.

11. Rosalie Murphy, "Why Your Yoga Class is So White," *The Atlantic*, July 8, 2014, https://www.theatlantic.com/national/archive/2014/07/why-your-yoga-class-is-so-white/374002/, para. 3.

12. After the assault, Ananya learned Shaq was a 23-year-old who was *not* an MU student. While Shaq did not attend the institution, he was very popular within and connected to the MU Indian community. Shaq attended a nearby community college and was often on the MU campus.

13. Kimberlé Crenshaw, "Mapping the Margins: Intersectionality, Identity Politics, and Violence against Women of Color," *Stanford Law Review* 43, no. 6 (July 1991): 1241–1299.

14. American Psychological Association, "Apology"; Kimberly Gordon-Achebe et al., "Origins of Racism"; Derek H. Suite et al., "Beyond Misdiagnosis, Misunderstanding, and Mistrust: Relevance of the Historical

Perspective in the Medical and Mental Health Treatment of People of Color," *Journal of the National Medical Association* 99, no. 8 (August 2007): 879–885.

15. American Psychological Association, "Apology," para. 8.

16. American Psychological Association, "Apology," para. 8.

17. Luona Lin et al., "How Diverse is the Psychology Workforce?" February 2018, https://www.apa.org/monitor/2018/02/datapoint.

18. Suite et al., "Beyond Misdiagnosis."

19. Monae eventually found yoga and meditation as a source for healing. She did not enroll in the MU yoga program, but her friend, who was a survivor and a past participant of the program, told Monae how yoga had supported her healing. Monae tried yoga on her own and found that it was exactly what she needed to continue to heal from violence.

20. The student health insurance policies and Counseling Center procedures were similar across the three institutions.

21. Richard Kadison and Theresa Foy DiGeronimo, *College of the Overwhelmed: The Campus Mental Health Crisis and What to Do about It* (San Francisco, CA: Jossey-Bass, 2004); Victor Schwartz and Jerald Kay, "The Crisis in College and University Mental Health," *Psychiatric Times* 26, no. 10 (October 2009): 1–5.

22. "The Vagina Monologues," VDAY, accessed May 9, 2023, https://www.vday.org/art-activism/the-vagina-monologues, para. 1.

23. VDAY, "The Vagina Monologues."

24. Although Carrie later worked for RU SVRC as a peer educator, she did not use the campus unit to gather resources or gain support for the campus sexual violence she experienced her first-year at RU.

25. Sabina et al., "Campus Responses to Dating Violence."

26. Maysa Akbar et al., "Psychology's Role in Dismantling Systemic Racism: Racial Equity Action Plan," American Psychological Association, July 15, 2022, https://www.apa.org/about/apa/addressing-racism/racial-equity-action-plan.pdf, 14.

27. Xhercis Méndez, "Beyond Nassar: A Transformative Justice and Decolonial Feminist Approach to Campus Sexual Assault," *Frontiers: A Journal of Women Studies* 41, no. 2 (2020): 94.

28. Sara Kershnar et al., *Toward Transformative Justice: A Liberatory Approach to Child Sexual Abuse and Other Forms of Intimate and Community Violence*, generation Five (June 2007), https://azinelibrary.org/zines/Towards-Transformative-Justice-Generation-Five; Xhercis Méndez, "Beyond Nassar."

29. American Psychological Association, "Apology."

30. Ginwright, *Hope and Healing*.

Conclusion

1. Women of the World Festival 2016. "Kimberlé Crenshaw—On Intersectionality—Keynote—WOW 2016," YouTube Video, 30:46, March 14, 2016, https://www.youtube.com/watch?v=-DW4HLgYPlA&t=245s.

2. MAKERS. "Kimberlé Crenshaw. The 2020 MAKERS Conference," YouTube Video, 1:48, February 14, 2020, https://www.youtube.com/watch?v=cSTf89pLclo.

3. Kimberlé Crenshaw, "Mapping the Margins: Intersectionality, Identity Politics, and Violence against Women of Color," *Stanford Law Review* 43, no. 6 (July 1991): 1241–1299.

4. Leila Wood et al., "Exploring Advocacy Practices for Interpersonal Violence Survivors on College Campuses: Approaches and Key Factors," *Psychology of* Violence 11, no. 1 (2021): 29–30.

5. Kelly Hayes and Miriam Kaba, "The Sentencing of Larry Nassar Was Not 'Transformative Justice.' Here's Why." *The Appeal*, February 5, 2018, https://theappeal.org/the-sentencing-of-larry-nassar-was-not-transformative-justice-here-s-why-a2ea323a6645/.

6. Shaun Ginwright, *Hope and Healing in Urban Education: How Urban Activists and Teachers are Reclaiming Matters of the Heart* (New York: Routledge/Taylor & Francis, 2016).

7. Carrie A. Moylan et al., "Campus Sexual Assault Climate: Toward an Expanded Definition and Improved Assessment," *Psychology of Violence* 11, no. 3 (2021): 296–306.

8. Carrie A. Moylan et al., "Campus Sexual Assault Climate Surveys: A Brief Exploration of Publicly Available Reports," *Journal of American College Health* 66, no. 6 (2018): 445–449; Moylan et al., "Campus Sexual Assault Climate."

9. Moylan et al., "Campus Sexual Assault Climate," 296.

10. Sylvia Hurtado, "The Campus Racial Climate: Contexts of Conflict," *The Journal of Higher Education* 63, no. 5 (1992): 539–569; Sylvia Hurtado et al., "Enacting Diverse Learning Environments: Improving the Climate for Racial/Ethnic Diversity in Higher Education," *ASHE-ERIC Higher Education Report* 26, no. 8 (1999): Washington, DC: The George Washington University, Graduate School of Education and Human Development.

11. Emily A. Leskinen et al., "Campus Climate Assessments: Limitations of Siloing Sexual Violence and Diversity Surveys," *Journal of Evidence-Based Social Work* 19, no. 5 (2022): 557–573; Moylan et al., "Campus Sexual Assault Climate."

12. Leskinen et al., "Campus Climate Assessments," 557.

13. Moylan et al., "Campus Sexual Assault Climate."

14. Hurtado et al., "Enacting Diverse Learning Environments."

15. Jennifer M. Gómez, "Microaggressions and the Enduring Mental Health Disparity: Black Americans at Risk For Institutional Betrayal," *Journal of Black Psychology* 41, no. 2 (2013): 121–143; Jennifer M. Gómez and Robyn L. Gobin, "Black Women and Girls & #MeToo: Rape, Cultural Betrayal, & Healing," *Sex Roles* 82 (2020): 1–12.

16. Women of the World Festival 2016. "Kimberlé Crenshaw—On Intersectionality—Keynote—WOW 2016."

17. MAKERS. "Kimberlé Crenshaw. The 2020 MAKERS Conference," 2:07.

18. Kimberlé Crenshaw et al., "What Does Intersectionality Mean?" March 29, 2021, in *1A*, produced by *NPR*, podcast 2:04, https://www.npr.org/2021/03/29/982357959/what-does-intersectionality-mean.

19. Crenshaw et al., "What Does Intersectionality Mean?" 43:15.

20. Kimberlé Crenshaw, "Postscript," In *Framing Intersectionality: Debates on a Multi-Faceted Concept in Gender Studies*, eds. Helma Lutz et al. (Farnham: Ashgate, 2011), 221–233.

21. Jennifer C. Nash, "Intersectionality and its Discontents," *American Quarterly* 69, no. 1 (2017): 118; see also Crenshaw, "Postscript"; Kathy Davis, "Intersectionality as Buzzword: A Sociology of Science and Perspective on What Makes a Feminist Theory Successful," *Feminist Theory* 9, no. 1 (2008): 67–85; Barbara Tomlinson, "To Tell the Truth and Not Get Trapped: Desire, Distance, and Intersectionality at the Scene of Argument," *Signs: Journal of Women in Culture and Society* 38, no. 4 (2013): 993–1017.

22. Crenshaw, "Postscript," p. 22

23. MAKERS. "Kimberlé Crenshaw. The 2020 MAKERS Conference," 11:10.

Appendix

1. Women of the World Festival 2016. "Kimberlé Crenshaw—On Intersectionality—Keynote—WOW 2016," YouTube Video, 7:00, March 14, 2016, https://www.youtube.com/watch?v=-DW4HLgYPlA&t=245s.

2. Carrie A. Moylan and McKenzie Javorka, "Widening the Lens: An Ecological Review of Campus Sexual Assault," *Trauma, Violence, & Abuse* 21, no. 1 (2020): 179–192.

3. Jessica C. Harris et al., "Who Benefits? A Critical Race Analysis of the (D)evolving Language of Inclusion in Higher Education," *Thought & Action* (Winter 2015): 21–38.

Index

Note: Page numbers ending with a "t" indicate material in a table.

racist systems against, 7, 127, 134; structures that oppress, 135; use of psychology to harm, 148, 149; violence against, 8, 34, 111

community-oriented campus, 65, 68, 72, 73, 168, 183

confidentiality, 48, 49, 74, 78, 108, 184, 218n3. *See also* privacy

consent, 58, 69, 73, 87, 113, 129, 221n42; in Aziz Ansari case, 66; in definition of rape, 53, 221n38; education on, 18, 22, 25, 33, 35, 37; in intersectional sexual health curricula, 40; prevention and, 38; toxic masculinity and, 67, 68

contraception, 22, 24, 39, 132

Cornell University, 96

Counseling Centers, 14, 149, 153, 189; help with healing, 164; policies and procedures of, 151; serving Women of Color, 152; SVRC works with, 184; therapy at, 150, 155, 159

Crenshaw, Kimberlé, 1, 5–6, 8, 12, 172, 175

criminal justice system. *See* justice systems

crisis centers, 7, 105, 201n2

cultural representations, 8, 171

culturally competent care, 152, 153, 155, 158, 162

Cuomo, Andrew, 121

Dartmouth University, 2

Dear Colleague Letter, 1, 36, 189

Department of Education, U.S., 1, 2, 36, 51, 202n4

DeVos, Betsy, 202n4

discrimination, 13, 92, 110, 171, 212n15; colorism, 105; intersectionality and, 6; sex, 1

Diwali, 139, 140

domestic violence, 7, 28, 29, 30, 153, 161, 162. *See also* intimate partner violence

domination, intersecting systems of, 4, 6, 13, 14, 112, 169, 173; institutional context and, 11; institutional structures and, 12; transformative justice and, 135

drinking/drunkenness, 42, 104, 130, 146; athlete students, 178; at fraternity parties, 93; toxic masculinity and, 67; victim blaming and, 58, 87, 115; of white students, 17–18. *See also* alcohol

drugs/drugging, 13, 48, 49, 94, 113, 146, 218n3; at fraternity parties, 96; role in campus sexual violence, 2, 17, 69. *See also* alcohol

Ellis, Lee, 88

empathy, 80, 81, 85, 167

empowerment, 109, 158, 161; approach, 83, 84–85, 166, 167; in feminist resistance movements, 7; of Latina women, 133; of rap music, 8; in reporting process, 76–81, 107. *See also* power

equity, 13, 55, 151, 169. *See also* gender inequity; inequity

evidence, court-room, 113, 116, 117, 119, 123, 135; evidentiary standard, 202n4

exclusion, 8, 13, 88, 92, 110, 125